Drawing the Line

W. E. Schluter
Pennington NJ
609-737-0561

Alan Rosenthal

Drawing the Line

Legislative Ethics

in the States

University of Nebraska Press

Lincoln and London

A Twentieth Century Fund Book

The paper in this book meets
the minimum requirements of American National
Standard for Information Sciences—
Permanence of Paper for Printed Library Materials,
ANSI Z39.48-1984.
Library of Congress Cataloging-in-Publication Data
Rosenthal, Alan, 1932–
Drawing the line : Legislative ethics in the states / Alan Rosenthal.
p.   cm.
"A twentieth century fund book."
Includes bibliographical references and index.
ISBN 0-8032-3919-X (cloth : alk. paper)
1. Legislative bodies—United States—States—Ethics.   I. Title.
JK2488.R66   1996   172'.0973–dc20   95-51513   CIP

To Patrick, Kelly, and Chas

Contents

Foreword

Today, the common opinion of government seems to be shaped less by direct personal experience than by the deluge of criticism that dominates media coverage and campaign propaganda. The best strategy for competing for public attention, either ratings or votes, appears to be emphasizing scandal, waste, fraud, and abuse of power. Whatever an individual's accomplishments in the private sector, for example, the minute his name is raised for a public post or she declares a candidacy, a race to discredit commences. And while Americans traditionally have been skeptical of their leaders and their government, it seems that neither has ever been held in such low esteem as is the case now.

It is possible, to be sure, to trace the deterioration of public attitudes to specific and substantive historical events that occurred during the last generation, Watergate being the most obvious. More generally, bad behavior, always the pattern for a minority of those in politics, today receives more extensive publicity because more aspects of the public and private lives of officials have become subject to scrutiny and exposure. Of course, this otherwise salutary development may foster a simple but important misreading of the difference between the way human beings act in public life and their behavior in the private sector. In fact, it is not at all clear that the incidence of routine moral turpitude in government exceeds the average in the balance of society. Indeed, one suspects that the greater transparency in the political arena might, on average, promote more rectitude. Whatever the case, the assault on government has been given added respectability by a new generation of antigovernment academics who argue that government, in the nature of the case, cannot be well-managed or even well-meaning.

In the face of these prevailing winds, there are serious scholars, guided by research and objectivity, who continue to amass considerable evidence that the reforms of the last quarter century have wrought substantial improvements in the ethics, operations, and efficiency of the public sector. Their work has attracted little attention, perhaps because it serves the interests of neither media competition nor campaign combat. And who can argue that it is unlikely that a headline will appear in tomorrow's paper that reads "No One in the Legislature Stole Anything Yesterday" or "All the Guards Showed Up for Work at the State Penitentiary." Without naïveté or apology, then, the efforts of these students of government provide a healthy antidote to the daily fare about public life available to most of us. It also has often been a blueprint for governmental reform.

Over the past several decades, Alan Rosenthal's extraordinary work has belonged in this constructive category. As probably the nation's leading expert on state legislatures, his publications have transformed our knowledge of how these bodies function and how they are changing. As director of the Eagleton Institute at Rutgers University, as professor of political science, and as consultant to numerous legislative bodies, he has been directly involved in the dramatic evolution and professionalization of this aspect of state government. Thus it was logical that the Twentieth Century Fund should turn to him to report on the state of legislative ethics across the nation.

The Fund has a long history of supporting studies of public ethics and has explored many issues related to state government. For example, since 1980, the Fund has published half a dozen studies of campaign finance, including Herbert Alexander's *Reform and Reality: The Financing of State and Local Campaigns* and Larry Sabato's *Paying for Elections: The*

Campaign Finance Thicket, and it has explored the ways in which different states provide welfare to their residents in *Turning Promises into Performance: The Management Challenge of Implementing Workfare* by Richard Nathan.

In this volume, Rosenthal explains the recent history and assesses the current condition of both legislative rules and actual behavior. His work is vivid and practical, with a substantial reliance on the thinking of those who actually serve in elected state posts. He provides a refreshing and, ultimately, optimistic perspective on the state of ethics in state legislatures in the 1990s. On behalf of the trustees of the Twentieth Century Fund, I thank him for his contribution to our understanding of this important topic.

Richard C. Leone, President
The Twentieth Century Fund
November 1995

Preface

This book is a by-product of the years I've spent studying legislatures wherever I could find them, teaching legislative politics to students who came my way, and consulting on legislative institutions and processes where I could be of help.

Some time ago, I became concerned about the inability of legislatures and legislators to assure the public that the legislative system had not suffered a moral breakdown. People seemed to believe the worst, having become increasingly distrustful of the individuals they elect, the institutions that represent them, and the entire political system. While legislatures bear some blame for what has befallen them, they certainly do not deserve the contempt in which they are currently held.

Ethics is one of the major dilemmas legislators face today. Try as they may, legislators cannot evade ethical issues. This book is intended to help members of state legislatures mainly but also legislative staff, lobbyists, journalists, and students of politics think about ethical matters in principled as well as practical ways.

I wish to acknowledge the help I have had in this enterprise. As a political scientist who makes house calls (and senate calls, too), I have had the opportunity to observe legislative ethics at close quarters. During recent years, I have delivered training in ethics for the California senate, consulted with the Washington legislature on partisan staff involvement in political campaigns, testified on ethics legislation in Kentucky, New Mexico, and Tennessee, held workshops on ethics for legislators in Vermont and Rhode Island, and chaired a commission on legislative ethics and campaign finance for the New Jersey legislature. All of this work has furnished grist for my legislative ethics mill.

I benefited greatly from fellowships in 1992–93 at the Kennedy School's Institute of Politics and in Harvard's Program in Ethics and the Professions. As an institute fellow, my colleagues were political practitioners; as an ethics fellow, my colleagues were scholars delving into ethics. They contributed mightily to my efforts. Special thanks are due Dennis Thompson and members of the Harvard ethics community, who did as much as they humanly could to get me to reason like an ethicist instead of like a politician. I could not have written this particular book without their stimulation. Thanks are also owed Ann Bailey, Michael Dukakis, Burdett Loomis, Michael Malbin, and Maureen Moakley.

The Twentieth Century Fund furnished encouragement, support, and critical comment, and I made good use of all of it. This project would not have been accomplished without the generosity of the Fund.

The Eagleton Institute of Politics at Rutgers has been my professional home for almost thirty years. It has enabled me to pursue my interests, whether on campus, in Trenton, or in state capitals throughout the country. I hope that I have done my part in carrying out Eagleton's mission of instruction, research, and applied research and public service. I am especially appreciative of the efforts of Chris Lenart, Chickie Charwin, Joanne Pfeiffer, and Sandy Wetzel, who managed to keep me going for such a long time.

Nothing is as important as the sustenance provided by family and friends. My four children, my son- and daughter-in-law, my ex, my old college buddy, and my significant other have been there when I needed them, and when I didn't. Only with John, Kai, Tony, Lisa, Garrison, Lisa, Vinnie, Hex, and Vivian firmly in my corner would I have had the courage to be so presumptuous as to write about ethics.

Drawing the Line

1

Introduction

Never before have American politicians and political institutions been held in as much contempt by the publics they serve. Skepticism, even cynicism, is not a completely new phenomenon in the nation and the states; nor is free-floating distrust of the political system. But the negativism of the American people appears to have reached new heights lately. If it persists, it can do grave damage to a political system that, for all its imperfections, still serves the nation well.

A good part of the problem, certainly as the public perceives it, lies in the ethical failings of the system and of the officeholders and other insiders who benefit from it. Held up for special censure are the legislators and legislatures, particularly the Congress in Washington DC but also the legislatures located in the capitals of the fifty states. Because these bodies are almost universally believed to be corrupt, Americans are losing confidence in legislative institutions that in this period of rapid societal change need public support.

The nation's state legislatures have been at the bedrock of representative democracy for over two hundred years, yet they are beleaguered and besieged today. The media stoke the fires, reformers fan the flames, politicians exploit the issues, the public buys in. Ethics has become a leading item on state legislative agendas, although most legislators wish the furor would die down and the subject of ethics would simply go away. For them, ethics puts the legislature squarely between the proverbial rock and hard place. In political parlance, it is a no-win situation.

Unethical and corrupt behavior by legislators is neither a figment of the media's imagination nor simply a manifestation of the public's uneasiness in turbulent times. It is an unpleasant reality, as is revealed by a number of scandals, both large and small, that have shaken legislatures throughout the nation.

Sins of the Few, Complicity of the Many

The legislatures of California, South Carolina, Tennessee, West Virginia, Arizona, New Mexico, and Kentucky have all been targets of stings, undercover operations that lured legislators and lobbyists into offering and taking bribes and extorting monies.

The first in the contemporary series of stings began in California in 1986 with FBI agents posing as businessmen offering bribes to ensure passage of a bill to benefit a fictitious seafood company. In August 1988 the operation, which became known as "Shrimpgate," became public, as FBI agents invaded the capitol, searching several legislative offices. Thereafter, Democratic senators Joseph Montoya and Paul Carpenter were convicted, and Senator Alan Robbins, also a Democrat, pleaded guilty to racketeering and extortion charges among others. Carpenter's conviction was reversed because of flawed instructions to the jury, and he was retried in 1993 and again convicted. Nearly five years after their offices were searched by the FBI, and not long before the statute of limitations was due to expire, Assemblyman Pat Nolan, a former minority leader, and Senator Frank Hill, both Republicans, were charged with extortion, conspiracy, and money laundering. In addition, Clayton Jackson, one of Sacramento's top power lobbyists, was indicted for racketeering and mail fraud. Nolan pleaded guilty, admitting he had used his leadership post to shake down political contributors. Jackson stood fast but was also convicted. Hill's conviction in June 1994 was the last of Shrimpgate, bringing the total to five sitting or former members, five former staffers, one lobbyist, and two others.

The South Carolina sting, known as "Operation Lost Trust," followed the same lines but with alarmingly widespread involvement on the parts of legislators. FBI agents worked under cover as lobbyists, offering money for votes on a gambling measure they had invented, and seized legislators' records in July 1990. After more than a year of investigation, a federal grand jury indicted twenty-eight people, including seventeen current or former legislators and five lobbyists. Most of them pleaded guilty. Only one legislator who was indicted escaped conviction and was subsequently reelected to the house.

At about the same time that South Carolina was experiencing its sting, Arizona was undergoing "AzScam," courtesy of the Phoenix Police Department and the Maricopa County Attorney's Office. This came in the wake of Governor Evan Mecham's impeachment and removal from office for financial irregularities and the involvement of both the state's U.S. senators in a scandal that involved their intervention in the affairs of a federal administrative agency on behalf of a campaign contributor. Among eighteen people indicted, eight were legislators accused of taking bribes, and seven pleaded guilty and were removed from the legislature.

Just as in Arizona, corruption was not unknown in Kentucky. There had been a string of probes into the administrations of the state's chief executives, Wendell Ford and Julius Carroll. Also investigated was Bill Collins, the husband of former governor Martha Layne Collins. Thus, "Boptrot," the FBI sting that surfaced in 1992 (named for the Business Organization and Profession [BOP] committees of the senate and house and for trotting races of harness horses), did not come as a complete surprise. This sting also focused on a fictitious bill, one that would have allowed thoroughbred tracks to carry simulcasting of thoroughbred races as well as harness races. The idea had been floated before by thoroughbred interests, but this time the FBI was pushing it with one of their operatives posing as a vice president of a harness track seeking to change state law. He paid bribes to legislators when they were at the Jockey's Guild annual meeting in Las Vegas, and the transactions were taped.

On the next to the last day of the legislative session, after the investigation had been going on for eighteen months, about thirty FBI agents went through the capitol and its annex, interviewing legislators and staff members and subpoenaing records. More than 1,000 audio and video tapes had been made surreptitiously, many at the Holiday Inn Capitol Plaza Hotel in Frankfort. They showed lawmakers taking bribes in exchange for their votes. In addition to lobbyist Jay Spurrier, who once worked for Governor Wallace Wilkinson, a top aide to the speaker of the house and three sitting and five former legislators were indicted. Several more former legislators were indicted by the end of 1993. All but one of the indicted legislators pleaded guilty. The biggest catch in Kentucky was Don Blandford, the house speaker. He was charged with accepting $1,500 in bribes and then lying to federal agents. He was further accused of a pattern of racketeering activity involving bribes and illegal payments from his campaign fund to his staff during the 1980s.

Louisiana is a state with a history of political corruption and public tolerance of it. That tolerance, however, may have worn thin as a result of an FBI investigation that was made public in the summer of 1995. According to the investigation, several key legislators took bribes in return for supporting truck-stop video poker interests.

Although the scandals noted above are the most dramatic examples, instances of questionable conduct occur just about everywhere. Legislative life is susceptible to abuse. The stakes for those groups contesting public policy can be high, and legislators have the authority to make decisions of enormous consequence. For the special interests, lawmakers are priority targets for courtship and flattery. On their part, legislators are tempted by the power they exercise and the opportunities that come their way. They are under the gun to raise money for campaigns and feel the pressure to do whatever is required to win reelection. Many are woefully undercompensated, considering the time they devote to public office and the sacrifice they make of outside careers and private lives.

Temptations to deviate from the straight and narrow path weigh upon legislators even more than they do upon most of us. To what extent do legislators succumb? Are those who are caught—indicted and then convicted—exceptions, or are they the rule? Are the minor peccadilloes more prevalent than the major ones? Are state legislatures more corrupt than they used to be?

The State of State Legislatures

The general position of this book is that legislators and legislatures, on the whole, are ethical bodies, considerably less corrupt than in earlier periods.

During the late 1960s, throughout the decade of the 1970s, and into the 1980s, state legislatures made substantial improvements in their operations and procedures. In most respects they became stronger and more effective institutions. If one compares the situation in the mid-1990s to that in the mid-1960s, the differences are striking.

Legislatures today are more representative. They are composed of larger proportions of women and minorities and a smaller proportion of attorneys, who once dominated legislative assemblies.

Legislatures today are more responsible. The federal government has devolved power upon the states, and the states have taken hold of it. Legislatures are on the firing line; they couldn't shirk responsibility, even if they wanted to. They may not solve all the problems that come their way, but they do address them.

Legislatures today are more capable. They have competent staffs and adequate facilities, and they are overloaded with information. They have the capacity to do their job, and they put it to use.

Legislatures today are more independent, particularly of governors and the executive branch. Although only in a few states is the legislature the dominant branch of government, in most it is truly a coequal or almost-equal branch.

Legislatures today are more involved. They are involved in making policy, in determining the budget, and even in overseeing, monitoring, and assessing the operations of government.

Legislatures today are more responsive. (Some observers would say they are too responsive.) They take good care of their constituents and give great heed to groundswells, to breezes, and even to a postcard or two.

Students of legislative politics would agree legislatures are significantly better than their predecessors, the premodern assemblies of the 1940s, 1950s, and 1960s. They may no longer be what they were in the late 1970s and early 1980s, after having just experienced reform and modernization movements. That may have been the high point for the nation's legislatures. There are signs today that the institutional fabric of the legislature is unraveling, as its responsibilities grow and its problems become more severe.[1] Still, legislatures are considerably more effective governmental institutions than they were thirty years ago.

The Reform of Legislative Ethics

I believe (and the large majority of veteran legislators agree with me) that legislatures are more ethical now than they have been in the past. These members, who can compare the present to the past, strongly feel that they do not deserve the criticism they have to endure because of a few rotten apples in the legislative barrel. Even in those places that have been hard hit by scandal, legislators defend one another and the institution in which they serve.

During a January 1993 session of ethics training for the California senate, for example, several members spoke up to affirm that the senate was a much more ethical body than it had been in the past. They were not speaking for the benefit of the media, since that part of the session was being held behind closed doors. One veteran member spoke at length on the integrity of his colleagues, in refutation of press and public images. A former member of the senate contrasted the present with the past. In the old days, he reported, catching legislators taking money "would have been like shooting rabbits with your auto headlights on them." Not anymore.

During task force deliberations on ethics legislation in Kentucky following the FBI sting there, Senator David Karem, who had headed the legislative ethics committee, said that, despite what Kentuckians thought, there was much less corruption in Frankfort than there had been in the past.[2] The reaction of New Mexico's legislators, in the wake of a scandal there, was similar. Those serving on the New Mexico Governmental Ethics Task Force expressed the feeling, at a hearing in August 1992, that most members of the legislature had nothing to apologize for and did not deserve the treatment they were receiving from the media and the public. Senator Les Houston spoke for colleagues when he said he was "in total shock" after having spent years making financial and other sacrifices. He and his fellow legislators were confused, frustrated, and angry at the assaults on their individual and institutional character.

Although it is virtually impossible to measure the actual ethical conduct of a legislative body, we can get an idea of the standards legislatures set for themselves, at least in the enactment of statutes and rules. Ethics laws and ethics codes have been on the agenda of state legislatures for some time now. The latest wave of reform spread through the states in the 1990s, with one out of every three legislatures adopting some significant measure to improve the ethical behavior of members and reassure the public that something was being done. Reform has been advocated by legislators, most of whom truly believe in the need to regulate themselves and their colleagues. It has also been pressed by legislators identifying with reform who sense that the ethics legislation is a good place for them to be politically. But in recent years the principal impetus for more stringent law has been scandal.

When a scandal occurs, the legislature has little recourse but to take action in order to gain redemption. It is under enormous pressure from the press and the public; it must do something; and it responds by doing what it normally does: it legislates. There may be no need for additional law, not at least to address the problems that provoke it; but law is what legislatures know how to make. Take the reaction, for instance, to the stings. Bribery, extortion, and racketeering laws, already on the books, address the corrupt behavior that occurred. Nevertheless, the legislature responded with additional law, because scandal provides the occasion for more intense pressure for ethics reform, mainly from outside the institution.

Especially after a major scandal, most legislators will do whatever

7

they have to do to get off the hook and hope that in time the heat will subside. They have little political choice. Take, for example, recent legislation in Iowa, where ethics regulation was the principal outcome of a conflict-of-interest case involving the senate president. Were it not for this scandal, there would not have been such an ethics package. But Iowa legislators were reluctant, to say the least, to vote against anything portrayed as ethics reform. That was also the situation in Minnesota following the "Phonegate" scandal there. Dozens of legislators protested that a ban on gifts from lobbyists was unnecessary, unworkable, and an admission of guilt. Nonetheless, the legislation won by a 64-0 vote in the senate and a 117-13 vote in the house.

In addition to being requisite politically, the enactment of law is a way in which legislators can hope to restore public confidence in the legislature. In Iowa, the senate ethics committee dropped its investigation of Senate President Joe Welsh because no formal complaint had been filed against him. But after an outcry by the media, Senator Jean Lloyd-Jones, who chaired the panel, reopened the investigation. She explained that although the committee had done the right thing from a legal point of view, "given the climate where everyone suspects legislators, we had to reopen it to restore confidence." Her experience had been a demoralizing one; she had truly been placed in a no-win situation. People, she felt, "don't trust us, so whatever decision we made would have been suspect."[3] Speaker Irv Anderson of Minnesota expressed a similar view when he explained that the ethics law passed in 1994 was intended as a big step toward "restoring public trust" in a beleaguered legislature.[4]

The restoration of public trust is one of the objectives of ethics reform practically everywhere. It certainly was in Kentucky. During hearings of the task force in Frankfort, Tom Loftus, the former speaker of the Wisconsin Assembly, testified: "Do something. It doesn't have to be Wisconsin's law. It's not the details of the law; it's whether you understand that there is a problem and you pass it willingly, hoping it will help, so the people see it as sincere and not a condescending gesture. So they know you get it. Because, now they think you don't get it."[5] The Kentucky legislature took Loftus's advice. It wanted to send a signal to the public. It worked first through a specially created task force on governmental ethics and then through the state government committees of the senate and house, legislative leaders, and majority party caucuses in a special session of the legislature. An ethics package passed both houses by unanimous votes. Kentucky's legislative leaders proclaimed the product a huge success and claimed that their state now had the strongest ethics laws in the nation.

Over the years, the standards of conduct that the public expects of legislators—and, indeed, that most legislators expect of themselves—have risen markedly. Many of them now are codified in statutory law and legislative rules. Ethics laws can make a difference. They tend to alter the cultures in capital cities, generally for the better. Tallahassee, Florida, and Columbia, South Carolina, are examples. The cultures of both of these cities have undergone change since the occurrence of scandals and the enactment of ethics laws that restricted the entertaining of legislators by lobbyists. In Tallahassee, gifts are limited and have to be disclosed. Legislators no longer travel at the expense of lobbyists, and they are less likely to eat and drink as lobbyists' guests. While lobbyists and legislators still socialize together, the freewheeling culture of the 1980s is gone. In Columbia, where a "no-cup-of-coffee" rule is in effect, relationships between lobbyists and legislators are dramatically different from those that existed before the 1990 sting and the passage of new ethics laws. There is much less socializing than formerly, and few members accept invitations of lavish hospitality. Receptions are not off limits, but because of a change in attitudes, fewer of them are held and fewer legislators attend. The transformation of capital cultures because of stings has widened the gulf between lobbyists and lawmakers, so that now in places like California, South Carolina, and Kentucky, they are waltzing at arm's length "instead of dancing cheek-to-cheek."[6]

Laws do curb some of the abuses that previously had taken place. But there is little indication that law, in and of itself, can address the ethical issues facing legislatures. Indeed, if one looks at the experience of the

9

U.S. Congress, there is cause for concern. Two decades of enacting ethics legislation and adopting ethics rules have not solved the ethics problems of Congress. Even with federal campaign finance laws, internal ethics codes, and ethics committees, many issues remain outstanding and others keep developing. As the Hastings Center pointed out, "The legislative ethics reforms of the 1970s have solved some problems, but they have also created new ones."[7] Among other things, they may have directed public attention toward examples of legislative corruption, in part by expanding prohibited activities and introducing far greater complexity into legislative life. Michael Malbin explains how this dynamic works in the case of Congress. New rules almost always bring a much broader range of behavior under official review. The new standards themselves are catalysts for bringing attention to situations that once might have been accepted without question. This attention, in turn, creates pressure for more changes.[8]

Ethics and the Legislative Institution

Law and regulation have certainly had an impact on legislative behavior. Yet they have not turned, or even stemmed, the tide of public opinion that presently is running against legislatures. Legislation may be a necessary response, but it is not a sufficient one to the problems that beset legislatures.

Legislative ethics has to be considered part of the regular business of legislatures. Not just the political dimensions but also the moral dimensions of ethics issues have to be addressed. The health and welfare of the legislature as a political institution demand no less. While legislators may argue that their ethics are a product of what they learned at their mother's knee, in kindergarten, or through life experience, their ethics are shaped to a considerable degree by the cultures in which they operate. This includes the wider cultures of both nation and state and the narrower culture of the legislature itself.

In years past, the legislative culture was the most salient one in defining what was appropriate behavior on the part of members. The institution was insulated from its environment, and informal norms and rules of the game governed legislative life. The culture of the legislature, however, fit in with the culture of its state. The Wisconsin legislature was rather moralistic, and so was the Badger State. The Louisiana legislature let the good times roll, and so did the Pelican State. These legislatures, like all the others, observed their own norms, but such norms were quite compatible with the state culture.

Legislative ethics seldom differed from societal expectations, but societal expectations were diffuse and rarely affected the legislature. Thus, legislative ethics were mainly the legislature's business. For the most part, the legislature defined its own standards for its members. Emphasis was on observance of certain norms such as reciprocity and keeping one's word that usually governed relationships among members. Less concern was given to members' relationships with lobbyists, their linkage to campaign contributions, and their conflicts of interest. A wide range of behavior was permitted and a wide range was indulged in, without strenuous objection from inside or outside the institution.

In the 1960s and 1970s ethics was not a major issue in state legislatures. There was conversation on the subject; legislators regarded a code of conduct as one improvement among others in the reformation of their institutions. But it was not a conversation that engaged the public.

More recently, the wider culture has begun to exert itself, so much so that it has actually become a dominant force in the internal affairs of the legislature. No longer is the legislative institution as insulated as it used to be. Nowadays the boundaries that separate the legislature from its environment are permeable indeed. Practically everything gets in; virtually nothing can be kept out. Legislators have less and less discretion to decide substantive issues on their own. They have less discretion, too, to decide management issues such as salaries, expense allowances, staffs, facilities, and ethics on their own. Legislative ethics has also become a priority item on the public's agenda. The legislature, therefore, is not authorized to control its moral or its institutional life, as was the case previously. Rather, a large measure of actual authority has been wrested from the legislature by outside forces, most notably the media.

Ironically, not long after legislatures, by means of reform and modernization, won their independence from governors, they began to lose it to the press and the public. No longer at arm's length from their environments, legislatures have lost much of their former institutional autonomy. This setting for contemporary legislatures provides the context in which this book has been written. Management of the legislative institution, particularly in the area of ethics, is still the responsibility of legislatures, but it is not their prerogative solely. The press and the public look over their shoulders, second-guess, and pursue whomever they believe to be guilty of transgression.

In part, because they cannot get ahead of the ethics curve, legislatures today are institutions at risk and possibly in decline. The direct impact of institutional decline on public policy outcomes may not be readily discernible, but the present course surely has negative results for the democratic processes by which public policy outcomes are determined.

First, it is not healthy for legislatures to lose the power to manage their own affairs. Legislators should best be able to judge how to organize their work. They, too, should know what activities are appropriate for their continuing education. They ought to be able to operate, according to their own rules, for the benefit of constituents and in behalf of policies they endorse. Finally, they should be able to serve as long as their electorates give them more votes than their opponents or until they voluntarily decide to leave.

Second, it is unfortunate that ethics as an issue has become politicized. Roger Moe, majority leader of the Minnesota senate, refers to the new "politics of ethics." Ethics today is a political issue, says Moe. "Candidates use it in their campaigns to get elected, and the idea that somehow corruption pervades [the institution], despite all our reform efforts, is a powerful one."[9]

Parties and candidates accuse one another of ethical violations, and the accusations are being carried over into the legislative process. All of this is contributing to a breakdown of trust among members and a diminution of civility in legislative bodies. The consequences are dire. On the one hand, governance becomes more difficult. When distracted by ethics controversies and provoked by the assassination of their character, members have a more difficult time developing the consensus required to resolve public policy disputes. Deadlock and gridlock are more likely, therefore, to be the outcomes. Politicization also does the subject of ethics an injustice. As Dennis Thompson writes, "When ethics charges become yet another political weapon, they lose their moral authority."[10] Under such circumstances, ethical conduct is less important than the points that can be scored; ethics is the means, winning is the end.

Third, the climate in which ethics plays a prominent part is having negative effects on people in the legislature and on those who might consider running for office. Although in the past politicians have reconciled themselves to the public view that their species is a corrupt one, there is no guarantee that they can do so today. People in legislative office are finding it more and more difficult to adapt to the contemporary atmosphere.

Take the effects of scandal on the membership of a legislature. On the positive side, scandals have a deterrent effect on some legislators, and they lead to a change in the immediate culture in which the legislature does its business. But scandals can also have harmful effects, at least in the short run. In the case of a sting, the harm is palpable. Legislators become demoralized as a result of the bashing they take from the press and the public. This does not help them do their jobs better. They walk on eggshells, afraid to do anything that might cast suspicion on themselves.

The effects of AzScam illustrate the institutional damage of a major scandal. As the Arizona sting broke, members became preoccupied with the question, "Did I ever say anything that could be misinterpreted?" The immediate feeling was one of fear. Subjects of the investigation were avoided by their colleagues. No one would risk being photographed with anyone else. The tapes that recorded members talking about one another were almost as damaging inside the institution as was the taking of bribes. Legislators said things about one another that were petty and mean-spirited; the reputations of a number of people were hurt as a result. All of this was embarrassing to individuals and destructive to the institution. Moreover, the news story kept running, and the pall did not lift from the capitol. Not only did members feel wearied by the aftermath of the sting, not only were relations chillier between legislators and lobbyists, but the entire fabric of legislative relationships was badly torn.[11] The house minority leader, who had been investigated and then cleared, carried scars from the experience. He stopped socializing with lobbyists, including those with whom he had a friendly relationship; he also decided that he would only meet with lobbyists in his office and then not without someone else present as a witness.[12]

Any legislature that has been stung is a wounded institution, none more so than California's. Aware that members were cooperating with authorities and hearing rumors of colleagues wearing wires to secretly tape conversations, legislators in Sacramento became distrustful of practically everyone. After the indictments and convictions of Senators Montoya, Carpenter, and Robbins, other members did not know who would be saying what to whom. The new style of communication in the capitol was to keep discussions brief and speak in official language. Joking, irony, and legislative humor were out; they could be misinterpreted if a grand jury were to get hold of a transcription of a conversation that had been secretly recorded.

Because of the hostile climate, the chilled atmosphere in which deliberations are more and more likely to take place, and the risk of being blindsided by an ethics issue, some legislators are voluntarily leaving office before they have to. It is my impression that among those departing are some of the ablest legislators, who no longer have the stomach for what they must endure. Those who can tolerate the environment better are people who represent particular interests or groups, who are driven by ideology, or who simply need power no matter what the cost. They are sufficiently motivated to absorb abuse as long as they can pursue their cause. Which type should be encouraged to stay and which to leave? We might be driving the wrong people out of office.

Many people undoubtedly will continue to seek legislative office, whatever the sacrifice. But there are those who might have been attracted to public life but will not be willing to pay the price. For them, the intrusions on their privacy and the assaults on their reputations are too high a cost.

Taking Ethics Seriously

This book is based on the belief that legislatures are vital political institutions and ought to be maintained and improved. They are not only the means by which we as a people deliberate and decide, they are an end in and of themselves. The democratic process itself is more important than any particular outcome, and we cannot afford to neglect it. Legislative ethics is central to the integrity of the legislature as an institution. That integrity is critical if trust in political institutions is to be rekindled and representative democracy is to endure.

The improvement of legislative ethics is no panacea. A number of problems currently besiege American legislative bodies, and they are likely to increase rather than diminish in the years ahead. Attending to matters of ethics may not help legislatures put other issues to rest, but no matter what the reward, ethics issues have to be confronted. The public and legislators themselves deserve no less.

No one would challenge the assertion that elected public officials should conduct themselves ethically. We all think we have a notion of what ethical conduct is and that it only takes common sense and decency to conform to ethical standards. When a person holds public office, which is a public trust, we expect more from him or her than we expect from ourselves, which is as it should be. We prohibit officials from using office improperly; we go further, insisting that they use it properly. On the negative side, this means, among other things, that officeholders ought not to allow their self-interest to affect their public decisions. They should not surrender their independent judgment for money, gifts, favors, and other benefits. On the positive side, ethical conduct calls for honesty, openness, due consideration, fairness, the fulfillment of obligations, and respect for the rights of others.[13]

Legislative ethics pertains to both the behavior of legislators and the integrity of the legislative process as a consequence of individual behavior. Important here are the relationships of legislators with one another, lobbyists, interest groups, campaign contributors, officials of the executive branch, and constituents and the larger public. As an abstract principle, the importance of morality in legislative life is evident. At the extremes, right and wrong are easy to discern. It is the in-between terrain that causes difficulty. It is usually in these gray areas that legislators have to make their choices. These are places where politics and ethics overlap and disagreements about what is right and what is wrong are common. Those in office, in performing their roles, tend to bend ethics somewhat to suit their purposes, arguing that the issues in question are really political and not ethical. Those on the outside, making moral judgments, tend to minimize the political and institutional contexts and see things in black-and-white moral terms.

In view of the incidence of cases of legislative corruption and because of the exploitative nature of media coverage and the negative nature of political campaigns, the public's assessment of its representative institutions seems to be at an all-time low. I believe that the public assessment is way off the mark, but it is having an enormous impact on the legislature as an institution. Legislatures are trying to reinstill public confidence by undertaking changes in the name of reform and by tighter regulation through law of the conduct of their members. The public cannot manage legislatures; the internal organization and procedure of such bodies have to be left to members, who, in turn, are accountable to the public district by district. The imposition of term limits is an instance of public management. Whatever its intentions, such a restriction is likely to have negative results for representative democracy. The media-led assault on so-called perks of office is another instance. It has deterred legislators from providing resources needed for the institution to function effectively, including the budget required for participation in the programs of the national legislative organizations, such as the National Conference of State Legislatures and the Council of State Governments.

My general defense of legislatures does not mean that no change is called for; it does suggest, however, that a number of the changes that enjoy current fashion do not promise to solve the problems they are supposed to be addressing. Rather, they may aggravate them or give rise to still other problems. One has to be careful in choosing reforms for legislative ethics or for other putative disabilities of state legislatures. Requirements for more detailed disclosure of financial interests, restrictions on legislators becoming lobbyists after leaving public office, the abolition of PAC financing of election campaigns are not the right answers. They will accomplish relatively little, while entailing substantial costs.

At the risk of disappointing those who are seeking clear-cut solutions, this account of legislative ethics shows that there is far more to ethical issues than meets the naked eye, particularly the eye of the media. The effects of unethical behavior are not always obvious; often, in fact, they are subtle. The "corruption" of legislators by campaign contributions, gifts, and perquisites fits into the subtle category. Legislators are neither entirely pure nor impure. A few of them are rogues or miscreants; a larger number are oblivious; and the overwhelming majority are well meaning.

This book attempts to put ethics in context, the context being the political system of the legislature. Reformers press forward with proposals for statutory and regulatory change. Such proposals appear unobjectionable. But closer scrutiny reveals some unacknowledged effects and necessary trade-offs. These need to be made manifest. Moreover, changing one element of the legislative system may have unintended effects on others. The point is that before adopting a reform agenda we ought to anticipate likely effects and weigh the trade-offs.

Take conflicts of interest, for example, which inevitably arise in so-called citizen legislatures, where members have to pursue private occupations in order to supplement low legislative salaries and support themselves and their families. Conflicts can be reduced by converting these citizen legislatures from part-time bodies, in which members receive little compensation, to full-time bodies, in which members are adequately compensated and need not earn income outside of legislative office. Congress exemplifies the full-time body. The trend, in fact, has been toward professionalized, full-time legislatures. But even if this trend ameliorates conflicts of interest, other problems arise as a consequence of professionalization. Political careerism is one of them. In examining possible remedies for conflicts, one must take into account the potential costs as well as the potential benefits and choose deliberately on a number of grounds.

Campaign finance is another illustration of the types of dilemmas that exist in the field of legislative ethics. The campaign-finance system has relatively few defenders but numerous critics. For many, money is the principal problem in American politics, and it ought to be eliminated from the field of play entirely. That is much easier to advocate than to accomplish. We want to be able to pay for modern campaigns in a way that reduces the possibilities for corruption. But we also want to achieve this without sacrificing other goals, such as the opportunity for candidates to reach the electorate with their messages and the possibility of challengers defeating incumbents (who, even in today's antigovernmental climate, have advantages that derive from holding office). What about the role of leadership PACs, which centralize fund-raising activities and thereby strengthen legislative parties? Such practices have spread throughout the states, accompanied by additional ethical concerns about the influence of money in legislatures. Are the benefits of stronger legislative parties, one argument for leadership PACs, worth the ethical costs that might be involved?

Interactions between legislators and lobbyists is another area deemed to be in need of reform. The purpose of lobbying is to influence legislators and legislation. The extent, nature, and means of that influence is in question, and the possibility of undue influence being exerted always exists. More law and regulation do not eliminate problems in legislator-lobbyist relationships; they merely change the dimensions. Moreover, in trying to regulate relationships, it is important that the integrity of the communications process not be jeopardized. Here, as with other aspects of legislative ethics, there are no guarantees that well-intended and carefully conceived reforms will not have unintended and deleterious consequences. In tinkering with the system, we have to think proposals through carefully and then maintain a guard against negative effects.

Despite the culpability of the media for their attacks and sniping and the distortion in pictures conveyed to the public, legislatures themselves have to bear responsibility for their situation. Members understandably are preoccupied with a host of problems—constituency, policy, and re-election being among the foremost. They have few personal resources left for the legislature itself, including the matter of legislative ethics. Yet if it is to heed the public's loss of faith in the fundamental trustworthiness of legislatures, the legislative community will have to engage seriously with the subject of ethics. If it does not, the role of the representative assembly will be even more endangered than it currently is.

Legislative leaders must set an example, and both leaders and members will have to accept responsibility for the actions of the collective community. The legislature cannot afford to allow its members to stray far out of ethical line before counseling them and trying to rein them in. Once a scandal occurs, the fallout is widespread; everyone suffers. At the same time, the legislature will have to do a far better job than it has in educating the public about the institution and the process. Right now, people's demands and expectations far outweigh their understanding. It is up to the legislature, as the representative assembly of the people, to take on the challenging job of teaching the public about the workings of a democratic system. This is a long-term endeavor and one that does not come naturally to legislative bodies. Greater familiarity, however, will result in a better understanding of, not contempt for, the legislature.

A critic may think that I am too kind to legislatures and legislators—an apologist for the first branch of government. I admit to empathy as well as understanding, having studied the politics of legislatures for many years and having associated with members of legislatures in many states. My perspective is an institutional one. I believe that the well-being of the legislature as an institution and the legislative process are vitally important to American democracy, and therefore my treatment of ethics takes this into account. This institutional perspective, which stems from my values and my experience, is one that is underrepresented in the public debate. The media and reformers are quick to condemn. Ethicists ordinarily give political factors short shrift. The arguments of legislators themselves are discounted as the pleadings of interested parties.

This book is certainly not an attack on the current practice of legislative ethics, nor is it a defense of it. Legislators, in my judgment, are treated unfairly, but that does not mean that they are as ethical as they should be. They are not. They can do a number of things to improve the ethical climate of state legislatures, and I specify what they should be doing and why they should be doing it. Some of my recommendations will not please practitioners; others will not please the public. The former are quite willing to settle for less than half of the full moral loaf; the latter wants it all.

Much of what is reported here is based upon the work I have done recently with legislatures on matters of ethics. I have conducted ethics training for the California senate, testified on ethics in Kentucky, New Mexico, Rhode Island, Tennessee, and Washington, and consulted on the ethics of legislative staff involvement in political campaigns in New Jersey. I have interviewed a number of legislators, staff members, and lobbyists along the way. As part of my research into public attitudes toward legislative ethics, which are considered in this study, I commissioned a series of focus groups, which were conducted by the Center for Public Interest Polling of the Eagleton Institute of Politics at Rutgers University. Two focus groups were held in each of these states, as follows: New Jersey, 30 March and 1 April 1993; California, 19 April 1993; and Minnesota, 3 May 1993. Also commissioned were several questions, which were administered by the Center for Public Interest Polling to 801 New Jerseyans between 10 and 16 February 1994.

My principal purpose in writing this book is to put ethics on legislative agendas in ways quite different from before. I would like legislators to take ethical considerations into account, be conscious of ethical questions, reason with ethics in mind, and incorporate ethics into their judgments.[14] Legislators, and other members of the capital community (staff, journalists, and representatives of interest groups and lobbyists), constitute the audience I have mainly in mind. If this book does not prove useful to their thinking, it will not have achieved its major goal. The book has another purpose as well. It is intended to provide more grist for the mill of political scientists who study legislative politics and other academicians who are interested in the application of ethics to political and professional life. Some of what is presented describes the ethics-related dilemmas legislatures presently confront. Some explores the scope of legislative ethics and its overlap with democratic politics. Most, however, involves reasoning through practical ethical problems and reaching judgments on proper legislative behavior.

Chapter 2 surveys a range of factors—including the nature of the process, the practices of politics, the press, and public opinion—that account for the ethical quandary in which legislators find themselves. Chapter 3 looks at legislative ethics from a more theoretical perspective, considers lessons from other professions, and concludes by offering as standards *appearance, fairness,* and *responsibility,* which should be used in judging legislative conduct and proposals for ethics reform. The major areas of practical concern to legislatures are taken up in the next three chapters. In chapter 4 I examine conflicts of interest and what can be done to minimize them. In chapter 5 I examine the interactions between legislators and lobbyists, mainly the relationships that develop, entertainment and socializing, and gifts. Chapter 6 probes the area of campaign finance, and what money buys in the legislative process. In chapter 7, I discuss a particular case, as well as other developments, in order to see what is happening to the management of legislative affairs in today's climate. Chapter 8 speaks to the limits of law and regulation and calls upon the community of legislators within a chamber and state to take on major responsibility for the ethical practices of the legislative institution.

2

What's the Beef?

Nearly anywhere one looks, it is possible to see signs of scandal—even in those states like Minnesota and Wisconsin that can boast long traditions of squeaky clean government and politics. It helps, of course, that nowadays practically any issue can be labeled an ethical one and be subjected to the moral judgment of observers. There is cause for the criticism that is leveled at the condition of legislative ethics. But the incidence of corruption uncovered does not fully explain the low assessment in which legislative character currently is held. Additional factors are at work. I discuss a number of them in order to show just why we are where we are and why legislators are being besieged as never before. While legislators are by no means saints, neither are they the sinners they are pictured to be.

Prosecution

More legislators are being caught with their hands in the cookie jar, but it is not because more legislators have an irresistible sweet tooth. There are simply more cookies, and we are doing a more aggressive job nowadays of guarding the cookies or, better still, seizing the hands that we invite to pilfer them. The apprehension and prosecution of public officials has become a big-league undertaking, not only of the federal government but of state and occasionally local governments as well.

The surge in prosecutorial fervor began with Watergate and the federal response to it. In 1976, the Public Integrity Section was formed within the Criminal Division of the Department of Justice. Thereafter, the FBI, the U.S. attorneys, and the Public Integrity Section were all making the investigation of public corruption a priority. The federal government increased its activity, with the nearly one hundred U.S. attorneys throughout the country increasing their staffs (to about three thousand prosecutors) and moving forcefully into areas of public corruption. As a consequence, between the early 1970s and late 1980s, the federal prosecution of public officials grew by a factor of ten.[1]

Not only has policy dictated a prosecutorial assault on suspect public officials, but the incentives for individual prosecutors have pulled strongly in the same direction. For federal, state, and county attorneys, legislators are fair game. For those who have elective or higher office in mind, legislators are big game. Bagging a legislator, and especially a legislative leader, can launch a prosecutor on a successful political career. One New Mexico legislator reported that the question asked again and again in the state attorney general's investigation was "Can you help us get legislators?"[2]

William Weld, the Republican governor of Massachusetts, formerly was a U.S. attorney and assistant attorney general in charge of the Criminal Division. He testified before the judiciary committee of the U.S. House that going after public officials "is where the passion of the federal prosecutors beats strongest."[3] It is also where the rewards, in terms of media exposure and public recognition, loom largest. Even in a state like Massachusetts, where the Democratic establishment has been protective of its own, the state attorney general, L. Scott Harshburger, has been vigorous in investigating fellow Democrats, and certainly more so than his predecessors. Despite the political risks he may incur at the hands of insiders, Harshburger has brought charges against thirty-seven present or former government officials (including two state legislators), seventeen of whom have been found guilty with the other cases still pending.

I am not suggesting that career ambitions propel prosecutors. They are doing their jobs, and, even if they wanted to, they could not afford to go

23

easy on politicians. They have to consider their own survival, and that alone can drive them to probe criminal activity on the parts of public officials. Once a charge is aired in the media, anything less than vigorous prosecution on the part of law enforcement authorities may seem like a cover-up. It is almost impossible for someone in public office to defend himself or herself against such an accusation. It is dangerous, therefore, to pursue an investigation informally or close one down too quickly. Investigations must be done by the book and carried on until there can be no dispute whatsoever that a case is too weak for conviction.

Currently, prosecutors, especially those operating with federal law behind them, have powerful tools available for making a case. They have statutes that give them ample leeway in the definition of corruption. By the end of the 1970s, the Hobbs Act, Mail Fraud Statute, and Racketeer-Influenced and Corrupt Organizations Act (RICO) were being put to use. The Hobbs Act makes it a violation for anyone to obstruct, delay, or affect the commerce "or movement of any article or commodity in commerce, by robbery or extortion." It has been interpreted by the federal courts to prohibit state officials from accepting payments or bribes "in return for the performance or non-performance of . . . official act(s)."[4] RICO, a law aimed at organized crime, relies on the concept of criminal conspiracy and has been used to compel defendants to offer to testify against others. An Arizona legislator involved in AzScam was advised by his attorneys that he might have beaten the criminal charges filed against him, but he could not take a chance on RICO, so he pleaded guilty to several misdemeanors.[5]

Along with the law has come the sting, a formidable weapon in the hands of law enforcement agencies. Although undercover methods had long been used to combat street crime, it was not until the 1970s that they were used against white-collar criminals. The sting was made possible by improved techniques of recording and videotaping transactions between undercover agents and the targets of an investigation.[6] The first big sting was ABSCAM, which employed over one hundred FBI agents, an undercover investigation, and videotaped transactions between bribe-givers and bribe-takers in Congress.

Since then, stings have been used a number of times in the states; for example, by the FBI in California, South Carolina, and Kentucky and by local authorities in Phoenix, Arizona. In each instance, an undercover agent lured susceptible legislators into a scheme involving them taking bribes in return for their support for legislation. Sting operations cast a wide net, with more than a single fish brought in on a haul. The Maricopa County attorney in Arizona, for instance, used an ex-convict as his undercover agent during a sting. Pretending that he wanted to legalize gambling in the state, he offered legislators campaign contributions or cash in return for their help. Everything was recorded on videotape or on tapped telephones. Audio and video technology, with hidden cameras and microphones, reproduces the sounds and pictures of legislators accepting money. All this makes for a very persuasive case when played to a grand jury or on television.

As lobbyists and legislators become implicated in the course of a sting operation, each in turn is given a chance to plea-bargain. In return for their plea and their cooperation, they have a good chance of having their sentences reduced. In a Wisconsin influence-peddling case, for instance, five lobbyists were let off with fines because they fingered legislators. In California, Senator Alan Robbins, who would have faced a long federal prison term, in return for some leniency was reported to have agreed to bring in some live bodies for the government. In so doing, he wore a concealed wire so that he could tape legislators and lobbyists and provide grist for the prosecutorial mill. His work was critical in the conviction of lobbyist Clay Jackson.

The pattern in Kentucky was similar. After being confronted with evidence against them, one after another legislator and lobbyist were persuaded to collaborate with the federal investigation. The FBI wired two people and sent them trolling Frankfort for incriminating conversations.[7] Then, John W. "Jay" Spurrier III, one of the state's most influential lobbyists, was caught giving and taking bribes. The FBI put Spurrier's skills to work during the 1992 session, rigging his private suite in the Capital Plaza Hotel with hidden mikes and video cameras. This ensnared a lobbyist and former legislator, Bill McBee, who pleaded guilty to extortion and bribery and promised to cooperate with authorities and testify against others implicated in Boptrot.[8] Similar deals were made with several defendants. As a result of these tactics, the number of legislators who were indicted grew, and the duration of the inquiry became extended.

If legislators stray from the fold, they may become sitting targets for vigilant prosecutors. And legislators do stray. Some are greedy; some are oblivious; some are simply sleazy; and some are just stupid. The corrupt ones who are caught are few in number, but they give the rest of their colleagues a bad name. The few, however, account for a large part of the public's perception of politicians today.

Politics

The nature of contemporary politics has even more to do with legislative ethics than do prosecutors and their stings. Political factors play only an indirect role, but they are responsible for putting an array of ethics issues on the legislature's agenda, whether the legislature is comfortable having them there or not.

The greater involvement of legislatures and legislators has been mentioned earlier. It leads to more, not fewer, ethical problems. As legislatures take on additional tasks, such as that of intervening with executive bureaucracies on behalf of constituents or exercising oversight over agencies and their administration of programs, the chances of an ethical issue arising increase. Just how far should legislators go in representing individuals and interests in their districts? Just how much pressure should they bring to bear if they think programs are being managed ineffectively?

In the 1960s and 1970s legislators were looking for respect. That is one reason why legislatures professionalized themselves. Now legislatures have power, but they have yet to achieve respect, because the exercise of power increases the stakes, and higher stakes are accompanied by additional ethical challenges. Kentucky illustrates the point. In earlier years, corruption in the Blue Grass State centered in the executive branch because the legislature, dominated by the governor, was too weak to matter. An attempt to purchase a legislator's influence would have been silly. In the mid-1970s, the legislature began to change, culminating in 1979 with the election of Governor John Y. Brown Jr., who had little interest in the legislative process and permitted the legislature to run its own show. Lobbyists then turned to the Kentucky legislature for favors, and some legislators did not have the strength of character to turn them down. In recent years, as the legislature gained in power, corruption became a problem that it had not been earlier.

Myriad interests wage contests in state capitals today. More groups, more lobbyists, and more pressures increase the opportunities for legislators to step over the ethical line. With increased opportunities, there are likely to be increased infractions. In the past twenty-five years the states, following the example of the national government, have seen an explosion of interest-group representation. The formation of one group has led to that of another—sometimes as a reaction, sometimes in opposition, and sometimes simply in emulation. More groups have led to the employment of more lobbyists. An Associated Press survey found that in 1990 there were more than 42,500 registered lobbyists at state capitals, an increase of 20 percent in four years.

These lobbyists, representing a broad spectrum of interests, have a lot at stake in state legislatures. They can gain, lose, or be held harmless by means of legislative action on appropriations, revenue, policy, and regulations. It is up to them to do whatever is in their power—within the limits of the law and political prudence—to defend or advance their cause. This leads to lobbyists' efforts to cultivate legislators in order to forge and solidify relationships and, thereby, gain some advantage in the legislative process. In contesting issues before the legislature, lobbyists and groups also participate in political campaigns, anteing up a large proportion of the money that both fuels and, to some degree at least, contaminates the electoral process.

Campaign contributions have assumed greater importance to legislators because incumbents want very much to maintain themselves in office. The modernization and improvement of legislatures have ushered in professional legislators who spend essentially full time on the job and are ambitious for more elevated positions in the legislature or, better still, more elevated elective office.

Despite the hardships of legislative life and the financial and familial sacrifices they make, many legislators still want to serve in office. A number walk away for one reason or another, but most choose to remain. They enjoy the opportunities they have to achieve some of their public policy goals, to exercise power, and to participate in the exhilarating game of legislative politics. In order to stay, however, they have to raise money for their campaigns. Some campaigns may not appear to an observer to require as much money as is spent. But the more money legislators raise, the more likely they are to discourage serious opposition and, thus, the better their chances of being returned. If seriously challenged, moreover, they must wage an aggressive campaign. Both the funding and conduct of the campaign seldom fail to roil the ethical waters.

The electoral contest for legislative office is not merely among individuals. The competition between the Democratic and Republican parties for marginal seats and control of legislative bodies around the country is intense. The party that has a majority of members in the senate or house enjoys the spoils that derive from control: leadership positions, chairmanships, management of an agenda, and the upper hand in shaping policies and budgets. In highly partisan states, like Illinois and New Jersey, it can honestly be said that although being a member of the majority may not be everything, being a member of the minority is close to nothing.

Partisanship is not a new phenomenon, but it is more vigorous now than it used to be. The partisanship of campaigns has worked its way into the legislative process. Now, campaigns do not end; they go on and on. Moreover, they are waged on the floor of the legislative chambers as well as in the constituencies throughout the state. That is one reason why partisanship within legislatures has been on the rise—not only in places like

Michigan, New Jersey, and California but also in Florida, Texas, and Maryland. Heightened partisanship has led to the exploitation of more and more issues for partisan purposes, including issues related to ethics and, of course, to the character of candidates.

Bayless Manning provides a persuasive account of the dynamic at work when two parties compete. Those out of power try to demonstrate the failures of those in power, while those in try to show the riskiness of choosing the outs. Ethics becomes part of the picture, Manning writes, because "the opposition, and especially the Ins, must be made to be personal scoundrels and dishonest men; that they might be proven to be incompetent or inert is not enough; they must be shown to have been morally delinquent." To demonstrate the perfidy of the Republicans, the Democrats "blow up isolated instances of impropriety so that they appear as illustrations of massive, pervasive hidden corruption." To demonstrate the perfidy of the Democrats, the Republicans do the same.[9] It is not surprising, therefore, that when there is the least semblance of a scandal in a legislature controlled by Democrats or involving Democrats, Republicans will play it up, and vice versa. There are exceptions, but in its desire to hang on to or to win control of the legislature, each party exploits whatever issues it can. And ethics sells well.

Given the competitive nature of politics and the appeal of office, individual candidates and the two political parties do what they have to in order to win. One thing they do is raise money for campaigns. Money does not win elections, but it usually helps. It can purchase some of the increasingly costly elements of campaigns—professional consultants, television and radio advertising, direct mail, and the like. Large accumulations in the hands of a candidate can also give the impression of strength and discourage opponents from throwing their hats into the ring. But money in politics does pose serious ethical questions. Even if it is not the root of all evil, it does arouse the suspicion of many Americans.

It is not only the amount of money that is needed for a campaign in a competitive district (and that is desirable from the candidate's point of view even if a district is less than competitive) but the nature of the campaign itself that is problematic. Campaigns have become increasingly negative and scurrilous, with many of them polluting the electoral atmosphere and encouraging further cynicism on the parts of citizens. The candidate who is trailing in the polls frequently will go negative, or worse, because that is assumed to be the only way to win. The front-runner may take the first step in the negative direction as a preemptive strike. Pretty soon both candidates are smearing one another in their attack ads and targeted mail. The system is inflation-prone. It escalates, because it is difficult for either participant to stop, to recognize a standoff, or to see the deleterious effects on the larger system.[10] And it works, at least for the short-term interests of candidates. The political parties abet the negative process, as do liberal and conservative operatives, who not only want to defeat each other but destroy each other. "When politics is about personalities," writes William Schneider, "there is only one way to discredit a politician. It has to be done personally. Character attacks, negative campaigning and scandals have become the normal mode of politics."[11]

If bashing one another were not enough, candidates are likely also to bash the system and the legislature. Challengers predictably run as outsiders these days; but so do incumbents. Everyone can run against the legislature. "I'm okay, it's the rest of them who are lacking and the system that needs to be overhauled." There is no penalty for unloading on the institution; quite the opposite, institutional trashing is in favor. Whatever the case, only one side is heard during the campaign. There are no defenders of the legislature as an institution—or of its character or ethics. It is hardly surprising, then, that Americans are suspicious, distrustful, and ever ready to believe the worst. That is what both sides tell them—the worst.

Politicians

Part of the explanation for the contemporary ethics crisis lies with politicians themselves. The point was made earlier that legislators are probably more ethical today than they used to be. Nevertheless, the very nature of public office and political power has effects—certainly on some legislators in many places. At the very least, a number of legislators live their political lives in the gray area between landscape we admire and that which repels us. Their world is very different from that of most Americans, and that is one of the reasons they do not look good to the public sitting in judgment.

Legislative life is unlike normal life. The environment is a heady and exciting one in which the egos of members are well nourished by those in their immediate environment. Staffs defer and lobbyists cater to members' whims and their needs. Citizens see legislators as being awash in perks, although in most places the perquisites of office are few and far between. Most often, what perks there are consist of those supplied by lobbyists, and they can have an insidious influence.

Florida and Texas are examples of states where things had gone too far. In Tallahassee and Austin, legislators took the freebies provided by lobbyists not only for granted but to excess. The belief among legislators was that lobbyists were there to pay the bill. Thus, on every possible occasion, legislators would seek out a lobbyist for a free lunch. Florida's legislators had become accustomed to these perquisites of legislative life; they felt entitled to them. Their attitude was "We're here to be served," or, in the words of one legislator, "I like people to kiss my ass." In Texas, as in Florida, the system has been stretched—or abused—by some members who signed the tabs with a lobbyist's name or who entertained on a lobbyist's account. In such environments, it is easy to lose perspective and wind up unable to distinguish between right and wrong.

To be fair to state legislators, many allow themselves to be fed at the hands of lobbyists, because they are so woefully compensated by the states in which they serve. The fact is that only in the larger states—such as New York, California, Michigan, Massachusetts, Illinois, and Pennsylvania (as well as Alaska)—do legislators earn $30,000 a year or more. Given the amount of time they devote to their jobs and the compensation they receive, legislators resent the way they are shortchanged. They are unhappy with the perceived need for further restrictions on themselves, despite their financial sacrifices in the service of the public. In New Mexico, for example, when ethics legislation was being considered by the ethics committee, one member characterized it as "a slap in the face" and another commented, "I would agree some of this would be necessary if we were well paid."[12]

Because of the imbalance in what they officially give and what they officially get, legislators can develop an attitude of "It's owed me." I am convinced that more than a few of them step over the ethical line because they feel justified in taking whatever favors come their way to make up in part for the unfavorable compensation they receive from the state. Their sense of victimization can dull their moral faculties and render them oblivious to even the shadiest of deals. One solution, of course, is to compensate legislators fairly.

Because of the peculiar nature of legislative bodies and the legitimate claims members have, it is not difficult for some to succumb. This is not very different now from what it has been in the past. The temptations are many and can be irresistible. The power, the wealth, and the blandishments of one's colleagues all are tempting. Everything works to soften the new legislator morally. While virtually all legislators can be sure that they will never engage in extortion or solicit a bribe, they cannot be sure that they will resist all temptations. Nor are they exempt from human weakness and the possibility that they will give in.

Beyond entitlement and temptation is the arrogance that at least a few legislators develop over time. Alan Robbins, a former member of the California senate who pleaded guilty to racketeering, bribery, extortion, and tax evasion, described what happened to him and to some others: "When you're in the middle of it, you don't feel that anything you're doing is wrong. You don't feel you have to be subject to any limits."[13]

Because of the intense nature of their work and the fact that they are constantly at risk, a sense of power and entitlement develops among members of a legislative body to which legislators become susceptible. In Kentucky, some were convicted for taking as little as $400. But they were not wheeling and dealing for money; they were doing it to exercise power. The convicted New Mexico legislator was described by a colleague as the type of person who was "always putting together a deal."[14]

One of the legislators involved in AzScam, characterized by a colleague as someone who had never been a major player, was flattered by being approached, and succumbed.[15]

To be in the legislature may encourage a different moral posture on the part of members. This has not changed over the years. If an amoral politician stance affects more than an isolated few, the legislature's collective sense of ethics will suffer. That is surely the time for serious reassessment.

Process

Changes in the political and legislative processes also bear some responsibility for the current ethics crisis. The norms that once served to hold Congress together have waned, reflecting the atrophying of core American values.[16] At both the national and state levels, during recent decades communitarian values have been on the decline while individual values have been on the rise. Political institutions, particularly legislative bodies, are more individualistic than formerly. They are divided into opposing parties, competitive houses, divergent caucuses, different blocs, and various and sundry jurisdictional committees. Legislative leaders, who once exercised some sway over party members, find their position to be much weaker now. The rank and file marches to a different tune, one composed of individual ambitions, current and possibly future constituencies, supportive interest groups, and the media. It is often difficult for legislators to agree on values, including where to draw the line in terms of what is appropriate and inappropriate conduct.

The current openness of legislatures complicates the moral dilemma facing members, because they have to be concerned as never before with how their behavior appears to the press and the public. In contrast to the past, today nearly everything hangs out—clean and dirty laundry alike. Legislators are condemned on those occasions when they meet behind closed doors or away from the capitol in order to negotiate with one another or possibly to engage in discussions with representatives of affected interest groups.

Several years ago, when the Florida legislature was in the process of enacting a major tax on services, legislators found it necessary to work out a final settlement in private. Leaders left their offices in the capitol for the privacy of an apartment some distance away. Once there, they sent out for pizza and made the compromises needed to achieve support for the proposed tax package. As soon as the media discovered the meeting, they referred to it in condemnatory fashion as the secret pizza meeting. The implication was that the public was being sold out. Years thereafter the media were still reminding the citizens of Florida of that allegedly shameless event.

New kinds of ideologically based interest groups have arisen in past years. They turn to the media to tell their side of the story. Their strategy relies less on relationships between lobbyists and legislators and more on grass-roots and media campaigns. Indeed, lobbying in state legislatures is moving in the direction set by groups espousing a cause. It is becoming much more of an outside game and less of an inside one. The result of all this is that "compromise and private agreement have declined as political strategies, while the use of publicity, litigation, and appeals to moral principle have risen."[17]

Even at its best, the legislative process is not a pretty one. It cannot be; it is not supposed to be. A major purpose of the enterprise is to resolve conflict, and there is plenty of conflict to be resolved. With government in the sunshine and media and grass-roots campaigns common, little opportunity exists to disguise what is a messy, disorderly, and sometimes chaotic institution. Nor is there much chance of smoothing over the rough edges of a highly political process and a polity that is divided into many groups with special, distinct, and conflicting interests. People do not appreciate the fact that when the legislature is doing its job, it cannot help looking bad. No doubt, public evaluations of legislatures and legislative ethics would become more positive if not a word were heard from or about legislatures, if legislatures simply never met.

Moreover, the public does not see the results that it wants. Legislatures seem unable to solve problems—traffic, uncontrolled growth, air pollution, crime, health care, welfare, education, and the rest that we have come to expect government to handle. The public, however, does not take into account that people themselves disagree in many cases as to what the solutions are and, in any event, are reluctant to pay higher taxes in order to deal with them.

The Press

If ethics is in disarray, the press bears substantial responsibility. In reporting on state legislatures, journalists and editors play a key role in determining just what issues will be labeled as ethical problems and brought to public attention, how these issues will be framed, how long they will run, and—to a considerable extent—what judgments will be made.

According to one view, members of the press function as agents of the public and help safeguard democracy. They are watchdogs and, as such, contribute to the maintenance of an ethical climate. A former speaker of the Wisconsin assembly maintains that fear of the consequences is the most salient deterrent to unethical behavior on the part of legislators, and fear of the press is paramount in this regard. In his view, "a watchful, picky, even vengeful—but consistent—muckraking newspaper is needed."[18] The public buys into this view, according to a *Times Mirror* survey. It finds the media to have a good influence on how things are going in the country. A large majority, moreover, feels that media criticism keeps politicians honest.[19]

Although most legislators would agree that the press ought to act as a watchdog, they would also say that it has overstepped its bounds and now acts as an attack dog. At any meeting of legislators from across the nation, inevitably one panel or discussion session focuses on the legislature and the media. Such a session offers legislators therapy; they can confront the reporters and editors who are participating. Legislators are frustrated and angry, and when given the opportunity, they vent their feelings. But they cannot prevail in their contest with the state press. Veteran legislators counsel new members on relations with the press: "You can't win with someone who buys paper by the truckload and ink by the barrel." Legislators, who visit editorial boards in attempts to get a fairer shake, get little satisfaction and characterize their discussions as almost a total waste of time. The real question for legislators is how much they lose. A New Hampshire legislator with whom I discussed the matter felt that he and his colleagues were relatively fortunate. "The press accuses us of being jerks, but not thieves," he said.[20]

In a survey conducted by the Josephson Institute of California, there was considerable agreement among the legislators and legislative staff who responded as to how the media had changed: 88 percent saw the media as more aggressive; 84 percent as more intrusive; 89 percent as more negative; 87 percent as more cynical; 64 percent as more prosecutorial; 68 percent as more biased; and 61 percent as more unfair.[21] In another survey, this one of 304 veteran legislators, 64.9 percent said that media influence had increased, while only 9.9 percent said it had decreased.[22]

While people attend to reports of legislative hanky-panky, they also suspect that they are getting a very distorted view from the press. A *Times Mirror* survey found that people were critical of the media for their lack of objectivity, emphasis on bad news, and sensationalism. Only 10 percent believed that the press was very responsible in the way it covered the personal and ethical behavior of politicians, while 56 percent thought it was fairly responsible in its coverage. Almost one third of the people surveyed believed press coverage was not very responsible or not at all responsible.[23]

The scandalous and the sensational drive out the more serious and positive news. In addition to muckraking and investigative reporting, the press corps today is investing heavily in what has been dubbed "gotcha journalism," the effort to catch public officials in seemingly compromising positions. The focus is on uncovering faux pas instead of reporting on what a person does on the job.[24] While the media may not have created the contemporary culture of cynicism, they thrive on it. "The press turns every scandal into another Watergate," writes William Schneider. "The challenge is to bring down the President."[25] A New Mexico legislator, from his bird's-eye view, accused the media of finding "that little bit of dirt" and building it up into "a mountain." According to him, "they make something out of nothing and destroy people's lives" in the process.[26]

The press may have no choice but to travel the route it does, partly because for the press good news is no news. Given the competitive situation today—with newspapers competing with one another and the print media competing with television and radio—the pursuit of dirt seems to be economically obligatory. A New Mexico legislator recalls that at an ethics task force meeting, which he was chairing, he asked a representative of the press how to get the media to be more appreciative of the legislative process. The reply was "Remember, we're a competitive business. We're here to sell papers and news time. Unless we give the public what they demand, we're out of business."[27]

Afternoon talk radio and television programs like *Hard Copy* and *Inside Edition* are now establishing the standard for journalists of all types, pressuring the media to elevate a story to the level of sensationalism or scandal to compete successfully for public attention. Anthony Lewis of the *New York Times* refers to this as the press's version of Gresham's Law—the tendency, in the competition for readers or viewers, to let the scandalous and sensational drive out serious news.[28] Initially, the media may play a story straight, exercising restraint and trying to be responsible. But as soon as one media outlet breaks away from the herd, the others feel compelled to follow. What may at first have been a one- or two-day story quickly becomes a continuing campaign. David Broder, the syndicated columnist, is a stern critic of the media's tendency to sink to the lowest common denominator. Increasingly, he feels, the standards and patterns for the entire media are being dragged down by the shoddiest parts of the community—radio talk shows, television "information" programs, and supermarket tabloids. They lead, and the mainstream press feels compelled to follow.[29]

Even without competition, the journalistic drive is to uncover what is hidden and to seek out the new, the dramatic, the aberrational, and the controversial. Watchdog journalism, which is very much in vogue, has as its purpose exposing flaws. It makes little provision for constructive commentary. Investigative reporting, moreover, is designed to prove a preconceived notion, with sources used to buttress the reporter's case.[30] Journalism is an aggressive and adversarial business, and reporters are distrustful of official explanations and want to bring to the public's attention the deficiencies in its institutions and its leaders.[31] Legislators feel the heat. A survey of 304 veteran legislators around the country revealed that 86.2 percent of them perceived a more confrontational press corps.[32]

As Gunnar Myrdal pointed out years ago with respect to race in American society, it is usually more difficult to discern signs of health than of disease. Similarly, it is seldom easy to find convincing representations of beauty, virtue, and dignity in our culture today. So it is not at all strange that the press gravitates toward the negative, virtually ignoring the positive. Since Woodward and Bernstein made reputations out of Watergate, investigative or watchdog journalism has been the model for statehouse correspondents. The big story—one that nails the legislature and legislators to the wall—is rewarded in the profession with front-page placement, peer recognition, and perhaps even a Pulitzer Prize. With this mode of journalism the rage, reporters have become intrusive, relentless, and judgmental.

In addition to these incentives, which help shape journalistic behavior, the beliefs of many reporters move the statehouse press corps in the same direction. Journalists ordinarily have a reformist bent and a skepticism of the major institutions of society. Vietnam and Watergate added fuel to the fire, so that now skepticism has turned sour. The view that reporters have of politics and politicians is a cynical one, that public officials and our political institutions cannot be trusted.[33]

Reporters believe that power corrupts and that legislators easily become corrupted. Most legislators, in their eyes, represent special interests and not the people, and many are on the take. One *St. Petersburg Times* reporter, in a conversation with me, described a colleague as someone who is "always trying to catch legislators doing things they shouldn't be doing." He himself had little sympathy for legislators. In jest, but nonetheless with a point, he suggested that every legislator in the nation should be put on a boat and sunk in midocean. Would anything be lost?

Another journalist, from Ohio's *Akron Beacon Journal*, called me to see if I had data on the indictment and conviction of legislators in states around the country. I could give him information for a number of states but not all. He indicated to me that the indictment and conviction of legislators just about everywhere but in Ohio proved what he had believed to be the case: Ohio legislators must be corrupt. This was demonstrated to him by the fact that none of them had been indicted or convicted, meaning they had covered up their illegal and immoral actions.

In view of the disposition of journalists and the imperatives of journalism, it is to be expected that the media will whip the legislature if they have any opportunity. And like other interest groups in the states, the press has its demands—and the capacity to express them forcefully. As a reporter for the *St. Paul Pioneer Press* acknowledged, "Sometimes we report, but sometimes we try to set the agenda."[34] One of their agenda items is ethics reform, which they repeatedly demand. In testifying before the New Mexico Governmental Ethics Task Force, a local television producer reflected the opinions of the newsroom when he said that it was about time the legislature came up with standards and accountability after doing nothing for the past ten years.[35] Meanwhile, the *Albuquerque Tribune* was running a series of articles headed "Whose Legislature Is It?"—the inference being that it surely was not the public's. In Iowa, the *Des Moines Register* played a large part in bringing to its readership the scandal involving the senate president, and in Minnesota the *Minneapolis Star-Tribune* was relentless in its pursuit of the telephone records of the legislature so that it could find out and publish data on just who made how many personal calls.

Imbalanced reporting of the legislature is the norm rather than the exception. On occasion the press goes further, abandoning any semblance of objectivity or fairness. The *Lexington Herald-Leader*, from the time the FBI sting became public until after the Kentucky general assembly passed an ethics package during a special session, was merciless in its treatment of the legislature. The newspaper was at the extreme, with an editorial headed: "Frankfort Fantasy—Can Legislators Reform Legislature? Can Pigs Fly?" The editorial went on to criticize the appointment of a task force that would be charged with proposing ethics legislation. Letting Kentucky legislators work on a legislative ethics law, it read, "is like letting Leona Helmsley write the federal tax code."[36] There was nothing subtle here.

The *Herald-Leader* could also be misleading, as is indicated by an editorial in response to the ethics bill passed by the senate. This one was headed "Ethics Gets the Ax." It took the Kentucky senate to task for allowing lobbyists to spend up to $250 a year on an individual legislator. Then it calculated that, since 429 lobbyists had registered at the previous session and since each lobbyist could spend $250 a year on a legislator, a total of $107,250 could be spent on each of 138 legislators.[37] While mathematically a possibility, there is no real chance that every one of 429 lobbyists or even half of them will be providing gifts to any, a few, the majority, or all of the legislators. More likely, there may be 50 to 100 lobbyists who do any entertaining at all and perhaps half that many who do it on anything approaching a regular basis. What, then, is the point of the editorial if not to make people think that much more is afoot than actually is!

Kentucky legislators were not the only ones to be upset by the *Lexington Herald-Leader*'s coverage of the legislature in the period following the FBI sting. Some journalists also felt that the press had gone too far. David V. Haupe, an editor of the *Louisville Courier-Journal*, wrote a column to that effect. He repudiated the media's condemnation of the entire legislature and their allegation that the legislature was owned by special interests. He criticized the media's insistence that the task force proposal be passed intact, even if some of its parts were unworkable. Without mentioning the *Herald-Leader* by name, he assailed what he called "hyper-journalism" as being opposed to the public interest by creating "a constituency for ham-fisted, counter-productive remedies, not for wise reforms." He was regretful of the unfortunate impact of the media's treatment of the Kentucky general assembly: "It is destructive to indulge in unfair, broad-brush criticism of society's basic institutions. Such tactics can turn support for reform into alienation from government, and from the whole process of governance."[38]

Legislators are frightened and demoralized, and the legislature as an institution is reeling under the blows. Legislators do not know where to turn for relief or help. At the annual meeting of the Council of Governmental Ethics Laws, held in September 1993, a journalist asked the legislators in the audience: "As bad as we are, what would you do without us?" "I don't know," replied a legislator from Nebraska, "but I'd like to try." Legislators will not have an opportunity to try to do their work without benefit of the press, so they will remain at the media's not-so-tender mercies. The wear and tear on legislatures that comes from this has become part of the routine of politics. While the public might not be aroused by any single story, the cumulative and longer-term effect is devastating. Ginger Rutland, a former television reporter and now editorial writer for the *Sacramento Bee*, stated, "This constant bashing, this constant negative rundown is because our editors want it, because we are competing for audiences, because we want conflict and we want corruption and we want all of those things we assume go on and are damaging to representative government."[39]

The Public

The scandal in Florida in 1990, involving the undisclosed trips of a number of legislators, led the Leon County Grand Jury to conclude in its presentment that "the abuses of a few have caused a negative light to be cast on all public officials." This is what has been happening not only in Florida but throughout the country. The media have been communicating negative rather than positive messages about legislatures and legislators, because the positive does not qualify as news. In this behavior, editors and journalists would argue, the media are simply giving the public what it wants. A Washington state television reporter put it as follows: "I think the electorate likes to smell blood in the capital. They like to look for that scandal, and when they find the scandal, it validates their search."[40] Whatever the media's negative message, the public has been buying it— wholesale.

People have always been wary of elected politicians. That is not new. But the popular climate seems to be worsening. One indicator is that of "trust in government," which has been measured by the University of

Michigan and the Gallup Poll since 1958. Trust has declined substantially, from 73 percent who felt they could trust the government in Washington to do what is right "always" or "most of the time," to only 19 percent who felt the same way in 1995.

Citizen distrust rests in part on the widespread belief that ordinary people have been shut out. Politics has been taken away from them by a system made up of lobbyists, political action committees, special interests, and the media. This is a central conclusion of the Harwood Group, which conducted a series of focus groups for the Kettering Foundation a few years ago.[41] It is reflected in the discussions of the focus groups we conducted a while later.[42] People are convinced that legislators are driven by special interests, are "on the payroll of somebody or many people," and will push for whatever policy a group that is greasing their palms wants.

People's distrust is also based on the view that politicians are dishonest and unethical. When asked in Gallup Polls to rate the honesty and ethical standards of people in a number of different fields, only 14 percent rated state officeholders as "very high" or "high" (rather than "average," "low," or "very low"). U.S. senators were "very high" or "high" in the judgment of only 18 percent. By contrast, druggists/pharmacists were rated highly by 65 percent. The ratings for public officials, it should be pointed out, have been low since the question was asked in 1981, although they had risen in 1985 and 1990.[43]

Minnesota's legislature has a national reputation of being serious, hard working, progressive, and honest. Scandals have been few and far between, although the so-called Phonegate affair had broken a little while before our two focus groups were held. When participants were asked what percentage of Minnesota legislators were good, honest, and ethical, as opposed to those who were corrupt, the responses ranged widely, from a few who said three quarters were ethical to a few who said three quarters were corrupt and one who thought 10 percent were at each end of the spectrum with the rest in the middle. Whatever the exact proportions, the feeling was that "they're all capable of being tempted." When members of one focus group in Minnesota were asked how they felt about legislators, the responses were short but not sweet: "cynical"; "downright disgust and distrust"; "I don't trust them—any politician, not a single one." Throughout the discussion, the descriptions of state legislators included "power hungry," "out of touch," "interested in personal gain," and "not representing the people."

It is not just that citizens question the ethics and integrity of members of their legislature, they believe that most or many members are, in fact, corrupt. In Utah, which had not been touched by recent scandal, over two thirds of people polled said that they believe legislators take bribes.[44] In New Mexico, before the legislative scandal there, 69 percent of people surveyed said that they thought that corruption was a "very" or "somewhat serious" problem in their state government.[45]

The population of New Jersey is only slightly more sanguine about its legislators than are people in Utah and New Mexico. In a poll conducted by the Center for Public Interest Polling at the Eagleton Institute in February 1994, several years after any scandal involving the legislature, New Jerseyans were asked several questions about the ethics of their legislators.[46] They were asked to grade, from A to F, the ethical behavior of those serving in the legislature. Only 3 percent rated them A, 27 percent B, 44 percent C, and 20 percent D or F, with the rest not responding. That is about a C+ average, not too bad for a legislative body these days.[47] Another question, however, tapped a more negative view. Respondents were asked not whether they thought New Jersey legislators took bribes, but what percentage specifically they thought took bribes. Five percent answered that none took bribes, and 4 percent thought all took bribes. Between these extremes, assessments were scattered. Of those who ventured an estimate, an astounding 36.6 percent thought that *half or more* of the legislators took bribes.

Nowhere is cynicism as high as in California. Participants in the two focus groups there had no doubts that the behavior of legislators was unethical, if not outright illegal. Typical were the opinions that over half of California's legislators act unethically in any given situation; 60 percent or so have empowered themselves in ways that are unethical; one third are intentionally or inadvertently corrupt; and 20 to 30 percent have consciously "gone out to break the law and enrich themselves." Californians feel so burned by the legislature that they are sure that no member will stand thorough scrutiny. In the words of one participant: "If I look through their financials and through all their dealings and saw who was giving them gifts, I guarantee I could find something. Pick one [legislator], it doesn't even matter whose."

Some allowance is made by people for their own legislator. Public opinion polls almost uniformly show that, although citizens view legislatures and legislators negatively as a species, they are more positive toward their own representative. A New Mexico poll, for instance, revealed that while almost two out of three people said they suspected that some legislators engaged in unethical behavior, only one out of five believed that their own representative did so.[48] New Jerseyans in the Eagleton Poll also gave their own legislator something of an edge. When asked how honest they thought members of the legislature were, only 4 percent said "very honest." When asked about the people who represented their district in the legislature, 13 percent thought them "very honest."

Scandals focus attention in a way that little other news of state politics does. The public has scant knowledge of what, other than scandal, is going on at the state level. Some people, as is suggested by the discussion in our focus groups, realize that they are getting only one part of a larger picture. "I guess it focuses a lot of negative attention," said a New Jerseyan. "You don't hear much about the positive." "You've got the good apples and the bad apples," commented a Californian. "We hear a lot about the bad."

Minnesotans, like Californians, New Jerseyans, and citizens of other states, generalize from those few cases of which they are aware. In Minnesota, it is the $90,000 telephone bill. In California and elsewhere, it is the stings, the audio and video tapes, and the convictions. If nothing scandalous or corrupt has happened in a state, people are still likely to have the same impression. They will have learned of scandals elsewhere, thanks to reporting by the national media. The videotapes of Arizona legislators being stung (with one senator stating that she wanted to die rich) and the *Sixty Minutes* television segment on the corruption of the South Carolina legislature serve to reinforce further what people think about politicians.

The news from Washington probably has an even greater impact. Citizens make little distinction between the behavior of congressmen writing overdrafts on their accounts at the U.S. House bank and what goes on in the capitol of their own legislature. The way members of one of the California focus groups saw things, congressmen had a swimming pool, free health care, limousines that drove them to and from the airport, "and it just goes on and on and on." The crossover from Congress to the California legislature is easy to make: "You name it, they have it. I'm sure at the state level it's exactly the same. I mean, I'm positive without knowing anything about it."

On the basis, then, of relatively few politicians and relatively few instances, people carry with them a picture of pervasive corruption. They are firmly convinced that whatever they do know is only the tip of the iceberg. The FBI sting in California, for instance, is just an example of what is going on—one among many more instances. For Californians in our focus groups the sting did not do more than merely scratch the surface. The popular attitude is that "if you haven't been indicted, it just means you haven't been caught yet."

Ethics has not only helped erode citizen trust and confidence, it has also led to a severe sanction being imposed on legislatures and legislators. The term limits movement, the goal of which is to restrict the terms of legislators to six, eight, or twelve years, has been sweeping the nation in recent years. In 1990, electorates of California, Colorado, and Oklahoma adopted in referendum term limits for their legislatures, and two years later twelve other states followed suit. Now term limits are in effect in twenty-one states, having been adopted by popular initiative in all but two of them (in one of the two, the legislature passed the measure under the pressure of an initiative). There can be little doubt that the public's perceptions of legislative ethics have helped fuel the term limits fire.

One other reason for discontent relates to public expectations of proper behavior by politicians. We no longer tolerate behavior that in the past would have gone unnoticed. It is not that there has been a moral decline among political elites but rather that there has been a higher attention level and elevated standards on the part of the populace.[49] Our appetites for scandal have grown, and our ethical sensitivities have become sharper. There was a time when public officials could stumble, could make a mistake. People considered them to be "only human." Now they are considered corrupt—damned for all time, without the possibility of atonement, redemption, or forgiveness.[50]

When we expect impeccable moral behavior, we set ourselves up for great disappointment. Nowadays we have it both ways: we demand the most ethical conduct while we expect the most unethical conduct. If by chance we are unable to uncover moral deficiency by standards accepted at the moment, then we can ratchet up the standards so that we will find moral deficiency somehow. Thanks to the media, the public can be educated to be horrified by the new sins just as they were horrified by the old ones.[51] Morality, thus, is in a state of continuous escalation. We now make large scandals out of what were once considered to be garden-variety misdeeds.[52] No wonder legislators feel unfairly judged by the public. They feel they are being judged by standards that are beyond their control and always rising.

If all this were not sufficient to poison the political atmosphere, it must be noted that Americans today are not confident of what the future holds. We have been taught by our political leaders to expect more from the government and the economy than they have been able to produce. Rising expectations and increasing unmet demands result in unhappiness and fear. Neither the economy nor the legislature has been able to deliver the goods.

At a 1993 hearing of the Joint Committee on the Organization of Congress, Representative James Hansen of Utah testified that in the history of the West, when people were upset they would take someone outside and just hang him. That succeeded in calming folks down.[53] It is not very different from what we are doing to politicians today. The rule, as far as their ethical behavior is concerned, is that they are guilty until proven innocent. And we have neither the time nor the disposition to try to reverse this verdict. Let their guilt stand.

3

The Quest for Standards

Not surprisingly, the reaction of the men and women in legislative office to public hostility is a pragmatic one. They try to do whatever they have to do in order to quiet the media and pacify the electorate. This certainly accounts for the frenzy of legislative activity after a scandal and for the curtailment of life-styles that loom as targets for media criticism. Having adopted reforms, legislators want to move on to other matters. They fail to appreciate that, whatever rules and regulations they enact, they are still left with considerable leeway as far as their behavior is concerned. How can they decide what they ought to do, from an ethical as well as a political standpoint? Legislators need some guidelines, some general standards—other than political prudence—that will help them navigate the reefs and shoals of legislative life today.

The Scope of Legislative Ethics
The typical attitude of legislators is, "The test of my moral worth is reelection." This is what makes the practice of democratic politics unique. Legislators are first and foremost representatives of their districts, which may range in size from fewer than ten thousand to three quarters of a million people. They are responsible to their constituents, and especially to those who elect them. They depend upon their constituents for support and for survival. As representatives, they act for their constituents and

thus have obligations that many of us do not have. In addition, they are members of legislative bodies that range in size from forty to four hundred members for houses and twenty to sixty-seven for senates. Their effectiveness as representatives, and just how much they can do on behalf of their constituents, depends in large part on the cooperation of their colleagues. Legislators are interdependent, obligated to one another for assistance and, ultimately, votes. In addition, they have particular obligations to legislative party leaders, to the governor (particularly if he or she is one of their partisan own), to the overall needs of the state, now and in the future, and to the well-being of the legislature as an institution.

One can appreciate, therefore, that legislative ethics and legislative politics fuse and overlap, and the varying strands are by no means easy to disentangle. As Amy Gutmann and Dennis Thompson write, since the principles of legislative ethics are not the same as those that follow directly from ordinary ethics, "the requirements of the role of a legislator distinguish the content of legislative morality from that of ordinary morality."[1]

The question is where politics ends and ethics begins. Is there an area of pure politics and one of pure ethics, as well as the extensive in-between territory in which the two cohabit? Legislative ethics is inextricably intertwined with legislative politics. Many would accord greater weight to democratic politics and conceive of ethics in a limited way. Especially for those who buy into ethical relativism, ethical questions dissolve into political questions that have to be relegated either to personal conscience or to constituent considerations.[2] For these people and other so-called moral minimalists, the legislature is properly a political enterprise, where ethics are outweighed by members' connections to constituents and members' relationships with each other. Legislators are conceived of as acting *for* others and *with* others and not as free moral agents. Minimalist ethics would allow pluralist politics the greatest leeway, proscribing only a small area of conduct, that of outright dishonesty. The best that can be hoped for is to try to keep each legislator honest, in accord with the Latin axiom "Primum non nocere" [First, do no harm]. The language of moral obligation, articulated by ethicists, does not fit the minimalists' conception of competitive, adversarial, democratic politics.[3] Moral minimalists, it should be noted, are not restricted to politics. They exist in law, where they argue that the "legal" perspective is objective and integral to the lawyer's professional role, whereas the "moral" alternative is subjective and peripheral.[4]

Naturally, the leading minimalists are legislators themselves. Their view is from the trenches, where obligations are multiple, pressures intense, and risks perpetual. Some would even maintain that to expect a legislator to be ethical in any philosophical sense of the word, given the competitive nature of political life, is foolish. If you behave "ethically," you lose out. You cannot count on others being ethical; if they aren't, you will be at a great disadvantage. This is certainly the rationale of negative campaigning. The majority leader of the California senate was asked by the U.S. attorney why legislators happened to have fundraisers just before critical votes. His answer was, "If you don't do it and your opponent does, you won't be around very long." Every legislator is impelled to compete by whatever means, although legislators rarely admit this. Like all of us, legislators want to do the right thing, but not at the risk of jeopardizing their political careers and the pursuit of other values they hold dear. They have to trade off and, thus, they constantly face the dilemma of doing what helps them stay in office as opposed to doing what they hold office in order to be able to do.[5]

In some instances, unethical behavior may not harm anyone and may, indeed, do political good. Then, what difference does it make? In other instances, behavior may be unethical, but everyone is doing it and benefiting from it; why shouldn't I? In any event, to weigh ethical factors in every conceivable instance could be debilitating. According to this line of thought, legislators have to juggle many balls in the air, move quickly, and make hundreds of key decisions. It is much easier, and more efficient, for individual legislators to operate without worrying about ethics, particularly where no operating rules apply. If legislators become immersed in moral concerns, the danger of paralysis looms. The legislature will not get its business done; it will not satisfy its constituencies; and it will not be deemed effective. Ethics is a long and uncongenial route, while politics is a much shorter and more familiar one—and more to the point as well.

Practitioners have a firm basis in asserting that democratic politics—with periodic elections, majority rule and minority rights, and a deliberative law-making process—provides strong roots for our ethical system. In my opinion, these conditions are necessary but still not sufficient. Today citizens insist on more, much more. No longer satisfied with results, they want to know about the peculiarities of the people and the particularities of the process. As much as some people may regret the current climate, it is one with which those in public life must reckon.

Although popular pressures constitute the fundamental impetus for ethics reform, other reasons also require that these issues be addressed. If we do not agree on ethical norms or rules, those legislators who behave morally may lose out to those who do not. Such outcomes would be unfortunate. Moreover, many issues that are primarily political in nature do have moral components. These ought to be faced, no matter how difficult it is to distinguish the moral from the political. When legislators take ethics seriously—and not only for the obvious political reasons—they will behave differently than they do today. Admittedly, their conduct will be constrained and they may not enjoy life as much as their predecessors did, but even with ethics in the back of their minds they will still be able to perform essentially political roles.

Legislators first must recognize that "common morality" and "political prudence" are two different things. Second, they also must appreciate that some of their decisions raise questions not only of politics but also of ethics, and they must take the latter into account. Third, they must acknowledge the broad scope of ethical considerations and recognize that although the area cannot be fully delimited by law, it must be acknowledged nevertheless.

The law, of course, is the starting point. It puts a range of behavior beyond the pale. Laws proscribing bribery, extortion, the theft of public funds, electoral fraud, and other types of transgressions are on the books everywhere. Violations of legal rules are not only matters of ethics; they are matters primarily of criminality or corruption. They are enforced by compulsion of the state through fines and imprisonment.

One advantage of law over other ethical prescription is that of specificity. Compared to many ethical rules or guidelines, the line separating the illegal from the legal is clear. Yet, it is not always as clear as we might think. For example, Daniel H. Lowenstein, in an analysis of bribery, compellingly demonstrates that the law is neither precise, consistent, nor clean cut. Legally, the elements of bribery generally require that a public official must be involved; the person offering the bribe must have a corrupt intent; a benefit—anything of value—must accrue to the public official; a relationship must exist between the thing of value and some official act; and the relationship must involve an intent to influence the public official in the carrying out of the official act. Each of these conditions is difficult to discern and even more difficult to prove.[6]

Despite the lack of certainty in the law as elsewhere, many politicians fall back on legality as the single standard for behavior. If it's legal, it's ethical; if it's permissible, it's proper. This approach assumes that anything not prohibited by law is condoned, leaving broad scope for politics to operate as the regulating mechanism.[7] Whatever the practicalities of the matter, few of us really believe that law and ethics are coterminous. Instead, we acknowledge that ethical behavior, however difficult to nail down, is not all that which is legal and not illegal. Legal structures are not designed to anticipate every possible human foible or temptation; that is where matters of ethics come into play. In its 1989 report, the Commission on Federal Ethics Law Reform maintained that "laws and rules can never be fully descriptive of what an ethical person should do. . . . Ethical government means much more than laws." Ethical government is "a spirit, an inbred code of conduct, an ethos."[8] The law establishes certain standards of conduct, perhaps minimal ones; ethics goes beyond that.

How far beyond is an issue on which ethicists and practitioners disagree. The Hastings Center, for example, is of the "maximalist" school:

its definition of ethics is so broad that it applies to the entire range of legislative actions and decisions. Hastings argues in support of its position that first, ethics focuses on questions of right and wrong, good and evil, benefit and harm; second, such questions arise whenever an individual or group exercises power over others; third, in legislative life, the exercise of power is ubiquitous; and fourth, ethical issues are unavoidable.[9] Daniel Callahan, the director of the Hastings Center, criticizes legislative ethics codes for being "narrow in scope and short on aspirational statements" and for failing "to deal with the full range of legislative and representative functions."[10] The problem, however, is that the broader the scope, the more ethical obligations will conflict with democratic politics, and when they do the former will probably lose out.

The questioning of Callahan by Senator Howell Heflin of Alabama during hearings before the U.S. Senate Select Committee on Ethics in 1981 is most instructive along these lines. Heflin is concerned both with the specificity and the vagueness of an ethics code proposed by ethicists at Hastings. The code calls for senators to promote the national interest, and Heflin inquires as to who will determine whether a senator's action is in the national interest. According to his view, Hastings had gotten into an area of democratic politics that had evolved historically: "I have real questions about your concept and your approach in these areas in the context of a legislative elected body," he said. Another academic witness came to the defense of the proposed code on the grounds that it attempted to set out ideals. The provisions were not enforceable, he added, nor were they intended to be. What concerned Heflin, however, was that such a code would just provide negative fodder to political opponents and to the media. Furthermore, because it got into areas that were essentially legislative in nature, senators would be inclined to seek even more rulings than presently from the ethics committee in order to obtain protection against a charge that they had violated a rule. The Hastings code, in the senator's opinion, would have a chilling effect on the legislative function.[11]

From Heflin's perspective, one of the difficulties with standards of broad scope is that they normally include affirmative as well as negative obligations. Legislators are not comfortable with the codification of either obligation, but they are more willing to deal with prohibitions on gifts, honoraria, conflicts of interest, campaign funds, and the like. They are particularly fearful of having open-ended duties imposed on them. Ethicists have suggested, for example, as positive obligations that legislators respect democratic processes; serve the public interest; and treat individuals with whom they deal with respect, honesty, and fairness.[12] Are such obligations workable? Can they be imposed on legislators? Can the ends legislators ought to serve be reduced to ethical rules? Is it worth trying to do so?

The proper balance between specificity and generality and between codification and informality in rules remains in dispute. A rule should be general enough to direct legislative behavior to a higher ethical level, but it should not be so vague as to present legislators confronting allegations of misconduct with procedural due process problems.[13] The tension cannot be avoided. Congress, for example, has been reluctant to establish formal rules of conduct for its members, and this has led to situations such as the case of the Keating Five. The Senate Select Committee on Ethics found that the senators involved did not violate federal laws or Senate rules but that their behavior violated general standards of propriety for the institution. Senator Heflin, the committee's chairman, said that the decision was based largely on the totality of circumstances instead of any single one. "Not all standards offer the opportunity to arrive at easy judgments through the mechanical application of a fixed formula," he explained. Alan Cranston's contention, however, was that he was being reprimanded for violating standards that never existed,[14] or at least were never spelled out. It may be the case, then, that broad and aspirational standards of conduct can introduce an ex post facto quality to legislative deliberations on the appropriateness of conduct.[15]

To what extent, then, should a legislative body codify what it expects of its members, and to what extent can society rely on informal standards to regulate conduct? The question has not yet been satisfactorily answered, but it is central to the discussion throughout this book.

Lessons from the Professions

The professions have also had to confront ethical issues. The way in which they have handled them may be instructive for legislators. The more the role of the legislator resembles that of the professional, the more relevant the instruction. But even if legislators are not professionals in the same sense that attorneys and physicians are, it should be possible to cast light on the ethical problems legislators face by looking at the professions. To compare legislators, we must establish the distinguishing characteristics of the professions and see how they fit the vocation of legislator.

First, professions are characterized by a body of abstract knowledge and prolonged training before entry. Professional schools draw on a large literature and provide two, three, four, or more years of specialized education. Legislators, however, have no such body of knowledge available, and nobody trains for office. The nearest thing to training grounds are the public policy schools, which grant professional degrees; but they hardly prepare people for elective office. Anyone can, and does, run for the legislature or any other public position without prior training.

Second, professions are characterized by self-regulation and considerable freedom from lay control. In law and medicine, self-regulation is not as unquestioned as it was formerly. The professions now have to negotiate their rights and obligations with the larger society. Lawyers are subject to sanctions, such as liability suits, institutional controls, and administrative regulations, and physicians are highly regulated by state agencies.[16] Nevertheless, by comparison with legislators, the professions still exercise significant self-determination. They themselves decide what credentials and training are necessary for admission to practice. The qualifications for legislators are few and are set down in constitutions, not determined on an ongoing basis by the legislature. Legislators have little to say about who enters their calling (although legislative leaders may play a role in the recruitment of candidates to run for legislative office). Legislators, furthermore, are subject constantly to control by their clients, having to stand for election periodically, respond to the demands of numerous interest groups, and fret over treatment by the media. Indeed, there are few people as dependent upon clients and kibitzers and regulation from the outside as are elected public officials.

Third, professions are characterized by a set of obligations. Most important in the case of law and medicine is the duty to client and patient—to the client's legal rights and to the patient's health. The professional is expected to serve patients and clients zealously. Recently, the public, as well as the private, duties of professionals have been noted, with an emerging sense that professions have obligations to society. Nonetheless, the fiduciary relationship of professional to client, in which the former works to serve the ends of the latter, is far stronger than any duty of the professional to the public at large.

Legislators are in a very different position, as has been discussed above. They have a strong obligation to serve the public and promote the public interest. They also have a strong obligation, perhaps an even stronger one, to their immediate clientele—their constituents. Unlike lawyers, however, legislators do not choose their clients (except, perhaps, in the sense of settling in one district rather than another). They have to represent the individuals, the groups, and the interests that reside in their constituencies. Another difference separates professionals and legislators, as far as clients are concerned. In the case of lawyer and doctor, for the most part, clients are individuals. Doctors serve to maintain or restore the health of specific patients; lawyers serve as "zealous advocates" for specific clients. Legislators, by contrast, represent many individuals on the same issues rather than single individuals on different issues. Moreover, many of a legislator's constituents have opposing interests—prochoice versus antiabortion, or the right to bear arms versus gun control.[17] It is not possible for a legislator to satisfy everyone, or nearly everyone, while it is possible for most physicians and attorneys to do so.

Members of professions have obligations to colleagues as well as to clients. Physicians on a hospital staff cannot operate independently of one another nor can attorneys who are collaborating in a law firm, especially if they are working on the same case. Other doctors and lawyers are more loosely linked. But few professionals are as interdependent as legislators.

No legislator can pass a bill or accomplish much at all without the support, or at least the acquiescence, of colleagues in his or her own house and members of the other chamber.

Fourth, each of the professions depends in part on trust, and especially the layperson's trust in the competence and concern of the professional. In medicine, physicians assert that both the body politic and their patients can trust them on the grounds that altruism and an ethical code protect against any abuse of professional authority. In law, the ethic of lawyer-client trust is claimed to be "the cornerstone of the adversary system."[18] In fiduciary relationships, where professionals use their expertise to work for clients' ends, relationships have to rest on trust, because the professional is using his or her position and skills to serve the client's interests, "possibly contrary to the client's wishes or desires and possibly beyond the client's ability to understand the procedures the professional recommends."[19] The basis of trust is becoming weaker in the professions, with people resisting paternalism, insisting on participation in the determination of their own fates, and questioning their doctor's and lawyer's authority. But the degree of trust between professionals and patients or clients is still stronger than that between legislators and constituents.

Fifth, members of a profession are autonomous, or relatively so. They are governed by professional norms and rules and by the wishes of the marketplace. Their colleagues can—but only infrequently do—sanction them. Their clients can—but not often do—leave them. Legislators are less autonomous. They are dependent upon their colleagues, and particularly those in leadership positions, for their positions within the legislative-influence structure and for their accomplishments. They are dependent also on their constituents, who, while reelecting most incumbents, manage to defeat some and throw scares into a number of the rest. It can hardly be said that professionals live in fear of their clients; yet it can be said that legislators do so. They feel unsafe, whatever their electoral margins in previous races.

Legislators, then, differ significantly from other professionals as far as their practice is concerned. But what about similarities and differences in the area of ethics? Each profession has its own set of differentiated roles, along with its own peculiar ethical principles. These principles are embodied, in good part, in the profession's code of ethics.

Codes of Ethics

Virtually every professional group has a code of ethics, the purpose of which is to provide guidance to members relative to actions that might arouse public suspicions of violations of trust, impairment of independence of judgment, and favoritism. Because these codes are general, they cannot be expected to cover every possible case. But agreement on general principles does constitute a beginning. Marked differences characterize the efforts of the various professions. The American Bar Association (ABA) has a relatively detailed set of ethical rules. It sets out in great specificity the standards of behavior and thus can be used for the purpose of disciplining members. By contrast, the code of the American Medical Association (AMA), titled Principles of Medical Ethics, consists of seven short and general propositions, each of which is aspirational in character.[20]

How different are legislative codes, and how different should they be? The development of legislative ethics codes has not been voluntary but rather forced on legislative bodies by outside pressures and inside reformers. Take Congress, for example. Congress was content to go without formal ethics guidelines until the late 1950s, when it reacted to the scandals surrounding President Eisenhower's chief of staff, Sherman Adams. In the 1960s, the Senate established its Select Committee on Standards and Conduct and articulated new rules governing the acceptance of campaign contributions. Meanwhile, the House adopted rules to help prevent conflicts of interest and established its own Committee on Standards of Official Conduct, adopting a code of conduct. In 1977, the House and Senate passed new and more stringent codes of ethics as a condition for a salary increase for members of Congress. These codes limited the outside earned income of members, abolished office accounts, and required full disclosure of income, financial holdings, debts, securities, and gifts. The Senate code also prohibited former senators from lobbying in the Senate for one year after leaving office. In 1978, Congress passed the Ethics in Government Act to enforce the new code and to accomplish additional purposes.[21]

In the late 1960s, state legislatures began to address ethics issues. In part, this momentum was a product of the nationwide legislative reform movement, which gained steam after the reapportionment revolution and subsided about fifteen years later. During the 1970s, for instance, thirty states adopted new ethics regulations of one type or another, with codes becoming increasingly popular.

No state has done as much in this field as has California. The state legislature enacted a code of ethics as early as 1966, subject to the adoption by the electorate of a constitutional amendment that provided for a full-time legislature. Then, California embarked on ethics law in a big way with the Political Reform Act (PRA) of 1974. This act was passed by an initiative that received 70 percent of the vote, largely because of the loss of citizen confidence in government institutions as a result of Watergate. Among other things, the PRA created the Fair Political Practices Commission (FPPC) to develop rules and oversee the new system. In 1990, stung by the FBI sting, Senate President Pro Tem David Roberti sponsored Proposition 112, which restricted gifts, prohibited honoraria, required ethics training, and further regulated conflicts of interest by legislators. The initiative passed, bringing about what could be considered the most far-reaching ethics reform of any state in the nation.

Most of the ethics codes that have been adopted focus narrowly on conflicts of interest, disclosure of income, and use of legislative privileges. Many maintain an "appearance of impropriety" standard. Some cast a broader net as far as principles of an aspirational type are concerned.

The California Senate Standards of Conduct offers an example of a well-constructed code that aspires high. It is worth reviewing in some detail. The first standard requires legislators to "exercise independent judgment on behalf of the public," rather than for personal gain or private benefit. Legislators should not accept anything that would interfere with their judgment. Nor should they accept outside employment that is inconsistent with the conscientious performance of their duties. Nor, of course, should they use their office for material or financial gain or private benefit. Here, we have a set of positive obligations, specified by prohibitions, but at a general exhortative level.

The second standard obligates legislators to provide "energetic and diligent representation." This is as aspirational as a standard can get. In their representational capacities, legislators are enjoined to be "informed and prepared," recognizing all sides of an issue. When intervening on behalf of constituents, legislators are instructed to ensure that decisions are made "on their merits" and "in a fair and equitable manner." According to this standard, legislators should be accessible to all constituents, "making a special effort to attend to the concerns of those who might not otherwise be heard." Finally, they are told to "fairly characterize issues" and "accurately inform" the public regarding their conduct in office. This certainly aims high.

The third standard obliges legislators to be informed about and abide by senate rules. This entails performing with courtesy, using the confirmation power with regard for the general welfare of the people of the state, and conducting legislative oversight with due respect for the independence of the agency under scrutiny. The fourth standard, similarly aspirational in nature, provides that legislators should enhance "reasoned and visible decision making" by the senate. The fifth calls for the fair treatment of staff; the sixth, the proper use of public funds; and the ninth, that legislators conduct themselves in a manner that does not discredit the senate.[22]

In California, many prohibitions on behavior are included in state law, so that the senate ethics code can lay out positive norms for members to follow. Whether written to appease the public or to guide members, or because it is the product of informed and creative staff, this code, which was influenced by the work of the Hastings Center, adheres to the prescriptions advanced by ethicists. The California senate covers all the bases, but so do other legislatures, even less professionalized ones. They, too, have absorbed the contemporary language and rationale of ethics.

New Hampshire illustrates the case of a legislature at the other end of the continuum from California. It is a citizen legislature, not a professional one. It has little staff, minimal resources, and as many as four hundred members in its house. In a ten-page booklet, the New Hampshire legislature sets forth its Ethics Guidelines and Procedures (dated July 1992). It begins with a section on "Principles of Public Service"—public office as a public trust, objective judgment, and accountability. The first principle commands that legislators use their office to advance public interests, not their own. The second specifies that legislators use objective judgment, deciding all matters on the merits "free from conflicts of interest" and "improper influences." The third calls upon legislators to assure that government is conducted "openly, equitably, and honorably" in a manner that permits citizens to make informed judgments and hold government officials accountable. New Hampshire's three principles are roughly equivalent to the first two standards of the California senate. The guidelines then go on to note the financial disclosure requirement for legislators and specify prohibited activities and the conflict of interest procedure. New Hampshire manages to be aspirational and disciplinary at the same time.

Codes range from those with general, broad, and aspirational ethical standards to those with narrow, legalistic regulations of conduct. Each extreme poses difficulties, but the language of aspiration versus that of prohibition is not what matters most. What is of great importance is the attentiveness of individual members and the legislative community to the rules that they adopt.

Standards for Judgment

Peter Brown delineates three categories of circumstance that result in moral dilemmas for public officials. First is simple moral disregard, where officials ignore doing what they know is right. Second is ambiguity, where there is an issue as to whether moral rules apply to the act under consideration. Third, the most difficult dilemma of all, is where the rules of morality that govern a particular action come into conflict.[23] Although dilemmas of the first and third categories do arise in legislative life, many issues that achieve ethical status are ambiguous in nature. In so many cases, black or white answers are lacking, and the right course of action is not clear. Indeed, ethical issues become ethical issues only when someone—usually the media or reform groups such as Common Cause or an opponent in a campaign—label them as such. Otherwise, different people have differing judgments as to whether or not an issue has much of an ethical component and just how significant that component is. An issue perceived by one legislator to have a weighty ethical component may, in fact, be seen by another as being without any serious ethical content at all.[24]

Policy decisions ordinarily do not raise ethical dilemmas, not in legislators' minds. Legislators are so well grounded in the practices of representation and so well equipped in the uses of policy justification that they have little room for an entirely different set of considerations. Furthermore, rarely do legislators have to decide between a policy that is just and one that is unjust. Nearly all the policies on which they act are subject to reasonable differences of opinion.[25] On some policies, such as abortion and euthanasia, moral considerations count heavily, and legislators cannot ignore them. A number decide mainly on moral grounds and hold fast to their positions. Some who have weakly grounded views bend with the political breezes, citing their representational role.

But for the most part, the ethical issues to which legislators are compelled to pay heed are more routine, mundane. These are not matters of conscience but usually questionable calls. They involve the relationships that legislators have with other people, the commitments they make, the favors they do, their life-styles, their efforts to make a living while serving, and their strong desire to hold on to their office until they themselves decide to leave for greener pastures.

Each case of conduct and each proposed change in statute or rule will be decided on the particular merits and immediate circumstances. In the case of behavior, legislators implicitly take moral considerations into account, but rarely do they reason morally. They have neither the time nor the inclination. They operate by instinct and habit. In more and more instances, they may check with legal counsel. They are concerned with how things will play politically. Rarely do they ask themselves what is right or wrong; they assume that they know instinctively. In the case of proposed changes, so-called reforms, legislators operate politically to arrive at some settlement. Usually, however, they do not get much beyond strategic and tactical considerations. Who is applying pressure? What are the advantages and disadvantages of acting? Of not acting? How can we appease the media and the public at the least possible cost to ourselves? Rarely do legislators ask themselves whether the proposal makes the best ethical sense.

Because judgments and decisions are ad hoc, the ethical perspective of legislators is either absent or lost. It would be of benefit to legislators and to the legislature if legislators were to make the moral factors more explicit in their deliberations. Principles or standards may not be determinative, but they can be of assistance to legislators here. Although seldom can they be applied unambiguously to specific circumstances, they can give definition and shape to legislative ethics.[26] They can help guide legislators in their assessment as to whether conduct passes ethical muster and in their decisions as to whether proposals have ethical promise. "Political ethics," Dennis Thompson writes, "consists of judgments or criteria for making judgments, not particular rules or general theories."[27] Such criteria do not negate the need for legislators to examine the particulars of a situation; rather, they help tell legislators what to look for and how to interpret cases. They cannot be applied automatically, without reflection. The purpose of principles or standards is to encourage moral judgment in the legislative enterprise, something that does not come without effort.

It is no simple matter to devise standards for ethical conduct in state legislatures and for the improvement of the institution and the process. For one thing, none of the standards that might be proposed are purely ethical in content; each has political as well as ethical loading. We cannot disentangle the political from the moral strands. Our purpose is to suggest a combination that would make sense to legislators and serve them in a practical way. Also, whatever their loading, moral standards have to be general and imprecise. Consequently, we cannot expect them to settle concrete cases. That does not mean, however, that they are unworthy of consideration. Quite the contrary. It is still useful to have standards in mind when assessing legislative behavior and legislative rules.

I submit that legislators already have in mind the three standards that I shall make use of in my treatment of ethics. They are general and imprecise, as indeed they must be. In practice, they may come into conflict with one another. On those occasions, we have to choose between "goods," for in the imperfect world that legislators inhabit ethics requires balancing standards rather than adhering to absolute principles, all of which point in one clear direction.

Students of political ethics have suggested several standards in the main. One of them is "autonomy." Moral philosophy accords great weight to the autonomy of the individual, and this carries over to standards developed by ethicists for application to legislators. As formulated by the Hastings Center, this standard dictates that legislators should act as "morally autonomous agents whose decisions are based on informed, unbiased, and uncoerced judgments." Moral autonomy requires that legislators "deliberate and decide free from improper influence."[28] The question, then, is, What influence is improper? Influence that stems from behavior proscribed by law, such as bribery, clearly is improper. But beyond that, what qualifies for proscription?

Gutmann and Thompson define such influence as that which is "irrelevant to the merits of the legislation."[29] What is that? Not much is irrelevant, even to the merits. Influence exercised by constituents, by colleagues, by party leaders, and by interest groups—all of it has much to do with the politics of the issue, but it also has something to do with the merits of legislation. Ordinarily, such influence is not deemed improper. Furthermore, ethicists insist that legislators consider issues on their merits, and legislators do, surely to a considerable extent. In part, that is because legislators rationalize, or justify, their actions on the basis of the merits. In any case, it is almost impossible on most issues to separate the merits from the rest of the fabric. Although legislators are used to having their autonomy restricted in the political sense, seldom do they feel that their autonomy is constrained in the moral sense. Perhaps they do not even realize that it is.

Despite its limitations, which would apply to just about any standard, autonomy does have its uses. The autonomy of legislators may be questioned when legislators go too far or neglect drawing the line in the appropriate place. If legislators are overly dependent on a special interest group or exceedingly narrow in their representational perspectives, their autonomy may be in jeopardy.[30] Accordingly, a legislator who is a spokesperson for a particular group, a single-issue representative, or a recipient of campaign funds from only a few interests is open to challenge by ethicists on the autonomy standard.

Autonomy is a very difficult standard to operationalize, for rarely can we discern behavior that is extreme enough to qualify as beyond the limits. Even Hastings realizes that it excludes very little: "Beyond these clear instances [bribery and extortion], we cannot say that any type of influence will always violate or will always satisfy the duty of autonomy."[31] For my purposes, autonomy is too broad, and if applied across the board it might preclude too much conduct that is desirable in politics. We will not be using autonomy as a standard, but we shall be paying the notion heed, implicitly at least, in our consideration of conflicts of interest, gifts, and campaign contributions.

Contemporary ethicists also beat the drum for "publicity." The ethical rationale for publicity is that, because social institutions must rest on the informed consent of members of the community, citizens have to know about legislators' decisions and also about the factors that influence them. Publicity is necessary, the argument goes, if government is to be accountable to the citizenry. The applications of such a standard are evidenced by open meetings, financial disclosure, campaign finance reporting, and so forth.

Publicity entails the provision of information to citizens. But applying this general standard is far from obvious. What information and how much of it has to be disclosed? When does the information have to become public? Granted the public's right to know, do we mean access to all information or only to some?[32] Does the publicity standard permit the negotiations and compromises outside of public scrutiny that normally take place in every legislative setting? The problem is to figure out what is needed for democratic citizenship, as opposed to what is needed for the conduct of democratic government. Full public discussion may inhibit governing by inhibiting compromise and encouraging acrimony and even chaos. How are these interests balanced; where should the line be drawn? We shall not deal explicitly with publicity as a standard, but it is captured to a considerable extent by appearance, which we cannot possibly avoid.

No standard today exercises the force on practitioners and citizens that appearance does. According to this standard, legislators must avoid even the appearance of impropriety. Like Caesar's wife, they must be above suspicion.[33] Other professions are also mindful of how things look. Take the legal profession, for example. If a judge's impartiality might reasonably be questioned, the practice is for the judge to recuse herself, even though she is not in fact biased. Lawyers are required to avoid even the appearance of impropriety. Public officials also acknowledge the importance of appearance, recognizing the potential political consequences of actions that seem improper, although they may not be. By now legislators have become used to being counseled by leaders and senior colleagues not to do anything they would not want to read about in the newspaper the next day. They nearly always take into consideration the political ramifications of their behavior, and they normally tailor what they do to meet public expectations.

Appearance has made its way into laws and rules at both the federal and state levels. As early as 1978, the Ethics in Government Act, based in part on an executive order, generally required that officials avoid conduct which could create the appearance of a loss of impartiality. Since then both the executive and legislative branches have adopted ethical standards which explicitly or implicitly utilize appearance. Appearance has also been adopted as a standard at the state level, particularly with reference to possible conflicts of interest by executive and legislative officials.

Josephson has written that in matters of public trust and confidence, appearances are crucial.[34] Most people are inclined to agree. In surveys of legislators, legislative staff, and journalists, the Josephson Institute asked whether they agreed with the following statement: "Because public trust can be undermined by perceptions of wrongdoing as much as by actual wrongdoing, public officials ought to avoid conduct which creates an appearance of impropriety, even though it requires them to refrain from conduct that is not actually improper." The statement is worded in a way that would seem to ensure a positive response. Thus, 91 percent of legislators and staff and 99 percent of journalists agreed or strongly agreed, indicating that practitioners either accept the standard or at least pay lip service to it.[35] Whatever they truly believe, they certainly are reluctant to argue against appearance in any public forum.

There can be no question that this standard is a prudential one for people in public life, where nowadays perception is reality. What is less indisputable is the claim that appearance also is a moral standard. In the view of ethicists, appearance matters ethically, as well as politically. Thompson goes so far as to maintain that "appearing to do wrong while doing right is really doing wrong." Officials who appear to do wrong, he continues, actually do several kinds of moral wrong: they erode confidence in the political system; they give citizens reason to act as if government cannot be trusted; and they undermine democratic accountability. All citizens have to go by is their perception of actions and events and the circumstances under which officials act. They cannot assess the motives of public officials, for the motives are many, mixed, and hidden from view. The appearance standard, then, points us in the right direction—away from motives and to "conditions that establish corrupt connections." For Thompson appearances are inferences from "objective circumstances" to subjective motives and institutional tendencies.[36]

It is unfortunate that an official's proper behavior may appear improper and thereby erode citizen confidence and trust in the political system. But that does not, in my judgment, mean that the official is acting unethically. If he or she knows that an action will have a negative impact on citizen confidence, then he or she will have to bear some responsibility for that outcome. Just how much will depend on what the purpose and the substance of the action are. Appearance itself focuses the legislator on the perceptions others have of his or her action, not on any special characteristics of the action itself. However, it may be a legislator's moral obligation to do something, even if it looks wrong and has negative political effects. Suppose, for instance, that a legislator truly believes in the position taken by a powerful, local corporation, and one that also contributes generously to his campaigns. He knows that the company's well-being will benefit his district, and he judges that its case is a good one. Local media have conveyed a different picture. Can we claim that, since his procorporate position *appears* to be a result of campaign contributions, the ethical thing for him to do is to act contrary to his basic conviction? We would have to stretch the argument for democratic accountability absurdly to make such a claim.

If current conditions—as they appear—are the kind that citizens know from past experience tend to lead to improper actions, then citizens will be justified, according to ethicists, in concluding that the current action is also improper.[37] At times, of course, a pattern may be clear, but more often there is considerable room for doubt as to ethical transgression. The question is, How persistent and clear a pattern does there have to be in order to justify an inference of unethical behavior? Too often, I believe, people generalize from past experience to current action on the basis of flimsy circumstantial evidence. That is a very far reach for the purpose of ensuring democratic accountability.

Presently, considerable information is available for citizens to use in deciding on issues or on candidates. It includes party affiliation, votes, declared positions on issues, constituency service, and much more. Such information is more direct and more substantial than are inferences that rest on how things look—or how they are painted to look.

It should be readily apparent that there is a fundamental and very disturbing problem with the application of appearance as a standard; that is, who—in fact, not in theory—determines what appearance is? This determination is extremely important, since morality and immorality will hinge on it, in that an action that is not immoral in itself can, in the language of ethics, be immoral because it resembles an immoral action. Practically speaking, appearance is that which is communicated by the media and, as we have discussed, the media are inclined to portray actions as scandalous whenever possible. Suggestion, inference, innuendo are the mainstays of much (although by no means all) coverage of the legislature. Accounts are one-sided, with the preponderance of illustrations, exclamations, and quotations running in the direction of establishing the immoral or, at best, questionable practices of the legislators involved or of the legislature as an institution. Such a standard allows the press to be the judge and the jury, while the public has little recourse other than to go along.

It is one thing to ask how a legislator's action would appear to the public as interpreted by the press. It is quite another thing to ask how the same action would appear if the legislator could explain what he or she did and why. The two perspectives are better than either one alone. Moreover, what public do we have in mind to sit in judgment? Everyone, no matter how ill informed? Or only a select group? In legal ethics, the judgment is presumed to be that of "a fair-minded" person. In ethics, generally the judgment would be that of "a reasonable observer" or "a reasonable person."[38]

Even though it may not be linked to behavior, appearance is a standard that cannot be ignored. There is no avoiding its widespread currency and practical application. President Clinton, for one, exhibited his awareness of its force. At his press conference on Whitewater (24 March 1994), he took on appearance: "There may or may not be a different standard than I have seen in the past, not of right or wrong—that doesn't change—but of what may appear to be right or wrong." Moreover, citizen confidence and trust in the political system, which may be affected by the appearance of improper behavior, merit serious concern. Legislators do have a moral obligation to consider the appearances to the public of what they do, because of the impact people's perceptions will have on their trust and confidence in the legislature itself. If their actions can be misconstrued and lead to unfortunate consequences, legislators normally exercise caution. That is as it should be. All of this means that we have to take appearance into account in assessing not only conduct but also proposals for reform.

Currently, appearance is virtually the only standard actually being used in debates over ethical conduct and ethical rules. I would argue that it is being overused or even abused. I do not deny that appearance should be given weight, but how much? If no other standards are brought into play, appearance will be given all the weight. I suggest that the standards of *fairness* and *responsibility* must also be weighed. They may be no easier to apply in specific cases than other standards, but they are too important to be overlooked.

Fairness is not dealt with in the contemporary literature on political ethics, but it ought to play a part in the assessment of both legislative conduct and ethics proposals. One of the most basic ethical theories, to which all of us subscribe, is the Golden Rule: "Do unto others as you would have them do unto you." Treat them as you would want to be treated. This requires putting yourself in the other person's shoes, or changing places with the affected person, in order to see things from his or her perspective. In that way, one can become more sensitive to the fairness concerns of others.

Fairness to constituents, to other citizens of the state, and to the myriad of organized interests—and particularly those who are not usually heard—is important. But for present purposes the fairness standard is meant to apply mainly to legislators themselves. They, too, have a right to be treated in certain ways: to be able to maintain some degree of privacy; to be granted due process; to receive adequate compensation for their services in public office; and to have at their disposal the wherewithal to do the job for which they are held accountable.

Legislators as public officials are expected to give up some of their right to privacy, because the public has a prevailing right to know. But that doesn't mean that legislators should surrender all of their privacy. Certainly in many states, excepting perhaps a few like New York and California, legislators also are expected to sacrifice income. If they do so, in their capacity as "citizen legislators," they must be permitted to make a living outside of the legislature. But while doing so they cannot engage in practices that would conflict with their public duties. When accused in the press of unethical or corrupt behavior, legislators like anyone else are entitled to due process and a presumption of innocence if they are to receive fair treatment. Just as citizens have their rights vis-à-vis their representative, so representatives have their rights vis-à-vis the public, the press, and other agencies.

Responsibility is the third standard—along with appearance and fairness—that we shall bring to bear in subsequent discussions. The notion of responsibility, specifically responsibility to a community, carries less weight in moral philosophy than that of individual autonomy. But, as pointed out by Gutmann and Thompson, legislators are responsible not only for their own activities but also for the well-being of the institutions in which they act.[39] Legislators rely upon one another in the process of enacting laws; no one could achieve anything without the cooperation of others. Thus, legislators have mutual responsibilities. Democrats have special obligations to their caucus and Republicans to theirs. Rank-and-file and legislative leadership have reciprocal responsibilities. Beyond such ties, legislators have a duty to the office they hold, to the legislature as an institution, and to the legislative process. They are special custodians of representative democracy and are responsible for its working properly and for its maintenance.

These institutionally focused responsibilities show up in legislative ethics codes, whereby members are directed to conduct themselves in a manner that does not discredit the senate or the house. It is no simple matter, of course, to determine just what responsibility entails in particular instances and just what behavior is likely to discredit the institution. Nonetheless, responsibility, primarily in the institutional sense, is a standard that cannot be ignored. Legislators ought to ask questions regarding fairness to themselves and colleagues, appearances to their constituents and to the public, and also responsibility to the institution in which they serve. Will their conduct tend to diminish the standing or image of the legislature? Will a proposal to achieve reform prove harmful to the process? Not all legislators ask such questions. But many do. They believe that legislators have to do their jobs and cannot always please the press. They feel the need to walk a tightrope between what the public seems to want and what they believe is best for the institution. In my opinion, institutional responsibility should be at the core of the ethical reasoning of members. As legislators they have a special obligation to the institution. For legislative leaders, the obligation increases.

The three standards that will prove most useful to us are differently oriented. Appearance relates mainly to the public (and to the press); fairness is concerned with individual members of the legislature; and responsibility has to do with the institution. In the chapters that follow, we examine conflicts of interest, legislator-lobbyist relationships, campaign finance, and the management of the legislature, all with these standards in mind. Occasionally, none of the standards will furnish much help, and judgments will have to be made on other grounds entirely. So be it. More often, one, two, or all three standards will be applicable. Where several standards apply, the likelihood is that they will not work in the same direction. Not infrequently, appearance and fairness or appearance and responsibility will come into conflict. In such instances, it will be necessary to assess which standard should prevail and where a balance ought to be struck.

4

Interests Are Always in Conflict

Conflicts of interest are one of the several problematic areas in the field of legislative ethics. The possibility always exists that a legislator's personal interests will come into conflict with the public interest, and inevitably there is the danger then that the legislator will choose to promote the former while sacrificing the latter. Even if legislators do not pursue personal ends at public expense, it may appear that they are doing so. The appearance of conflict—as well as any actual conflict—has to be avoided in contemporary politics.

Appearances Can Be Deceiving
During the course of working on this book, I was called by a reporter from the *Atlantic City Press* to respond to a case involving a conflict of interest. What did I think, she asked, of the hiring of Lynette Dilbeck, the wife of the state tourism director, to work on a $12 million advertising campaign for the Atlantic City Convention Center Authority? According to the story that appeared on 3 June 1993, Kohm Associates won the contract after telling the authority it would hire her if it got the account. Previously, however, members of the authority's selection committee expressed concern that the hiring of the wife of the state tourism director might appear to be both a conflict of interest and the result of political maneuvering, so the committee recommended that she not be part of a proposal. But after

the contract was awarded, Kohm Associates persuaded authority staff to permit Lynette Dilbeck to work on the project because she was uniquely qualified for the job. The authority agreed.

There did not seem to be much question about the qualifications of the Kohm Associates firm or of the process by which the contract had been awarded. The agency had been chosen from among the twenty-four companies that had submitted proposals and the three that had made the finals. The story that appeared in the *Atlantic City Press* reported that while Kohm's plan dealt with Atlantic City's problems head-on, the other two finalists focused more on gaming and entertainment, coming up with little that was new. Among Kohm's clients were the Meadowlands Racetrack, Meadowlands Arena, New Jersey State Aquarium, Rutgers University, New Jersey Bell, Public Service Electric & Gas, and Blue Cross & Blue Shield of New Jersey—a blue-chip list. The *Press* followed up on 13 and 15 March 1993 with an editorial that praised the authority for commissioning an advertising firm that had a promising idea for selling Atlantic City as "a happening place."

However, the publicity surrounding Dilbeck's role in the project proved too threatening to the Convention Center Authority and to Kohm Associates. The wife of the state tourism director was removed from the Atlantic City account. A story on 4 June 1993 ran under the subhead "Ethics: The Convention Center Authority's advertising firm reassigns Lynette Dilbeck to avoid an appearance of a conflict of interest." A managing partner of Kohm explained, "We know it [a conflict of interest] does not exist, but we're forced for the sake of the way it looks to take her off the account." The advertising firm that, in its presentation to Atlantic City, had counseled the authority, "It's the image, stupid," took its own advice and retreated.

The reporter who sought my opinion was surprised when I responded that in my opinion no conflict of interest was involved. There is always the potential for impropriety and the appearance of impropriety, but I thought that in this case disqualification was a long stretch. Just because the woman's spouse headed the state tourism division was not a sufficient reason to disqualify her from working on the Atlantic City account. The division, in fact, had little directly to do with Atlantic City, and the tourism director had no role whatsoever in the affair. The reporter insisted, however, that even if there was no problem with practice there was a question of appearance. What would people think?

What people would think depended in large part on how the issue was communicated by the media. The 3 June 1993 story might have suggested to readers that undue influence was being used, that Ms. Dilbeck was hired only because of her husband's position, and that the affair was being handled as secretively as possible. Although it is unlikely that many citizens even read the story, let alone were aroused, members of the Convention Center Authority became skittish, and the Kohm management made the decision not to run any further risk.

The results in this case were several. First, the woman who was considered the most qualified person for the job did not get it. Kohm had received about seventy-five résumés, and none equaled hers. Thus, a legitimate process had been undermined. Second, an injustice was done to an individual who deserved the opportunity to work on the account. Instead, she was disqualified because her husband had a job with the state, although no nepotism was involved. Third, the advertising campaign and the interests of the client, Atlantic City, might have been adversely affected, as someone less qualified had to be substituted in the job. Fourth, the appearance standard, by which so much is measured nowadays, was given another boost—unfortunately, in my judgment.

This is not to suggest that conflict of interest is not a problem in government today, whether it is in the executive or legislative branch. It surely is. But the point of the Atlantic City case is to bring out the ethical standards that come into conflict. Most obvious was the standard of appearance. It played the decisive role. But the standard of fairness—principally to the woman who, on the basis of qualifications, was assigned to the account—was neglected. The standard of responsibility, in this case the advertising firm's ability to do the best job possible for the client, could also have been a factor. But it did not prevail. Judgments on this case will vary, but mine is that the appearance of conflict was given too much weight. There was little evidence to cause concern, except for possible guilt by marital association. Nonetheless, Kohm Associates made the politically correct decision in finding someone else to do the job, thereby reducing its risks at the outset. The advertising firm had to be worried about its own image and that of its Atlantic City project.

A conflict of interest, in fact, involves appearance and not necessarily conduct. For a conflict to exist, there need not be evidence of corruption or undue influence. A conflict of interest can occur even though no actual impropriety has occurred or will take place. Thus, a conflict of interest can be nothing more than a "potential" impropriety or an "appearance" of impropriety. How great is the potential, and how strong must the appearance be before remedial action is taken? In the Atlantic City case, the potential seemed slight and the appearance minimal.

Nothing in legislative life is entirely unambiguous. Conflict of interest situations are probably among the most ambiguous ones that a legislator faces. Almost everything a legislator does raises the possibility of conflict. Ambiguity inheres in this area, because conflicts of interest are an inescapable aspect of life. The question arises with regard to "inherent conflicts," which occur by virtue of a legislator's being a homeowner, taxpayer, or member of one or another occupational group. It also arises with regard to "politically dictated conflicts," such as that of a farmer from an agricultural district who, in representing the interests of his constituents, also advances his own interests or may seem to advance his own interests. And it arises in instances of "personally necessary conflicts," which primarily involve citizen legislators pursuing jobs and income outside of public service.[1] These conflicts, to one degree or another, are virtually unavoidable.

The only way to dispose of the thought of a conflict is for legislators to take positions that are contrary to their self-interest (and perhaps to that of family and friends as well). Then, legislators would be above suspicion. In some cases, it is true, legislators' self-interest is not at all involved, not even politically. But much of the time, legislators may be promoting their personal interests concomitant with their activities as public officials. Self-interest is not the crucial factor, even in such instances. "Democratic representation itself," writes the Hastings Center, "inevitably serves to entangle a legislator's own interests with the broader interests held by the members of the various communities he or she represents." Ideally, legislators should not be able to separate the promotion of their constituents' interests from the promotion of their own. Conflicts arise not when interests coincide but when "a legislator's personal or political self-interest pulls in one direction, and his or her duty to serve broader public interests pull in another."[2] That is when a legislator, in order to maintain the integrity of his or her judgment, must override self-interest for the public interest. Put another way, whatever one's theories of representation, roles, and allegiances, "they are not to be neglected for personal gain, whether financial *or* political."[3]

The prohibition is clear at the theoretical level, but applying it is something else entirely. In dealing with the issue over the years, legislatures have concentrated on personal financial gain while ignoring personal political gain. It would be virtually impossible, anyway, to demonstrate that a legislator was seeking political gain to the detriment of constituents or in conflict with the public interest. Each issue has too many sides for legislators to be unable to justify the political position they hold. "Good politics is good government," as the old cliché goes. Seldom, if ever, is the situation so black and white that a legislator can go only one way, and no other—at least in ethical terms.

Thus, legislatures opt for rules that prohibit conflicts of interest of limited scope. Most states restrict or ban members from using their official positions for personal gain, taking part in outside business activities that may conflict with public service responsibilities, or favoring relatives, friends, and cronies. The fundamental prohibition applies to the legislator who would personally benefit from some piece of legislation in a way or to a degree that other people would not. But if others of similar standing or in the same category benefit, then a legislator is allowed to benefit as well. For example, Washington state prohibits promoting legislation or

77

voting on it if the legislator derived benefit to a greater extent than that afforded to any other member of the legislator's business, professional, or occupational group. This means that a teacher-legislator can support legislation advocated by the education association that would raise teachers' salaries, a banker-legislator can support legislation advocated by the banking industry that would deregulate aspects of banking, and a lawyer-legislator with business clients can support legislation advocated by the state chamber of commerce that would reduce the business income tax. Many reform-minded people question such an arrangement. But the provision that legislators can benefit, if people who are in the same occupations also benefit, is essential for states with citizen legislatures.

The Problem of a Citizen Legislature

Unlike in the U.S. Congress, in most states most legislators have outside employment and earn income in addition to their legislative compensation. Only ten or so states have full-time, or virtually full-time, legislatures, with members receiving salaries of from about $35,000 to over $50,000. For example, in California, legislators receive a top salary of $72,000, while in New York the salary is $57,000. Michigan, Ohio, Pennsylvania, and Illinois all pay their legislators $40,000 or more. The large majority of members in these legislatures derive nearly all of their earned income from their legislative compensation. Most legislative bodies, however, are still composed mainly of citizen legislators, people whose primary income is derived from positions outside the legislature. Given the levels of compensation in these states, it would not be possible for most citizens to serve without deriving income from outside employment. The salaries in so-called citizen legislatures are as low as $100 a year in New Hampshire, with most states paying annual amounts between $10,000 and $25,000.

Consequently, the large majority of the 7,461 legislators in the 50 states have occupations in addition to that of legislator. Only about 14 percent of the total acknowledge that they are full-time legislators, although probably another 10 percent who do not acknowledge it also are. The rest report occupations in law (17 percent), business (22 percent), education (8 percent), agriculture (8 percent), insurance, real estate, medicine, engineering, and state or local government employment.[4] Any of these occupations pose the potential for a conflict of interest.

One way to reduce the incidence of conflict situations is to do away with the citizen legislature, making legislative service a full-time occupation, as it is in Congress. Those who advocate such a transformation do so for a variety of reasons, not the least of which is that conflicts of interest are much greater in a part-time legislature than in a full-time one.

During the past decades, all of our state legislatures have been requiring more time of members. Much of the additional time is spent by members on political and constituency tasks and not on lawmaking itself. But legislator salaries have not been raised to compensate for the extra time required. Outside income is still critical, albeit more difficult to sustain, given the greater demands of the legislative job. The majority of state legislatures continue to be citizen bodies, in part because the public is not at all disposed to pay members what the job is worth, and legislators are reluctant to raise their own salaries in the face of vocal opposition by the citizenry (if they are constitutionally permitted to raise them at all).

It is not only compensation that restricts legislatures from becoming full time but also the belief by many legislators and some of the public that there is value in preserving the citizen legislature. Proponents of the citizen legislature maintain that its members are closer to their constituents because they have an occupational, as well as residential, presence in their communities. Moreover, citizen legislators can easily resume their outside careers and, therefore, need not stake their economic as well as psychological well-being on continuing in office. In short, they can afford to lose; and it is an advantage in public life to be willing and able to lose, if it appears necessary to take an unpopular position.

The question is whether it is worth jettisoning what is left of our citizen legislatures in order to avoid or reduce conflicts of interest. Do we want full-time careerists with the possibility of fewer conflicts or part-time citizen legislators with the possibility of more conflicts? Relatively few states have opted for the former. After all, the Congress, California, New York, and other full-time legislatures—no matter how they may minimize conflicts—have not been exempt from ethical problems.

If eliminating the outside employment of legislators is not a viable solution for conflicts of interest, then what is? Legislatures have yet to work out ideal arrangements, but they have devised a number of ways to manage situations and reduce conflicts. The first is to acknowledge that a problem exists and set general standards of behavior. The second is to disclose information about legislators' financial and other interests and permit people to draw their own conclusions. The third is to disqualify legislators from certain positions or actions within the legislature. The fourth is to restrict or prohibit them from engaging in certain outside activities.

Facing Up to the Situation

If legislators are to avoid, or minimize, conflicts of interest, they must first admit to the problem. Legislatures have done so and have been addressing conflict situations through legislative codes of ethics. These codes proscribe behaviors that would pit a legislator's financial well-being against a legislator's public duty. For instance, Washington's code, among other things, bars legislators from "exercising influence where one's personal interest is in conflict with the proper discharge of one's duties; accepting compensation other than one's legislative salary for services rendered in connection with one's legislative duties; and receiving anything of value upon the understanding that one's behavior will be affected thereby."[5]

Codes not only proscribe, they also provide guidelines for members. How seriously these guidelines are heeded is another question. For the most part, legislators are so preoccupied that they have little time, energy, or incentive to explore the meaning or the application of conflict of interest provisions. Some legislatures will review their codes in new member orientation sessions. A few will attend to codes as part of ethics training that they provide to freshmen and veteran members. Every now and then, a legislature will devise a different method to raise the consciousness of members. New Mexico's method, after the state legislature recovered from the censure and then conviction of a member, merits attention. An oath of ethical conduct was adopted by the house and senate, and at the opening of the 1993 legislative session all 112 lawmakers in New Mexico recited: "I shall not use my office for personal gain and shall scrupulously avoid any act of impropriety or any act which gives the appearance of impropriety." In the opinion of the house speaker, Raymond Sanchez, "If you have to say it and read it, then it forces you to think about it."[6] The speaker has a point.

The New Mexico oath requires legislators to declare that they not only will avoid acts of impropriety but also acts that give the appearance of impropriety. Other legislative codes specify that appearance has to be taken into account and that legislators ought to avoid taking anything under circumstances where it can be reasonably inferred that such action would influence their actions.

Legislators, in our view, have a responsibility to take conflict of interest issues very seriously. This probably cannot be done in the abstract but rather as cases arise. In many instances, there may be no simple answers. But a process of self-examination can and should be undertaken.[7] Legislators first ought to ask where their own direct private interest lies. If an act does not benefit their own interest, directly or indirectly, or is contrary to their own interest, cause for concern is unlikely. If, however, the act does benefit their own interest, they should be on guard. This raises the question of where, in the perception of legislators, the public interest lies. If it is in conflict with their own interest, the choice is clear. If not, as is the likely case even with legislators who are most honest with themselves, further scrutiny is still in order.

Even if one's contemplated action survives this process of self-scrutiny, it is probably wise to go further. It usually helps to seek advice. One can turn to one or a few trusted colleagues to see where they stand. Legislators frequently do so. Tom Loftus, the former speaker of the Wisconsin assembly, recalls how the then-minority leader (and later governor), Tommy Thompson, sought collegial advice about his outside law practice. He told Loftus that a chiropractor had sent his will to him and asked him to look it over and send him a bill. This occurred a few days before a vote on legislation mandating that private insurers cover chiropractic visits, legislation that Thompson had always opposed. Loftus advised his colleague to return the will and vote no on the bill (suggesting, I suppose, that where there's a will there's a nay), and Thompson did so.[8]

Today, there are institutional means for legislators seeking advice. Ethics committees within the legislature or independent commissions outside the legislature, when requested, will provide legislators with advisory opinions. More and more legislators are making such requests in order to enjoy the protection of an opinion from an authoritative agency. Some legislators may refuse to request advisory opinions in order not to hear the bad news and be restricted. They feel that there is ample protection in not knowing. Most, however, are aware of the advisory process when an occasion arises, and they are not averse to using it.

Revealing One's Interests

It is now standard practice in the states to have legislators disclose their financial interests. The rationale for such a requirement is that citizens have a right to know just where public officials stand financially so that they can judge for themselves whether these officials' private interests affect their public activities. The purpose of financial disclosure laws is to make available sufficient information to allow citizens to judge whether officials are favoring personal interests or not. Thus, if a legislator has large holdings in real estate and if that legislator also sides with real estate interests, people may draw their own conclusions as to motivation and behavior. Some would assume a coincidence of interests and nothing more; but others would conclude that the legislator's public behavior is being influenced by his or her private holdings.

Requirements vary. Information subject to disclosure may include assets, income, transactions, liabilities, and gifts. It usually pertains also to members of one's immediate family. Some states have more stringent disclosure provisions than others. In New Hampshire, all legislators have to do is fill out a simple form naming professional, business, or other organizations from which they derive in excess of $10,000 income as officers or employees. New Mexico, which recently amended its law, requires disclosure of all sources of income of $5,000 or more for members and spouses. This includes real estate, business interests, board memberships, and dealings with state agencies. If the legislator is a member of a law firm, anyone represented by the firm for lobbying purposes must also be listed.

The argument favoring financial disclosure of one's interests is rooted in the notion of democratic accountability. Only when citizens know where their representatives stand in their private dealings and with whom they are linked financially will citizens possess the information necessary to hold representatives accountable for their public actions. Thus, the fuller the publicity, the better. Some would argue that if legislators do not reveal their holdings, the public will—and has a right to—suspect the worst. A lack of information thus gives an overall appearance of impropriety.

Ethically, it is difficult to maintain that full financial disclosure is good because otherwise people might suspect the worst. That is equivalent to saying that legislators are guilty until they can demonstrate, by baring all, that they are innocent. Prudence may oblige legislators to respect the suspicions of the public, but ethical reasoning will not justify such suspicions. If fairness is one of our standards, then public officials, including legislators, are treated unfairly compared to the rest of us. Those legislators who are also in business may have to reveal important financial information to their competitors. Those who practice law may have to specify the clients they or their firms represent. All of them risk embarrassment by either having too much wealth or too little. After all, aren't legislators, as citizens, entitled to the right to privacy like others? No, not to the same extent. Public officials, by virtue of their roles in a democracy, have to sacrifice some of their privacy. One argument along these lines is utilitarian in character—that the interests of the larger number of citizens outweigh those of the smaller number.[9] Another argument is that legislators, by the very act of seeking public office, implicitly consent to the limitation of their privacy. In other words, they know what they are getting into and voluntarily surrender a measure of privacy.

If we accept the theoretical benefit of disclosure in a democratic system, we should ask ourselves two further questions. First, just how much is enough, and second, does the provision of such information in fact do more good or more harm? Legislators, of course, would opt for less intrusive requirements, while the press and reformers would opt for more intrusive ones. Exactly where the proper balance lies between fairness to legislators, on the one hand, and the public's right to such information, on the other, comes down to particular situations and cases.

Certainly, the public is entitled to know something of the financial standing of its representatives as a means of assessing what it is getting in the way of interests and possible biases. But what ought, in my opinion, to temper further inroads into legislators' privacy rights is the fact that no evidence exists to suggest that the disclosure of financial information is particularly well used. There is certainly no public clamor for it after it is filed. The press sometimes reports it but frequently in a distorted or misleading way—often as if to imply that one's private interests determine one's vote. Moreover, a legislator's opponent in the next election will probably go further. Election campaigns rely heavily on a strategy of tearing down the opposition, impugning an opponent's integrity, undermining an opponent's character, and questioning an opponent's probity. Financial disclosure information becomes grist for the attack mill, since it can easily be given a spin that benefits a challenger. What does the public learn as a result of all this? Is democratic accountability really advanced?

What Shouldn't They Do?

Disclosure is the bedrock in the regulation of conflicts of interest, but other tools are also available. One is prohibition, another is discouragement. Many private activities of legislators are barred; others are suspect, if not specifically off limits. Everyone agrees that legislators should not use their public positions to advance their private interests. But there is considerably less agreement as to what specifically should be regarded as illegal, as inappropriate, and as proper in a legislature that is less than a full-time one.

What about a legislator who is a lobbyist? A number of states prohibit lobbyists from serving in the legislature, but some do not. Defenders would argue that as long as a legislator's outside employment as a lobbyist is known, fellow legislators can take that into account. In such cases, however, the conflict is so direct and so severe that a legislator will be under inordinate pressure to reconcile a client's interest, on the one hand, and the state or constituency interest, on the other. Even if a legislator disqualifies himself or herself from voting on an issue of concern to a client, that legislator's influence still may be felt. Moreover, the appearance of influence in such instances is unavoidable and even logical. All of this would raise doubts about the legitimacy of any transaction in which a lobbyist-legislator was involved.

Take the case of someone who is a paid lobbyist, say, for a local utility company and is running for the legislature. If he wins, should he quit his job as lobbyist?[10] This was a question posed to me. It is truly hypothetical, since it is inconceivable to me that a utility lobbyist could win an election anywhere for anything today. Should lightning strike, however, the lobbyist would have to kiss lobbying good-bye in order to behave ethically. Some legislators are known by their colleagues as perennial advocates for certain causes and groups. They may be in the pockets of those they zealously represent, but presumably they are not on their payrolls. It is hard, if not impossible, to justify a legislator's outside occupation as that of lobbyist. The standard of responsibility would preclude that.

But what about legislators who are not lobbyists per se but rather are employed as executive directors of state associations or work in the public affairs division of large companies that have an interest in matters before the legislature? In Mississippi, for example, several legislators also work as executive directors of statewide associations, such as that of convenience stores and petroleum marketers. A former speaker of the house here was in the public affairs department of a utility company. Although these legislators were not registered as lobbyists, their outside employment could well raise questions. But since their associations did not receive public funds, their employment was not prohibited by statute. Since it had not been shown that they were using their legislative office to advance private interests, such employment has been permitted. The propriety in such cases, rather than the legality, would depend on particular circumstances. An executive director whose association had a substantial legislative agenda clearly should not also be a member of the legislature. However, an executive director whose association had no legislative issues would seem to stand on firmer ethical ground. The problem, of course, is to figure out how to treat those in the middle. It is relevant, too, whether the outside position precedes or follows the legislative one. In the latter instance, the impression that someone was offered a job with an association because of his or her position in the legislature is inescapable. It would not be at all appropriate for a legislator to accept such an offer. It looks bad, it is bad.

Lobbyist-legislators and association director–legislators are few and far between. But probably a larger number of legislators are on the payrolls of companies with legislative interests as "consultants." Allegations are made that they are not required to do much for their money but are expected to be sympathetic to the company's interests in the legislature. If the disclosure of clients were required, the problem would be addressed. But usually disclosure is more general, by category instead of by client. In some way, disclosure should try to get at such arrangements. They are cause for concern and should be made known to one's colleagues and to the public.

A more common ethical problem, and one that provokes a serious division of opinion, concerns lawyer-legislators. What aspects of a legal practice should be denied a legislator because of actual or potential conflicts of interest? Thirty-two states restrict lawyer-legislators from representing clients before state agencies.[11] Although such a provision may not be entirely fair to citizen legislators who earn a living practicing law, it is a proper limitation. A legislator possesses the ability to help or hurt an agency of the executive branch by supporting or contesting the agency's appropriations and in other ways as well. Legislative leaders and the chairs and members of appropriations committees are in the best positions to exercise such influence, but no member is without at least some ability. How, then, will an administrator respond to some client's attorney who also happens to be a member of the legislature? Whether the legislator has any intention of exercising influence, his or her position will cast a big shadow; and an administrator who wants to protect an agency may lean too far in the lawyer-legislator's direction.

The more a legislator relies for a living on income outside of legislative service, moreover, the harder it is to justify a complete ban on practicing before administrative agencies. The line should be drawn at a different place in states like California, Illinois, Massachusetts, New York, and Pennsylvania, with their full-time legislatures, than in smaller states, with their citizen legislatures. In those states where legislators receive ample compensation, it is not at all unreasonable or unfair to limit their outside practices.

Recently, in enacting new ethics laws, legislatures in Kentucky and New Mexico found this issue to be one of the most contentious facing them. Although there had been no indications of abuse, legislators admitted that subtle influence may have operated. Some legislators in Kentucky wanted a complete ban, others—mainly lawyer-legislators—wanted none at all. The resolution was a compromise based upon the law in New York, which prohibits legislators from representing clients before the Public Service Commission and agencies involved in licensing, permitting, contracting, and rate making. It does allow them to practice in the fields of workers compensation and unemployment insurance. It also allows a partner in the firm to practice before any state agency, but such activity must be reported, and no money can accrue to the legislator from a partner's work in this area. In New Mexico, where legislators receive no salary but $75 a day for expenses while in session, the legislature debated the issue. It decided to allow members to appear before state agencies but not to use their title or legislative stationery in connection with their legal work. Given the lack of compensation for legislative service in New Mexico, it is understandable, and would seem to be fair, that lawyer-legislators are given greater leeway than elsewhere.

The same moral logic that applies to representing clients before state agencies could also be applied to trying cases in the courts. After all, legislatures control judicial budgets and set judicial salaries, and lawyer-legislators may influence judges, just as they may influence bureaucrats. Should legislators who are attorneys be kept out of the courts? Should other members of their firms also be barred? This would appear to be an extreme solution to what is probably not a perilous problem. Judges are not apt to be swayed by legislators appearing in their courts, nor would legislators be able to get away with penalizing a judge for an unfavorable ruling. In all likelihood, any legislator who did so would be taken to task by the media and by colleagues as well.

All sorts of occasions can arise in which lawyer-legislators try to influence judges. For example, is it proper for a legislator to announce publicly that he or she will seek to raise judicial salaries and then, after the raise is enacted, continue to appear as an attorney in the courts? According to Washington's ethics commission, it is entirely proper. It is up to judges, on their part, to resist showing favoritism to those who have promoted their interests. It is up to legislators to decide on issues such as judicial salaries, regardless of their outside interests.

While no one would disagree with the proposition that legislators should not use their office specifically to advance their personal fortunes, we cannot be sure whether they are doing so. Even if they do gain personally while in office, it is by no means evident that what motivates their public action is private gain. They may benefit as a by-product of being in public office, of having high visibility. Attorneys, in particular, tend to attract clients after being elected to the legislature. Those who achieve leadership positions attract additional clients. It may be that some clients hope, directly or indirectly, to tap into the political influence of legislators who represent them. (Some clients, it should also be noted, avoid the controversy that can arise when they are represented by a political figure.) What can be done about this? It is hardly feasible for states to regulate the intake of lawyer-legislator clients. For the most part, the benefits accruing to legislators are marginal and not terribly different from those that would accrue to anyone who has differential visibility or celebrity status.

But some cases do arouse suspicions. One member of the New Jersey legislature had a small law practice before being appointed to the Senate Labor, Industry and Professions Committee in 1983. Within a few years, his practice had grown substantially. Among his clients were Allstate Insurance, Midlantic Bank, Prudential Insurance, and the Money Store. While the senator's committee was considering an overhaul of New Jersey's automobile insurance system, his law firm was defending insurance companies in auto negligence cases.[12] All of this is circumstantial. To demonstrate that the senator was using his public office, certain conditions should be met. It should be shown that the companies his law firm represented had interests in legislation; that such legislation came within the jurisdiction of his committee; and that he supported the legislation. Even then, the case could not be proved. The senator might have supported the legislation on what he thought to be its merits. It is possible that the companies gravitated to his firm because they felt he would appreciate their position and be favorable to them legislatively. That cannot be demonstrated either, although such motivation is not hard to believe. The senator–insurance company connection, however, is too close for comfort. The appearance of undue influence is inescapable. Although I do not advocate more and more regulation, I do believe that the individual legislator must be conscious of the nature of his or her practice, on the one hand, and his or her legislative role, on the other. In this case, the senator had crossed the line.

There is not only the danger that legislators will use their office on behalf of clients, there is also the danger that they will use it on behalf of their family. Some states have antinepotism provisions that preclude legislators from hiring members of their family or bar family members from working anywhere in the legislature. In some states today, and in many states in the past, a legislator's wife might work as a staff member in her husband's office and be included on the state payroll. Because of their relationships, these women knew what their spouses wanted and did excellent jobs. The legislature and the legislators benefited overall. This kind of arrangement is no longer deemed proper. If a family member were to receive a job through the intervention of a legislator, the public conclusion would be that connection, rather than merit, was mainly involved. Because of appearance, more than anything else, legislators have to be wary of what they do on behalf of relatives. This goes not only for hiring but also for inquiring and other minor matters.

There is always a risk that legislators will use their office to benefit not only clients and family but also friends. In the smaller states in particular, everyone who is prominent in public and private life knows everyone else. According to David E. Rosenbaum, President Clinton's Whitewater difficulties stemmed in part from the culture in which he operated: "Political incest is the rule in the less populous states like Arkansas, where the talent pool is small, the hand of Government weighs heavy and the politicians, lawyers and business executives are like pups from the same litter."[13] With a small leadership class, the possibility exists of giving special preference to people with whom legislators have built up relationships, and trust looms large. The question is what should be done about it. I see no fair way to regulate such relationships, and no way without transforming the basic culture of a state.

In many instances, ethical judgments must be made without law or rules to draw on for guidance. It is very much a matter for individual conscience, but a conscience guided by the possibility of negative exposure in the media. For their own political good and for that of the legislature, members had better take into consideration the appearance factor, even when an issue appears trivial. Take a citizen legislator who has an outside job but is seeking new employment. Should the legislator be able to write letters to prospective employers on legislative letterhead? What if the letterhead stationery is not printed at public expense? Generally speaking, legislators should not use legislative letterhead for private purposes, since their public role ought to have no connection to their private occupation. One might object, however, that at some point in their search for employment they would have to reveal to a prospective employer that they were serving in the legislature, so why make a big deal of the letterhead as long as the state is reimbursed for the cost of the stationery? There is a difference, albeit a subtle one, between identifying oneself as a member of the legislature by writing on official stationery and reporting that biographical fact, along with others, with an enclosed résumé. The latter is necessary, the former goes too far.

It is the use of office, not the use of office supplies, that really matters. Take the case of a senator in the New Mexico legislature. He sent a letter to lobbyists and others, thanking them for their help in his campaign, reminding them that he would be chairing a new revenue committee in the senate, asking them for their ideas on how the legislature could increase revenues without raising taxes, and inquiring as to what government could do to help their program or their industry. In the next paragraphs, however, the senator asked for leads on leasing an office building he owned and help in finding a job for his nephew. The letter came to light and was published in the *Albuquerque Journal* on 5 January 1993.

When asked by a reporter for his views on the matter, the cochairman of a task force working on ethics legislation to propose to the New Mexico legislature said that it was a mistake for the senator not to have thought about the conflict. "More care should be taken to separate the private from the public business," he said. In this case, such separation would have meant that the senator would have sent two letters, one dealing with state business, soliciting ideas for revenues, and the other dealing with personal business, asking for assistance with the leasing and locating a job for a nephew. Even then, of course, the connection could have been made. But the senator would not have been the one to make it.

An important and controversial issue in this area involves members of a legislature (whether a citizen or full-time legislature) who leave office and go into lobbying. They may become independent or contract lobbyists or take positions with trade associations, businesses, or other groups.

The question is whether or not legislators might use their current office to set up future jobs and what can be done to guard against it. People believe that many of those legislators who become lobbyists after retiring from the legislature have spent the last year or two of their term in office cozying up to the interests they are seeking as clients or employers. While there is little substantiation for such a popular belief, a number of legislatures have enacted revolving-door provisions intended to keep this from happening. Such provisions prohibit legislators from lobbying for one or two years after leaving office. California, for instance, has a one-year prohibition on lobbying in order to prevent legislative bias in favor of prospective employers while in office, as well as to prevent legislators from exploiting past connections, friendships, and inside information to gain undue and unfair advantage for their clients.

There is no doubt that revolving-door laws make the adjustment for some legislators from public to private life even more painful than otherwise. There is a serious question as to whether putting still another obstacle in the path of legislators meets our fairness standard. Many of them have sacrificed their outside careers to serve in public office. After leaving the legislature, they have nowhere to return. Their skills tend to be political and not managerial. The positions for which they qualify are limited. Moreover, they like the legislative process and are skillful at it. Why shouldn't they seek a career in lobbying? It promises to bring them not only income far beyond their legislative compensation but also the satisfaction of remaining part of the process.

In my opinion, revolving-door provisions are unduly unfair to legislators. True, if revolving-door restrictions applied not to current but only to future legislators, it would not be unfair in one sense. Candidates could choose whether to run or not. But discouraging legislators from going into lobbying fails the test of responsibility. It hurts, rather than helps, the legislative process. Let us say that lobbyists who have served in the legislature have "privileged" access with former colleagues. If that indeed is the case, it is only because these lobbyists already have proved themselves under fire. In their legislative lives, they were able to demonstrate their trustworthiness, so now there is no need for them to develop such a relationship from scratch. Their former colleagues start out trusting and respecting them. If, as legislators, they had proved to be unreliable, as lobbyists they would not be received with open arms by their former colleagues. Thus, only the better legislators are able to make their way as lobbyists. As lobbyists, they have less need than others to entertain as a means of building a relationship. Why should they be prevented for one or two years from entering the lobbying profession? After all, I would think that we would welcome lobbyists who have demonstrated in prior careers their good character and qualifications. Other lobbyists—those without legislative experience—might lose out in a competition for clients, but the process and the public would not.

Sitting It Out

Legislators may be prohibited or discouraged from affiliating with certain interests outside the legislature, or, if affiliated with outside interests, they may be prohibited from engaging in certain activities inside the legislature. They have to sit it out—refrain from sponsoring a bill, voting for a bill, or even serving on a standing committee. Normally, legislative codes of ethics provide that a legislator may disclose a personal interest and state that he or she can cast a fair and objective vote, and then vote; or a legislator can abstain and inform the presiding officer, and then not have to disclose.[14] This means that as long as legislators disclose their interests, they are legally permitted to participate throughout the process. The question for many people is whether they should.

Again, the decision must reside with the individual. There are many tough judgments, many close calls. Take the case of a New Mexico legislator, the owner of a land company, who introduced a bill to let developers like herself subdivide housing lots served by septic systems into half-acre parcels. The state environment department opposed the bill, because septic systems on lots that small could contaminate surrounding water wells. Yet, allowing septic systems on smaller lots would increase the value of her land. She maintained that she introduced the bill not to enrich herself but to help developers market small lots for low-income housing. Is her claim believable? New Mexico lawmakers, like lawmakers elsewhere, are allowed to introduce legislation that benefits the class of citizens to which they belong—in this case, developers—even though it may also benefit themselves. The developer-legislator was within her rights, but in this case she put herself in an awkward position. "It's a good bill," she said, "but it looks like a conflict of interest. I don't feel comfortable with it."[15]

Assuming that she believed in the merits of the issue, the representative in question probably would have suffered no discomfort had the issue not become visible. But because of the way it looked, or might have looked or was made to look, she did feel uncomfortable. Had she anticipated the repercussions, she might have limited her participation to voting on the bill rather than sponsoring it. There are notable differences in the participation legislators can engage in, and she might have chosen a lesser form to avoid the appearance of personal gain. She could have asked one of her legislator colleagues to carry the bill. If she were owed a favor, if it made sense as public policy, or if the developers had other friends in the legislature, this would not have been hard to accomplish. Such behavior on her part would have been something of a subterfuge, but a little distance from the issue would have been advisable for this particular legislator.

We can also examine several examples of possible conflict from Kentucky as they were reported by the *Lexington Herald-Leader*.[16] One representative, a liquor salesman, sponsored a number of bills dealing with alcoholic beverages during his dozen years in the legislature. Many passed, including one that helped protect liquor distributors from liability for the actions of drunken drivers. A committee that the representative chaired also killed Governor Brereton Jones's bottle-recycling bill, which would have placed a deposit on beverage containers. Another representative, an insurance salesman, led a fight in 1992 against a provision that would have required insurance companies to lower their rates. He maintained that the proposed rates were inadequate.

In each of these cases, legislators did not recuse themselves; they participated fully. They took positions that legislators with different outside occupations also took. One does not have to be a liquor salesman to believe that liquor distributors should not be liable for the actions of drunk drivers or that so-called bottle bills are not good public policy. The liquor salesman–legislator may have been doing what he did for private reasons. We cannot know for sure. But we can assume that, being a liquor salesman, he had a different perspective and could be expected to be sympathetic to the industry. Nor does one have to be an insurance salesman to believe that claims and settlements are the problem, not high insurance rates. The industry's argument was persuasive to a number of legislators. No doubt, the insurance agent–legislator was more knowledgeable and more likely to see things from an industry perspective. How should we judge the behavior of these legislators? It depends on their motivations, which we cannot know. Thus, it often comes down to one's sense of a legislator's character and integrity and one's overall trust. It is important, however, that one's colleagues and the public know what one's perspective is.

A third case from Kentucky is of a different nature. One senator had graduated from a South Carolina school that Kentucky did not accredit for licensing chiropractors. He backed legislation to expand the state's list of accredited schools, which would have allowed him to take the chiropractic exam in Kentucky and become licensed. His colleagues pushed the legislation, apparently in an attempt to help him out. A window of opportunity was created so that the aspiring chiropractor-legislator—and a few other people from heretofore nonaccredited schools—would be eligible to take the test. After the bill passed, the legislator took the test and got his license. Nobody was hurt by the passage of the legislation, but one legislator and maybe a few other people benefited. Why make a fuss about it under the circumstances? Because if there was little public policy justification and the purpose of expanding the accredited schools was to benefit a colleague, then the action was an unethical one. It was unethical, no matter that it involved no cost to the state or harm to individuals. While we cannot know for sure what the motivations were, on the face of it there would seem to be adequate reason for doubt.

Generally speaking, both the proximity of a legislator's outside employment to public policy issues and the nature of a legislator's participation within the institution have to be taken into account. If a legislator is employed as an executive secretary of a trade association, that legislator probably should abstain from sponsoring legislation or even acting on bills that are advocated by the association. In such circumstances a legislator ought to abstain, even though participation does not violate an ethics code in his or her state. If they hold other employment, however, legislators should feel free to participate. Take legislators who are teachers or who are married to teachers. Why shouldn't they vote on education issues and school-aid formulas? Representative Barbara Casey of New Mexico, a schoolteacher by profession, defends her participation in the vote on education spending. She supported additional spending, she states, not because she would benefit but because "the voters in my district, knowing of my occupational background and my stands on the issues, sent me to Santa Fe in part to fight for more money for education."[17]

The problem, of course, is that Representative Casey and others like her can be accused of feathering their own nests. It is impossible for them to prove differently. The alternative to participation—abstention—is not the solution. It may be safe, but it is not responsible. In this respect, the response of colleagues to an abstention, as recounted by a former Washington legislator, is informative.[18] He recalls a time when a senator took the floor with a point of personal privilege, asking to be excused on a bill to raise the pay for teachers. The senator said that he was married to a teacher. In reaction, members of the Washington senate split into three equally divided groups. One group believed that if the senator had an ethical problem, colleagues should simply take it on good faith; another thought the senator was grandstanding; and the final group figured he was trying to duck a controversial vote.

Legislators today tend to play it safe and not risk being accused of a conflict of interest by the media or by an opponent. Therefore, whenever a conflict appears to exist, a legislator might be disposed to abstain from involvement in an issue. Sometimes it is more courageous to vote, despite the impression it creates, than to abstain. The major problem with abstention is that, under such circumstances, the recused legislator's constituents are denied representation. It would be ironic if citizens voted for a candidate who worked as a teacher, in large part because he was a teacher, only to find that after being elected as a teacher he would not vote on education legislation. In some states, moreover, abstentions have negative, not neutral, effects. New Jersey's legislature, for instance, requires a constitutional majority to pass a bill (forty-one of eighty votes in the assembly and twenty-one of forty in the senate). If several proponents recuse themselves because of the appearance of conflict, a bill that might otherwise pass could instead fail, not having achieved a constitutional majority.

Voting on the floor is rarely the most significant activity in which a legislator engages. By the time legislation is calendared for a vote, disagreements have been worked out and sufficient support has been aggregated. That is why the overwhelming number of bills pass without serious division, although several bills and a number of amendments each year become contentious and go down to the wire. More critical participation by legislators usually occurs at the committee stage of consideration. It is understandable, therefore, that the composition of standing committees has come under criticism. The grounds are that committees fall under the control of those legislators who are affiliated with the interests in whose areas they are supposed to govern. Typically, the criticism has been directed at judiciary committees, which in the past had been dominated by attorneys. In the present day, with fewer practicing lawyers in state legislatures, the judiciary committees in some places have only a few lawyers as members. Legislators who are elementary and secondary school teachers or administrators tend to gravitate to education committees, while those in banking head for banking, those in insurance, for insurance, and so on.

What are the ethics of such committee memberships? It is natural that

97

people with experience and knowledge in a particular area would want to put it to use in the legislature. Teachers, because of their experience and perspective, have ideas for education policy. Doctors have a peculiar interest and expertise when it comes to health policy. To keep these people from serving on the standing committee that has jurisdiction over their area of concern is to deny them the opportunity to use their skills. More important, it is to deny the legislature and the public the benefit of their experience and knowledge. The only way to ensure that there is no appearance of conflict would be to appoint to a standing committee only members who have no experience, no knowledge, and no interest in the subject within the committee's jurisdiction. Even the most zealous reformer would not want to go that far, I think. The more responsible solution is for the appointing authorities to try to ensure a fair balance in making committee assignments so that no occupational interest dominates.

Informed Consent

In order to deter members from using public office for private purposes, legislatures have adopted rules to minimize conflicts of interest. Some people argue that the rules do not go far enough; others maintain that they go too far.

In a climate of distrust or even skepticism, just about anything can look bad or be made to look bad, and much of the behavior of public officials is viewed as suspect. The remedy, if there is one, is to insulate legislators from all financial interests outside of their service in the legislature. At the very least, this would necessitate a full-time, professional legislature with salaries high enough to make membership possible for those without unearned income. Deprived of private professions and employment, legislators would be heavily dependent on politics, not only for psychological satisfaction but also for economic well-being. If they lost their seats, they would have little or nothing to return to on the outside. More than citizen legislators, professional legislators need the offices they hold and cannot risk jeopardizing their reelection.

Is it worth opting for a full-time, careerist legislature in order to enhance the appearance of ethical behavior? Is it worth it, especially in states like New Hampshire, North Dakota, Wyoming, and many others, where the public clearly is in favor of retaining a citizen legislature? Is there any evidence, moreover, that the careerist legislature is more ethical than the citizen legislature? The answer to each of these questions is no. Although there may be reasons to choose a full-time legislature, avoiding conflicts of interest is not a principal one. Only a little will be gained, but a great deal can be lost. As far as actual ethics are concerned, an apparent reduction of conflicts does not a moral legislature make. The California, Illinois, Massachusetts, New York, and Pennsylvania legislatures—all of which are composed of full-time or practically full-time members— have at least as serious ethical problems as do most citizen legislatures. These ethical problems are less likely, however, to involve conflicts of interest and more likely to involve campaign contributions.

This is not to minimize the damage that can be done by conflicts of interest. According to the appearance standard, outside occupations of legislators will be problematic. But just how heavily should that all weigh? Not as heavily, in my opinion, as fairness to legislators, who are woefully undercompensated for the time they spend and the work they do. Generally speaking, some allowance has to be made for their earning a living on the outside.

Going to a full-time legislature, with more adequate compensation, in order to reduce conflicts is certainly not the answer. Changing an entire system to address a relatively narrow issue would be a mistake, even if it were possible, which it is not. Few electorates today would permit their legislatures to professionalize further. Term limits is meant to be a giant step in the opposite direction.

According to the standard of responsibility, representation should matter more than appearance. There is the belief that if legislators practice other occupations the representational function of the legislature will be enhanced, not diminished. Such legislators, the reasoning goes, will have a better understanding of public perspectives, since they continue to earn their livings like other citizens. They are not as insulated as they would be if their only profession was that of legislator. Moreover, they bring expertise to bear that serves the legislative process well. There is nothing wrong, according to this thinking, with teachers serving on education committees, attorneys on judiciary committees, and so forth. Nothing is served, moreover, for members to recuse themselves on a frequent basis, thus leaving their constituents without representation on those matters and denying the legislature the product of their experience and expertise.

It is my belief that when legislators truly feel there is a conflict, they ought to step back. But it is a disservice for them to be intimidated by what their action may be made to appear. It does not take much to imply a link between one's own personal interests and one's behavior. If members of a citizen legislature or a full-time legislature could not participate in matters that *might* affect their outside interests, then the legislative process and democratic representation would be the losers. It is preferable to risk some conflict situations than to severely encumber the legislative process and those who are trying to make it work.

Disclosure is by no means ideal, but it may still be the least objectionable remedy available. The purposes of financial disclosure laws are to make available sufficient, relevant information to allow citizens to judge whether legislators are favoring their personal interests or whether citizens want persons with such interests to represent them. If citizens are informed, their representatives can be held accountable for their actions. This is not unlike the doctrine of informed consent in the legal field. It confers on affected clients the power to waive conflicts of interest on the part of their attorney, as long as they act voluntarily and with full knowledge of all the risks of the conflict.[19] Information is seldom perfect, and client knowledge, in practice, is usually incomplete—in the field of law and also that of representation. Nonetheless, informed consent doctrines can be operationalized more effectively than any others.

The issue with which legislatures have to deal is not theoretical but practical—how much disclosure ought to be required? Legislators in many places, and particularly lawyers and business people, think that financial disclosure has gone too far. They believe that they are being treated unfairly. Their privacy is being invaded. Their outside interests suffer a competitive disadvantage because of the publicizing of their sources of income and their assets and liabilities. A number of legislators also resent disclosure requirements as an insult to their integrity.

A question in dispute is whether new and stringent financial disclosure requirements discourage good people from running for legislative office. Robert McKay of the American Bar Association, in testimony before the U.S. Senate ethics committee, warned that "if the balance is tipped too far in the direction of disclosure, we may defeat the high purpose of representative government by dissuading the best candidates from submitting themselves for elective or appointive office."[20] Thus far, there is no convincing evidence on this point. Some people do leave the legislature because of conflict of interest provisions. About twenty members left the Kentucky legislature in part because it passed a stringent disclosure requirement and tough rules on conflicts. In the words of Senator Joseph Carraro of New Mexico, "If you have 4,000 pages of ethics law, you won't have legislators. We'd have to give up our businesses."[21] The decline overall in the number of practicing attorneys holding legislative office is attributable, in part, to new rules governing conflict of interest.

But there are candidates to replace those who leave and those who step aside. Legislative office still is desirable, although perhaps not to the same people it appealed to before. Are the newer types—the full-time careerists, the single-issue advocates, the young and the retired—any less qualified for service than the older types? They are different from those we have traditionally thought of as citizen legislators.

Requiring strict financial disclosure alone will not discourage many candidacies, although it may discourage some good ones. In conjunction with other restrictions and together with a hostile press and distrustful public, financial disclosure does affect the recruitment and retention of people in legislative office. Yet, disclosure is ethically necessary if citizens are to be provided with information on which to make a judgment about the behavior of representatives. That information cannot be conclusive; no information can be. Moreover, it is subject to distortion and misuse by the media or by opponents.

In all of this, appearance and perception will count heavily, but primarily in political and not ethical terms. Does it appear to a legislator's constituents or colleagues that a conflict exists and that a legislator is using public office to advance private ends? If that is or appears to be the case, the legislator's standing with constituents and with colleagues may suffer. The legislator risks having to pay a political price for his or her private gain, and for most legislators the risk is not worth running. The political system itself works to restrain the most questionable behavior.

5

Lobbyists and Their Largess

In one of the focus groups we held in Minnesota, the subject of lobbying and lobbyists was brought up. Among comments expressing criticism and distrust, one participant showed keen insight into the system: "The lobbyist is there for one purpose and that is to push his issue through. If I was a lobbyist and I had wanted this to go through, I would do everything in my power to get it through. How far do they go and where do we draw the line?" The advice from ethicists regarding lobbyists is simply that legislators should not vote or take other action solely on the advice or request of lobbyists but "should always apply independent judgment to their duties based on all available information."[1] Every legislator would certainly claim to do so, but legislators cannot escape the problems posed by their dealings with lobbyists.

Lobbyists want something from legislators, and they try their best to get it. The job of the lobbyist is to persuade or influence legislators to support a client's cause. That usually gets down to passing a bill that benefits a client's interests or killing a bill that harms a client's interests. How lobbyists persuade and influence legislators raises ethical questions. What are legitimate methods of persuasion? What are illegitimate? What practices should be disallowed? In this chapter, we set our sights on entertainment, gifts, and various other inducements provided to legislators by lobbyists. In the next chapter, we deal with the matter of money in a system of campaign finance where lobbyists play a part.

Images of Lobbyists and Legislators

If Americans are suspicious of legislators, they are doubly suspicious of lobbyists. When legislators and lobbyists come together, citizens believe that the public interest is being sold out. The contemporary image, as suggested by public opinion polls and the focus groups that we conducted, is that of special interests having their way with legislators, naturally at the public's expense.

Not many citizens—including those in our focus groups—travel to Sacramento, St. Paul, or Trenton to visit with legislators or argue for or against some bill. Lobbyists don't have to travel; they reside in the state capital. They know the legislators; indeed, according to our focus groups, they have wined and dined them to excess. Toadying up to them constantly, lobbyists have achieved "access" to legislators that is denied to the rest of us. It is unfair, according to a focus group participant from New Jersey, who pointed out that while people do not know how to get their views heard, the lobbyists are "down there in Trenton talking to the right people, knowing how to get to the right channels." Lobbyists, according to this view, are the only ones who get to talk to legislators. Another New Jerseyan was of like mind, noting that the expertise and gifts of lobbyists give them a huge advantage: "I'm sure that if an assemblyman could be phoned by a lobbyist or me, the lobbyist would certainly have a better chance to talk to him."

These opinions are not without foundation. There is certainly a basis for them in history, as there is a basis for almost anything in history. There is also a basis for popular views in contemporary practice. The business of lobbying is not without abuse. Everywhere one can find a few lobbyists whose reputations are highly questionable, even in capitol communities that are known for their tolerance. Everywhere one can find a few who spend too much on entertaining legislators and servicing their various needs. On occasion, lobbyists who cross the line are caught. It is no coincidence that where legislators were implicated in stings, lobbyists were also involved. In Kentucky and South Carolina, several lobbyists were convicted. In California, Clay Jackson, the state's premier lobbyist, was convicted of racketeering, conspiracy, and mail fraud for bribing a senator. Elsewhere, too, lobbyists and legislators were inextricably intertwined in scandals of one sort or another.

But America's distaste for lobbyists and lobbying is a consequence not only of patterns of the past and practices of the present. More is at work. The press and politicians themselves combine to demonize lobbyists.

The press today is relentless in its condemnation of the lobbying system. In many states of the nation, at least one of the major dailies wages a crusade against lobbying. In Florida, several newspapers keep up a drumbeat of criticism. Not atypical is the following account from the *Pensacola Journal*: "The Florida Legislature is a wide-open playland for lobbyists armed with unlimited expense accounts. And so many of their playmates—who in their spare time make this state's laws—have become so openly greedy that it's not clear that they even recognize greed anymore" (1 July 1990). The editorial press is illustrated by the *Star-Ledger* in New Jersey, which declared that "the power of the lobbyists cannot be overestimated" (31 August 1991). It went on to set up lobbyists as the enemy of the public interest: "Many lobbyists pride themselves not in the legislation that's enacted but in the legislation that's killed—particularly if it's legislation that would aid the public but hurt their clients." The implication of many of the editorials and analyses that appear in the press is that lobbyists are trying to buy legislators' votes with campaign contributions, gifts, entertainment, and other blandishments. On their parts, legislators are all too willing to sell. An editorial in the *Santa Fe New Mexican* makes the point. "The New Mexico Legislature," the editorialists write, "long has labored in a shadow of suspicion that its leaders are likely to vote on behalf of the last person to buy drinks" (19 March 1993).

No matter how much they personally might rely on lobbyists for information, advice, and campaign contributions, politicians who are up for election find it advantageous to run against lobbyists. This should occasion little surprise, because incumbents and challengers alike have become used to running against the system. Lobbyists are part of the system; furthermore, they are sitting ducks, supposedly representing special interests, peddling influence, and collecting large fees just for their connections. Ross Perot and Bill Clinton denounced lobbyists during the 1992 presidential campaign, as did many candidates for statewide and legislative office throughout the country. Once elected, however, the same candidates who were so adept at demonizing lobbyists were now appointing them to important posts on their transition teams and to policy-making positions in their administrations. Apparently, lobbyists serve a variety of purposes for politicians, one kind in their quest for power and another kind in their exercise of power. The reputation of lobbyists certainly is not enhanced by the manner in which they are used.

The lobbyists that the public considers prototypical bad guys are the "contract lobbyists." They are also known as independent lobbyists, "guns for hire," or just counsel. What distinguishes these individuals is that they are not employees of a single organization but instead have a number of clients, usually ranging from half a dozen to thirty or forty (some may have as many as fifty to one hundred clients). They are much like attorneys in that they represent a variety of interests on any number of issues, not because of their beliefs in the merits of the case but because of the nature of their business. This is not to say that some contract lobbyists do not turn away clients whose cause clashes with their own beliefs but only that such actions are relatively rare.

Contract lobbyists depend more on their relationships with legislators than on the associations, companies, or other clients who employ them. Furthermore, they are more likely than other types of lobbyists to be heavily involved in entertaining, gift giving, and contributing or arranging for contributions to legislative election campaigns. These are the lobbyists who are identified with the uses of money in politics. They are the ones who tend to be implicated in scandals and act as informants in stings.

When people think of influence peddling and corruption, they tend to think of these guns for hire.

The public's perceptions of lobbyists are probably limited to a relative few of the many who buttonhole state legislators. But the few are important in state capitals and in the legislative process.

What Lobbyists Do

This is not the place to examine in depth the job of the lobbyist. But if we are to deal with the ethical issues that arise in the practice of lobbying, it will be necessary to consider one aspect of the job in some detail. That aspect is the building and maintenance of relationships. We have to appreciate that a lot of what goes on in politics comes down to basic human relationships. The goal of the lobbyist is to make connections and develop close relationships with as many legislators as possible, and certainly with the most influential ones. Not all lobbyists subscribe to this goal, but contract lobbyists are true believers.

Relationships are significant because they put a lobbyist in a better position than otherwise to advocate on behalf of a client. A lobbyist wants to win a legislator to his or her side. But that can involve a wide range of activities, most of which are directly supportive, some of which are neutral or even oppositional (although less oppositional than they would have been without the lobbyist's efforts). We usually think of help as a vote for or against a bill, but help can come in an almost infinite variety of forms. A legislator may agree to take a leadership role on an issue with which a lobbyist is engaged. A legislator may be willing to recruit colleagues to a lobbyist's position. A legislator may manage a lobbyist's bill in committee. A legislator may agree to vote to report it out of committee, reserving the right to oppose it on the floor. A legislator may manage the bill on the floor or rally opposition against it. A legislator may provide a lobbyist with critical information as to how his or her colleagues stand on the issue and what might be the best way to win them over. A legislator who opposes a lobbyist's position may agree to remain inactive or vote on the other side without being vocal about it. There are numerous possibilities.

In order to win a legislator to his or her cause, a lobbyist normally must be able to make a case. Increasingly, contract as well as association and company lobbyists must present facts and reasoned argument as part of their case. They have to provide a legislator with information as to why certain action should be taken. Such information includes the benefits (and often the downside as well) of support—benefits to the public, to the state, to the constituency, to the legislator, to the client, and perhaps to the lobbyist as well. In many instances, it may be enough to show that support will not hurt a legislator in any way but still be advantageous and fair to the client. Many of the arguments relate to what lobbyists and legislators would agree constitutes good public policy. In order to make the case to legislators, lobbyists need access; that is, the ability to talk to the legislator and be listened to. Just as support takes on a variety of shapes, so does access.

Lobbyists claim that the relationships they forge with legislators do not get them preferment, only access. Since these experienced practitioners are anything but naive, they must be disingenuous in making such a claim. They must know that more than access is involved. They are seeking advantages that derive from relationships. Relationships count more when relatively minor issues have to be resolved in the legislature. These are issues that do not have much effect on public policy writ large but may have substantial effect on special interests writ smaller. On many of these issues, it is difficult to discern what the public interest might be or if a public interest exists at all. A legislator's constituents may not be concerned or affected. The legislator may have no position to fall back on. The legislator may not care much one way or the other. As Elizabeth Drew puts it, "If an issue doesn't involve a high moral principle, and if it doesn't directly affect an important constituency group, the member is open to persuasion."[2] That happens on a lot of issues. If a lobbyist with whom the legislator has a good working relationship—indeed, a professional friendship—asks for help under such circumstances, why not give it to him or to her? There is no reason not to, and that lobbyist's help may be needed in the future. The less salient other considerations are, the more the legislator-lobbyist relationship counts.

Relationships also count more heavily in the interstices of the legislative process and in the nuances of legislative behavior. A close relationship might not determine a legislator's vote, but it might well affect the vigor of a legislator's behavior at a committee session or the informal conversations a legislator has with colleagues on the issue. The strength of a relationship may also influence in the most subtle fashion how a legislator reacts to the accommodations reached by the affected parties. The less central the action, the more the legislator-lobbyist relationship counts.

I am certainly not arguing that relationships are the most important factors operating, and certainly not on each and every issue. The merits of each case are very significant, and by merits I mean those of a political as well as substantive nature. But when the "merits" are equal, or relatively so, relationships may turn the tide. On visible and controversial issues, it is more difficult for lobbyists to effectively tap into the good will fashioned by close relationships. That is because one or both of the sides in contention have resorted to "outside" strategies and techniques to supplement "inside" ones. These include grass-roots campaigns in which members, employees, and constituents are activated on behalf of a cause. They also include campaigns waged by means of public relations and through the media in an effort to appeal to members of the public and impress members of the legislature. These issues are settled by campaigns that involve the public and not by the relationships that lobbyists have with legislators.

Socializing with Legislators

In developing and maintaining their relationships with legislators, lobbyists try to demonstrate the worthy attributes they themselves possess. Personal ties make it easier for legislators to develop trust and confidence in and a liking for those who are trying to influence them. Like the rest of us, legislators are more apt to do things for individuals they like and trust. If, through a relationship, a lobbyist proves to be a credible, reliable, loyal, empathetic, and likable person, he or she will have made the grade. The path of direct lobbying will be smoother.[3] Furthermore, obligations likely will have been created. Both legislator and lobbyist feel inclined to help out their friends. To my knowledge, there is nothing unnatural in such feelings, but they do get in the way of the objectivity we expect from our public officials.

While their behavior in the actual process of making laws counts most, lobbyists tend to work on their relationships constantly. Particularly when building relationships from scratch, but also in maintaining those that already exist, lobbyists seek opportunities for socializing with legislators. Socializing fosters a sense of familiarity, trust, and sometimes friendship. It allows legislators and lobbyists to establish bonds that are not directly related to the issue or issues in contest. It enables them to agree with and express understanding and sympathy for one another as politicians, spouses, parents, and football fans. From the lobbyist's point of view, socializing pays off in relationship building.

Nearly all of the socializing between lobbyists and legislators takes place under conditions where the former are providing benefits to the latter. The credo of lobbyists is that it is better to give than to receive. Entertainment and trips provide opportunities to socialize and build or strengthen relationships. They also may foster among some recipients a sense of obligation, one that does not have to operate at a conscious level. "He is a pretty decent guy." "It's a pretty good group." "I'd like to help them out if I can." Not that the lobbyist was ever thought to be indecent or the interest group bad, but a legislator's assessment may be subtly shifted in a more positive direction.

For legislators, it is better to receive than to give, particularly for those legislators who are woefully underpaid for the jobs they do, cannot easily afford the cost of living away from home during the legislative session, or have gotten used to the perks that seem to be due public officials. Many legislators sincerely believe that they are entitled to freebies; it is little enough compensation for what they put up with. They are also insistent that they cannot be bought or rented for a drink, a meal, or even greater generosity. Some legislators are envious of the lobbyists' style of life, one that they cannot afford but feel entitled to because of the importance of their jobs. Some are simply greedy, trying to get as much for themselves as possible. A few legislators go way too far and insist on largess from lobbyists, including the use of their credit cards and charge accounts. In South Carolina, for example, some years ago a group of legislators, self-styled the "Fat and Ugly Caucus," regularly demanded food and drink for themselves. In most places now such instances are relatively few and far between.

The capitol community has changed markedly.[4] Lobbyists no longer preside at bars, dispensing benefits to legislators. Today legislative life is less like fraternity life; parties are fewer, wining and dining has diminished, and spending is down. The life-styles of legislators are different. They eat less and drink less. Those who live in the capital or its suburbs go home to their families after a session. Others retire to their condominiums, apartments, or hotel rooms to catch up on their mail and other work. Some jog and work out; they are too busy to be entertained. It should be noted that families and work are priorities not only for legislators but for lobbyists too, particularly the newer breed. Thus, there are fewer incentives for socializing than there used to be, and many more forces are pulling legislators and lobbyists in other directions.

The increased openness of the legislative process has also affected the capital culture. Legislators are constantly under the scrutiny of the media, whose drumbeat of criticism has become inhibiting. They are wary of what they do and with whom they do it. A splendid illustration of the new legislator wariness is provided by New York Assembly Speaker Saul Weprin's announcement, in response to an article in the *New York Daily News,* that he would no longer play poker with lobbyists because it could be perceived as improper. The article had described how the speaker occasionally took part in a weekly high-low poker game with other Democratic assembly members and two lobbyists at a Quality Inn in Albany. Although the lobbyists were old friends of the speaker, in a poker game money did change hands. Even though the speaker was said to have lost more than he won, the perception of improper behavior could not in today's climate be avoided. In the future, when he wanted to play poker, the speaker said, "I'll go and see who's playing, and if one of them is a lobbyist, I'll say, 'Gee, nice seeing you; I'm going to bed.' "[5]

Legislation that has been enacted in the past few decades has had a substantial impact on the community life of legislators and lobbyists. Probably nowhere has law had greater effect than in California. The Political Reform Act of 1974, Proposition 9 on the ballot, restricted the entertainment culture in Sacramento. The ethics law in California was tightened further in 1990 with the passage of Proposition 112 and a companion law enacted by the legislature. The new law barred honoraria, limited gifts, applied gift limitations to lobbyists' employers, and virtually eliminated free trips for legislators. Wisconsin probably has the most restrictive laws today, at least as far as gifts and entertainment are concerned. Except in limited instances, a Wisconsin legislator may not accept anything of pecuniary value—travel, a meal, even a cup of coffee—from a lobbyist or a lobbyist's principal.

The trend nationwide has been toward the limitation or in some places the prohibition of gifts by lobbyists and the disclosure of anything above a certain value given to legislators. The no-cup-of-coffee rule is in effect in a few states. Wisconsin has had it since the 1950s, and South Carolina enacted it after suffering an FBI sting. Minnesota reacted to its "Phonegate" scandal with a similar law in 1994. The new law, banning wining and dining and gifts, replaces one in which no limits existed and disclosure was required only for gifts of $500 or more. Massachusetts also went cold turkey in 1994, adding itself to the list of legislatures that felt they had no alternative.

More common are stringent limits and disclosure requirements. California prohibits legislators from accepting gifts with an aggregate value of more than $250 from a single source per calendar year. Lobbyists are not permitted to make gifts to an individual member of more than $10 a month. New Hampshire limits gifts from a single source to $250 per year, and Kentucky's limit is $100 per year. Iowa imposes a $3 limit on any meal or gift. Florida's new ethics law prohibits legislators from accepting gifts worth more than $100 from lobbyists, their principals, or PACs and requires the disclosure of gifts worth more than $25, but lawmakers in Florida can still accept all the food and drink they can consume in a single sitting. Texas's new ethics law bans pleasure trips and limits the amount that can be spent on entertainment to $500 and gifts to $500 per member each year, although food and drink are not counted under the limit. Ohio legislators since 1994 cannot accept more than $75 a year from any lobbyist. Mississippi used to allow gifts of under $25, on a single individual at one sitting, to go unreported. In 1994, the state enacted a law that allows lobbyists to spend only $10 per legislator per year before having to report. Thus, virtually everything becomes a matter of public record.

All of these limitations have taken their toll on the pleasures and perquisites of legislative life. Entertaining has declined, trips are few and far between, and incidental gifts have been curtailed. Take, for example, the situation in Massachusetts, where a gift limitation had been in effect before the prohibition was recently enacted. In a letter dated 4 May 1994 to individual members of the Massachusetts legislature, Andy Ireland, the Ringling Bros. and Barnum & Bailey Circus vice president for government relations, wrote:

> We recently sent an invitation to you to attend Ringling Bros. and Barnum & Bailey Circus as our guest while it is playing in the state of Massachusetts. Our standard corporate policy has been to offer four (4) complimentary tickets for you and your family.
>
> A recent review of Massachusetts State Ethics Law, however, indicates a fifty-dollar limit on gifts to elected officials. Although Ringling Bros. and Barnum & Bailey is not currently engaged in any lobbying or other activity within the state of Massachusetts, it is of course possible that we may, sometime in the future, have a legislative interest in your state.
>
> In order to comply fully with both the letter and the spirit of the Massachusetts State Ethics Commission, we are imposing a fifty dollar limit on the value of the complimentary tickets.

The letter went on to list ticket prices for circus performances in Boston, Springfield, and Worcester and indicate that the individual legislator could pay the difference between the ticket price and the limit.

The Ringling Bros. and Barnum & Bailey lobbyist had to make sure that his offer of a gift of free tickets conformed to the ethics laws of each and every state where the circus was performing. The laws, obviously, were far from uniform.

Regulating Relationships

It is not my intention to review the body of law regulating the relationships between lobbyists and legislators state by state. One can easily become mired in the details of legislation and lose sight of the principles being pursued. My treatment of relationships shall be in more general terms, taking into account what can be provided and proscribed by law but at the same time considering what withstands an ethical test and what does not. The standards that we have adopted—appearance, fairness, and responsibility—will be helpful in distinguishing between appropriate and inappropriate legislative behavior. I apply these standards to entertainment and gifts, trips, conferences, and other activities that help shape legislator-lobbyist relationships.

ENTERTAINMENT AND GIFTS

Most citizens agree that lobbyists should not be permitted to buy meals or drinks for legislators or to give them presents. Whatever else, it simply does not look right. In terms of appearance, there is no question that legislators suffer in the public eye by taking anything whatsoever from lobbyists. Many legislators see nothing wrong with a system in which lobbyists pick up the tab, but even they cannot argue that it looks acceptable to the public. According to the appearance standard, there can be no question as to the propriety of lobbyists' gifts to legislators. It is improper, ethicists maintain, because it gives people the impression of being so.

Critics of the free exchange between lobbyists and legislators also summon up the standard of fairness. It is unfair, representatives of many groups state, because only certain interests and certain lobbyists can afford the entertaining and gift giving that are required in a nonregulated environment. Business and monied interests attain a position of advantage over other groups, especially as far as gaining access is concerned. In fairness to the contestants, the playing field should be a level one, according to this view. That means outlawing monetary favors.

I find this argument to be less than persuasive. Other groups may have other advantages, ones that are not directly based on the merits of their case either. For example, a number of groups espousing a variety of causes have preferred access to the media, which is certainly an advantage. Their positions tend to be controversial and, thus, appeal to the press. Yet, no way can be found to equalize access by groups to the media. Resources are differentially distributed and exploited. Some have more of one commodity and some more of another. Some groups have a greater arsenal overall and some have precious little of anything. Equalizing resources among the groups should not be an ethical requirement. If some lobbyists are favored—by personality, skill, or socializing—then, so be it.

An appeal to fairness is made not only by representatives of less wealthy groups but also by citizens. People in our focus groups, for instance, pointed out that they were not eligible for similar freebies. A Minnesotan who worked for the phone company reported that employees were prohibited from taking favors from salespersons or others. "If business won't allow this because they're afraid of something," she said, "then why should we allow our representatives to do so?" People are envious of the life-styles of their representatives, whether they have reason to be or not. "There are all kinds of perks that they give themselves that aren't in their salaries" is the way one Minnesotan felt. The popular notion is that legislators cash in on public office. As a California focus group participant explained, "The reason they go into political office and come out with five times the income they went in with is because they have accepted all kinds of favors." These are favors for which the rest of us do not qualify.

Many more legislators lose income than gain it by serving in public office. Furthermore, I find the idea that everyone should benefit equally or not benefit at all unpersuasive. Neither salaries nor working conditions have to be equal. They are not equalized in other areas of economic life. While people seem to have no problem with the life-styles of the rich and famous, they give very little slack to public officials. I return to the subject of the perquisites of office in chapter 7, but for now the point is that the fairness standard does not require us to intervene in the relationships between lobbyists and legislators.

Legislators, on their part, maintain that limiting relationships would be unfair, but unfair to them and not the public. They point out that business executives continue to entertain and be entertained and that journalists are not reluctant to freeload. They can point to those like Sam Donaldson of A BC News who receive huge honoraria for addressing industry groups. Why should legislators be singled out? Their argument has little merit, however. In the case of business executives, entertainment and gifts are a two-way street. People give, and they receive as well. In the case of lobbyists and legislators, the transactions all run in one direction, from lobbyists to legislators. As for journalists, a number do accept food and drink. But such practices have been on the decline since major newspapers have instituted policies to bar fraternizing at the expense of those a reporter may be covering. Those who accept honoraria are subject to criticism from their colleagues.

The principal contention of legislators with respect to fairness is more persuasive. In view of the meager compensation they receive, legislators in many places require and, indeed, deserve the supplementation that lobbyists provide. Take Texas legislators, for instance. Their annual salary is $7,200, and their per diem expenses amount to $95. Although the Texas constitution limits the legislature's regular session to 140 days every two years, special sessions occur with frequency, and members have to spend considerable time in Austin on committee work even when they are not in session. Living is expensive, and the fringe benefits from lobbyists have made legislative service possible for those who might otherwise not be able to afford the financial sacrifice. Legislators from New Hampshire,

Rhode Island, New Mexico, and similar states can also make a strong case along these lines. Given the demands on legislators' time and the limits on legislative compensation, members of most state legislatures have at least some reason to seek redress.

There is little doubt in my mind that, except in a few states, legislators are not paid adequately for their labors and, thus, not treated fairly. But that does not justify them taking other kinds of compensation. Although I can sympathize with their plight, I do not believe that a fairness standard supports the benefits they receive from lobbyists. They have the authority either to raise their pay and increase per diem allowances and other stipends or put such proposals on the ballot where constitutional change and/or a referendum is required. This admittedly offers nothing in the way of a practical solution. It has become politically risky to vote for higher legislative pay, and it is very unlikely that the electorate anywhere would authorize it in a state referendum. However, that is the law, and legislators ought to be able to live with it, if they cannot change it. If they can do neither, they can choose to leave office. To admit that legislators are treated unfairly, therefore, is not to condone any form of compensation. The case for lobbyist largess needs a much sounder basis than that of fairness to legislators.

The responsibility of legislators to the offices they hold and the institutions in which they serve is the final standard to be taken into account. Critics of the gift system argue flat out that legislators can be bought, rented, or, at the very least, influenced by lobbyist benefactors. The public overwhelmingly believes this. A poll of the citizens of Utah by the *Salt Lake Tribune* is illustrative of the public mind-set. It found that eight of ten people surveyed believed that free meals, gifts, and tickets to sporting events influenced lawmakers.[6] One of the questions asked on the *Star Ledger*/Eagleton Poll in February 1994 turned up similar attitudes. It asked New Jerseyans, "What percentage of state legislators are willing to sell out to lobbyists in return for free meals, free trips, or campaign contributions?" Only 3 percent responded "none of them," while 6 percent said "all of them," and 17 percent replied "half." As many as 58 percent of

New Jerseyans believe that half or more of the state's legislators are willing to sell out. Although "sell out" varies in meaning from person to person, we can be sure that for hardly anyone does it have positive loading.

If anyone attended to the debate on gifts that took place in the U.S. Senate, they would have heard member after member emphasize that no senator would be unduly influenced by a gift.[7] The same affirmations can be heard in state legislatures, where gift restrictions or bans are being deliberated. I question this judgment, however. It is difficult for legislators not to be influenced at all, although they might not recognize that what they are undergoing counts as influence. What happens usually is more subtle than any quid pro quo. John T. Noonan, who has written a history of bribes, noted that the Greeks did not even have a word for bribes, because all gifts could be considered bribes. "All gifts," Noonan writes, "are given by way of reciprocation for favors past or to come." Gifts engender expectations on the parts of givers and receivers. But these expectations tend to be diffuse. What distinguishes a gift from a bribe is the nonspecific and tacit character of the request that accompanies the former as opposed to the latter.[8]

Mutual obligations inhere in relationships among individuals. If one person is kind to the other, the other will feel obliged to reciprocate. Obligations are not based only on financial assistance. I am not troubled that legislators feel obliged, but I am troubled by how the obligations are incurred. It is one thing for an obligation to come about through trust or in return for assistance. It is another thing for it to be purchased. Thus, those who criticize entertainment and gifts have a compelling argument to make. Legislators will not be bought for the price of a dinner, but even a free meal or two may incur some obligation, while the habit of taking is even more likely to do so. The results are not certain, but why run the risk?

Legislators and lobbyists declare that the risk is negligible and worth running in the interests of communication. Lobbyists, especially, are concerned that their ability to develop and maintain relationships will diminish. Lyle Cobb, a veteran contract lobbyist in Frankfort, Kentucky, is typical. He believes that entertainment helps him "build rapport and get to know individual legislators." If there was a prohibition, it would limit his access. In Cobb's view, paying for food and drink are "just part of doing business." But why shouldn't legislators pay their own way? "I'm taking up their time," Cobb said. "I think that's part of it."[9]

A prohibition, or even limits, on entertainment and gifts affects different lobbyists differently. Those who rely on other techniques will suffer least; they will gain an advantage over others as a result. Those who already have well-established relationships, such as former legislators, do not have to rely as heavily on socializing to pave their way. Nor do the very knowledgeable have to resort to wining and dining. It should be noted that a number of lobbyists were not unhappy with the restrictive law of Kentucky and South Carolina. They felt that limitations protected them; they were not as likely to be subject to shakedowns. Some of them, reacting to scandals, adopted a no-cup-of-coffee rule for themselves.

A stricter regulatory environment definitely affects the way lobbyists do business. Some lobbyists come out ahead and some behind, as far as adjustment costs are concerned. No doubt, too, lobbyists will have a tougher time establishing a connection with newly elected legislators if they cannot make their time worthwhile in social terms. Legislators are not the ones pursuing relationships; lobbyists are. In fact, with restrictions on lobbyist spending, legislators are more likely to develop camaraderie among themselves. Under the old set of rules, the lobbyist decided whom he or she would invite out. Under the emerging set of rules, legislators will choose, and they are more likely to choose one another than lobbyists.

Without lobbyists to pick up the tab, socializing in general declines. A Kentucky lobbyist who had previously served in the legislature expressed regret for the changes that had come about in Frankfort. "In the past there was trust between government relations people and legislators," he said. Now, however, lobbyists no longer have the opportunity to cultivate a relationship, "so you have to rely on facts and data when you are trying to convince them that you are right," he concluded.[10] A decline in socializing is sure to weed out relationships based on the ability of one party to foot the bill. But firmly rooted relationships will not be seriously affected. Trust may be less easily established, but it will be based on factors more fundamental than conviviality. Its maintenance will depend on one's behavior under fire, not on one's choice of restaurants or wines.

No matter if entertainment and gifts go, communication between lobbyists and legislators will continue. Lobbyists are afraid that if they cannot pay, legislators will refuse to talk to them. There is some danger of that. One lobbyist, a former legislator in Nebraska, informed me that the only time during a session he had to meet with lobbyists was at meals. If lobbyists did not buy, he would not have been able to afford eating out. Instead, he would go home to his capital apartment for lunch and dinner and, thus, save money. This might happen, but I believe that lobbyists and legislators will still manage to come together under a new set of rules.

Another possibility under new rules is that lobbyists will have even greater incentive to use grass-roots campaigns to get their messages across. If they can't socialize with legislators, to make themselves heard they will resort more and more to mobilizing the people back home.[11] Grass-roots campaigns, like candidate-centered campaigns, have their own dangers. They can result in manipulation and deception, instead of the communication of substantive and political information that has been the principal method in dealings between legislators and lobbyists. But, even without the regulation of relationships between lobbyists and legislators, grass-roots campaigns would have become more salient in the current political scene. Resort to grass roots and media is one direction in which lobbying is moving.

Communication will continue because legislators need lobbyists for the information they communicate more than for the gifts they offer. Legislators are well aware that their capacity as lawmakers depends on the perspectives lobbyists bring to the enterprise. They do represent the most affected and the most intense interests. If not offered, their views would still be sought out. The style of communication will change, since fewer professional encounters will be buttressed by prior social engagements.

Legislator and lobbyist interactions may not be as smooth as before, but the two parties will still be able to talk to one another.

Banning entertainment and gifts is easier said than done. Indeed, most states have not seriously considered an outright ban but instead have settled for disclosure. Legislators maintain that letting people know who is getting what from whom is sufficient and sensible. Then the electorate can draw its own conclusions. Otherwise, they warn, some of their colleagues may try to get around a flat ban by taking gifts from advocates who are not registered as lobbyists or lobbyists' employers.

There are ways, of course, of evading disclosure. Several lobbyists may combine to entertain a legislator, with each contributing under the amount where disclosure comes into effect. With several cooperative lobbyists pooling resources, a legislator can partake of much more in the way of benefits. For example, if legislators can accept up to $25 a meal from a lobbyist without having to disclose, four lobbyists may join together, spending $24 each and buying the legislator a $96 meal. The occasion would not have to be reported if the lobbyists divided the tab. Or the cost may be divided among a number of the lobbyist's clients (a loophole in the Maryland law that was closed in 1995). Imaginative and skillful individuals can find loopholes in any law. A few will do so, but most use their energies for more productive purposes. Evasion is always a possibility, but that is not a persuasive reason for wanting to go further than disclosure in regulating transactions between legislators and lobbyists. There are better reasons that I have lately come to endorse.[12]

A few years ago, when I chaired New Jersey's Commission on Legislative Ethics and Campaign Finance, I voted with the majority of commission members to require lobbyists to report what they spent on individual legislators. We did not give too much thought to adopting the so-called no-cup-of-coffee rule, which prohibits legislators from taking anything of value from lobbyists and their principals. More recently, I had occasion to testify on ethics legislation in New Mexico and then in Kentucky. In New Mexico I opposed the no-cup-of-coffee rule; in Kentucky I supported it. The switch was not because legislators in New Mexico are more trustworthy or more needy than legislators in Kentucky. It was just that in a period of less than a year I had changed my mind.

My conversion stems in part from the embattled position in which legislatures find themselves today. Since they are besieged by the media and suspect in the eyes of the public, it is prudent for legislators and legislatures to throw in the towel. Their individual and institutional reputations will continue to suffer unless they abstain from accepting favors from lobbyists. I empathize with those legislators who sincerely believe that prohibiting lobbyists from buying them a drink or a meal is overkill. But, as I have discussed above, the elimination of such transactions rests on ethical, as well as prudential, grounds.

Disclosure may be a reasonable approach to the problem, but it works too unevenly for the well-being of the legislature as an institution. Many members, while believing that they are not doing anything wrong, fear the negative consequences that flow from having made public how much lobbyists spend on them. When New Jersey's new law went into effect, for instance, the press reported on gifts to legislators item by item and legislator by legislator. Everything was grist for the mill, from trips to Bermuda to address state groups to tickets given legislators by lobbyists to attend the annual Legislative Correspondents Club Dinner. The reporting implied that those who accepted such gratuities were doing something wrong; editorials hammered the point home. The same happened in Georgia as a consequence of its 1992 law. With every report of lobbyist expenditures, legislators were taken to task in the press. Those who are willing to accept anything of value are fewer and farther between. After a while, the press may cover lobbyist expenditures on legislators less diligently; but the political danger to a legislator from the press and from political opposition is ever present.

Many legislators in states where disclosure is the rule will only accept gifts below the limit for reporting. Many others decide to take nothing, thereby avoiding the problem altogether. Kentucky's house speaker, Joe Clarke, has gone cold turkey, even though he was not required to do so. "It's reached the point that I don't even let a lobbyist pay for my coffee these days," he said.[13] For many, a disclosure requirement works the same way as prohibition. Other members, however, may choose to continue to take what is legally offered. They may feel safe in their positions and willing to live with having such information made public; they are less concerned about their reputations or political opposition. We do not have to be concerned as much about the individuals who freely choose to take gifts and are willing to run the risks of bad publicity. But we should be concerned about the legislature as an institution whose image will likely suffer further from the fallout. People, unfortunately, are not apt to draw a distinction between the few who continue to take and the many who deny themselves.

I think that legislatures ought to ban gifts, rather than resort to limitations and disclosure. Yet, I am under no illusion that figuring out what to prohibit and what to permit is a simple matter. It is complicated, indeed, and leads to inconsistencies and contradictions. Here are a few of the problems that arise.

Who is proscribed from giving legislators gifts? Registered lobbyists, of course. But if the principals—that is, those who employ the lobbyists—are not covered as well, then the lobbyists' clients can easily fill in for the lobbyists themselves. That would be a sizable loophole, but it is doubtful that many people would exploit it. In regulating principals, it is necessary to specify just who the principal is. In a large company, is it the chief executive officer, the chief operating officer, the vice president for public affairs, or any employee? The problem of definition is a dicey one. Assuming the definitional hurdle is overcome, legislators may still be uncertain and, thus, at risk. A legislator might be having dinner with a high school friend, who picks up the check. That friend may have a position, unbeknownst to the legislator, that would by law be defined as a "principal." Therefore, legislators have to think defensively, lest they open themselves up to criticism in the press and attack by opponents.

What should qualify as gifts? It would be possible, as Florida and some other states do, to exempt food and drink that can be consumed at one sitting. In my judgment, food and drink should not be excluded, even though reasonable exceptions can be made. One category of exception is that of the reception or dinner held by a group, association, or organization which legislators are invited to attend and perhaps address. During the legislative session, three or four nights each week a number of state-wide groups hold receptions in the capital. Each member of the legislature has constituents who belong to a group and attend the affair. Legislators generally feel that they have little alternative but to accept any such invitations. It would be bad constituent relations and bad politics not to. It is difficult to conceive of most receptions as "entertainment" or "socializing." For legislators, they are work.

It makes little sense—practically or ethically—for legislators to be treated differently from others at these large receptions. In Iowa, legislators are limited to under $3 in what they can accept as a gift. Therefore, at morning receptions accompanied by breakfast, two lines will form: one line for juice, muffins, and bacon and eggs and another line, a legislators' line, for juice and muffins only. If legislators in Iowa were to breakfast like other reception-goers, they would have to reimburse the organization for food and drink consumed, and that would require that the organization be able to prorate the costs. Imagine the following case: Representative Jones is invited by the x y z trade association to attend its annual legislative reception held at the Golden Goose one evening. He has a bill up late in committee and another engagement that same evening. But he wants to be seen at the association's affair, so he stops in for fifteen minutes, during which time he eats seven carrot sticks and six broccoli florets and has a soft drink. If there is a no-cup-of-coffee rule, Representative Jones would be in violation. If there is a limitation, the charges would have to be figured out.

A distinction can be made between a lobbyist's entertainment and an association's reception. The only thing they have in common are food and drink, but the quality differs markedly. I see no reason, except for slavish conformity to a general principle of prohibition, to bar legislators from accepting what they are offered at receptions. As far as ethics are concerned, no obligations are likely to be engendered, no advantages conferred. Legislators may feel close to the groups that invite them to attend, but what they receive at their receptions has nothing whatsoever to do with their attachment.

Wisconsin, which arguably has the strictest laws of any state in the nation, provides that no lobbyist or client may furnish anything of value to a legislator unless it is furnished to the general public as well. That might make for even larger receptions than otherwise. The city of Superior, Wisconsin, puts on a feed for the legislature in Madison every year. The purpose is to acquaint members with the city and its people with the obvious hope of advancing the Superior legislative agenda. The ethics board predictably ruled that the event had to be open to everybody, so it was opened up to the public, many of whom came. Minnesota's new law makes an exception: if legislators speak at a gathering, they can accept food and beverages, but they still must disclose. Under their new law, Ohio legislators are not limited in what they eat and drink if it is provided as part of a conference to which the entire house or senate is invited. South Carolina, which also has a no-cup-of-coffee rule, also makes an exception. Receptions here are exempted if particular legislators are not singled out for invitations but rather all members of the legislature, or all members of the senate or house, or even all members of a specified standing committee are invited. South Carolina's seems to be an eminently reasonable approach.

Problems inevitably arise when entertaining and gift giving involve lobbyists and legislators who are friends. Should legislators be prohibited from accepting gifts from friends if the friends happen to be lobbyists? Suppose, moreover, the friendships developed before one became a legislator and the other a lobbyist? Legislators argue that a no-cup-of-coffee rule will unfairly restrict relationships among people who are friends. I know legislators and lobbyists who are friends, independently of their respective roles. But these people are relatively few, and their friendships should be able to endure the regulation of gifts. Most legislator-lobbyist friendships—as friendly as they might appear—are primarily professional in nature. The test of friendship is to pose the question, How many legislators are invited out by lobbyists after they are no longer in public office? The answer is, precious few.

Ethically, there should be no problem, but operationally, distinctions are tough to make. In some states, gifts among friends are exempted from restriction. This can, and does, lead to evasion. A lobbyist may entertain a legislator as long as the lobbyist is not reimbursed by his firm or client for the expenditure. But a loophole exists if the lobbyist, instead of being reimbursed, simply bills his clients more or draws a higher salary. California has also tried to make distinctions, but not without avoiding loopholes. Legislators there are permitted to take "home hospitality" as a gift as long as the lobbyist is the host. Thus, lobbyists can invite legislators to catered house parties without any restrictions on the monetary value of the entertainment applying. Yet, from the lobbyist's perspective, home entertaining can be the most desirable method of building relationships. A lobbyist has reason to believe that if legislators partake of hospitality in the lobbyist's own home, a relationship can be enhanced. Under California's home hospitality provision, a lobbyist cannot lend his or her place at Lake Tahoe to a legislator for a skiing weekend. That would constitute a gift, if the lobbyist wasn't there. With the lobbyist present, however, friendship can be invoked—despite the fact that such circumstances are the most beneficial for lobbyists, who rely heavily on socializing.

With regard to friendships and home hospitality, as with regard to many other instances, regulatory rules can do only so much. They are open to manipulation and evasion. Someone surely can figure out a way around them. But most will not make the effort. They will be willing to conform to the spirit of the law.

Although entertainment constitutes a large share of what most legislators receive, numerous gifts are also offered. In Tallahassee, for example, lobbyists roamed through the legislative office buildings, leaving in their wake gumdrops, popcorn, peanuts, and other tidbits. The gifts also come larger: car alarms, auto repairs, cuff links, jackets, football tickets, and the use of a lobbyist's credit card.[14]

Relatively few of these gifts have any bearing on the legislative process, but some do. I have less trouble, from an ethical point of view, with the smaller gifts than I do with wining and dining generally. Many gifts that legislators receive are simply tokens of appreciation, and nothing more. To refuse them would appear discourteous, a rejection of the person offering the gift. Take as an example the gift baskets delivered to the hotel rooms of legislators from five states in the region attending a conference in Sheridan, Wyoming. The products included a wrapped piece of pound cake, a jar of pure honey from a store in Kaycee, a bottle of Johnny Midnight steak sauce and a pad of sticky notes and a ballpoint pen from Buffalo, a pad of paper from B.J.'s Art in Wheatland, and a pen and a paper napkin inscribed with the names of ranchers and ranches produced by the Cattlewomen of Johnson County. There was little danger of creating obligations here.

Although I endorse a ban on gifts, exceptions ought to be made for things of little or no value, items that are not useful to the recipient. The operating rule might be "The more a legislator likes what he or she receives, the less right the legislator has to receive it." This kind of self-denial does not come easily to people in general nor to legislators in particular.

Among the most prized gifts in many places are tickets to sporting events—collegiate and professional football, basketball, baseball, and hockey games. Tickets for University of Kentucky basketball games were a major bone of contention during legislative deliberations on an ethics reform package in 1993. Members did not see why they should have to give up that one perk. As one legislator put the issue, "The cost of ethics is higher during basketball season than during football season." The Kentucky solution was to allow for tickets to the sporting events that counted. In its definition of anything of value, it specifically excluded the costs of attendance and food and beverage at events sponsored or coordinated by a state or local government entity, including a state institution of higher education. However, several universities, and most importantly the University of Kentucky, have adopted policies that require legislators to pay for their tickets, but they are still accorded preferred access and get

VIP seats for the basketball games of the Kentucky Wildcats. This appears to be a reasonable solution, even though legislators are receiving a benefit that other citizens normally do not get. Ohio State University followed suit when the state legislature was shaping its ethics bill. The university president announced that OSU would not finance a trip for legislators who traveled to a football bowl game at the end of the 1993 regular session. The previous year, eight legislators and their guests were part of the OSU delegation.[15]

Washington passed a law placing limits on gifts at its 1994 session, with exceptions for unsolicited flowers, plants, and floral arrangements; unsolicited advertising or promotional items of nominal value, such as pens and notepads; unsolicited tokens or awards of appreciation in the form of a plaque, trophy, desk item, or wall memento; informational material, publications, or subscriptions related to the recipient's performance of official duties; food and beverages consumed at hosted receptions where attendance is related to the state officer's official duties; and admission to, and the cost of food and beverages consumed at, events sponsored by or in conjunction with a civic, charitable, governmental, or community organization. Each legislature, and each legislator as well, will have to decide just where to draw the line on gifts. In Wisconsin, anything of value is ruled out, but that leaves plaques, calendars, and pens—items of token value. Other states limit gifts to $400, $200, or any specified amount but require disclosure. Still others have no limits but rely on disclosure. In some places, anything goes. The taking of gifts by public officials has no ethical foundation, but prohibiting everything may be going farther than is reasonable.

GETTING THERE IS HALF THE FUN

The trips that legislators take, compliments of lobbyists or the groups they represent, constitute one type of gift. Twenty-four Florida legislators who had accepted hunting, fishing, and pleasure trips all over the country and to Mexico, France, Switzerland, the Caribbean, and even Florida neglected reporting them as statutorily required. The legislators claimed, as a matter of fact, that they did not regard trips as gifts. One of them, at the adjournment of the 1989 legislative session, on exiting the house chamber had asked two lobbyists in the rotunda area if they had had a successful session and if they got what they wanted. The legislator then unabashedly solicited a white-winged dove hunting trip to Mexico.[16] That may be as blatant as it gets.

In most states, trips are covered by the same ethics laws that cover gifts. Trips occasionally go unregulated, but more likely they have to be disclosed and are limited as to dollar cost. In some states, they are prohibited just as other gifts are prohibited. Given the discussion of standards earlier, it is appropriate to ban trips, or at least pleasure trips with lobbyists or ones paid for by lobbyists. But in the domain of travel, exceptions have to be made.

Not all travel is the same. Some legislative travel is truly a broadening experience. It is work related rather than pleasure inspired. If such trips are curtailed, a legislator's performance of his or her representational role will be adversely affected. I have in mind here trips that legislators take in order to communicate and teach. They are invited by statewide or national associations, companies, or organizations to address conferences or annual meetings. They attend in their roles as state legislators—leaders, committee chairs, and specialists in one subject area or another. Presumably, these groups and their members have legitimate interests in the state. It is valuable for them to hear from legislators, even if they use the occasion to try to win legislators over to their positions.

Few would question the propriety of legislators traveling to such meetings in state, even if their expenses are paid by the group extending the invitation. Questions arise, however, when the meeting is held out of state at a resort area. Legislators may be accompanied by their spouses and make use of the occasion for pleasure as well as work. They may take a few days extra as vacation, partly subsidized by the organization that has paid for their travel. There is no doubt that, on occasion, legislators are invited by groups to meetings in resort locations not because of what they have to say but because of who they are. Such an invitation would be little different from the offer of a gift. There is no way to control these instances without completely banning speaking engagements. That would be a mistake.

I think it is important for legislators to address groups with an interest in legislation, even if these groups are meeting in a desirable location. That would not be possible unless the group extending the invitation were to pay the legislator's way. If legislators happen to enjoy themselves on the occasion, so be it. They will probably suffer on enough other occasions to make up for the enjoyment.

The benefits that legislators derive from these official trips can be regulated. California and a few other states limit the number of days for which legislators can be reimbursed by private parties, so that work and vacation cannot easily be combined. For example, if a California legislator is invited to address an interest group meeting in Honolulu, she will be allowed one day for travel each way and another day for the session. I believe that this is an extreme measure, and one that would apply to very few cases anyway.

New Jersey's Commission on Legislative Ethics and Campaign Finance had a better suggestion with regard to out-of-state travel at an organization's expense. Since individuals were invited by virtue of their legislative positions, the activity constituted a legislative function for which the legislature, as well as the member, should assume responsibility. What this would mean is that a group would not only invite the member but also request permission of the senate or house—through the leadership or a rules or management committee—for that member to participate. The member's expenses would be paid by the senate or house, with reimbursement furnished by the group. Thus the legislative body could, under unusual circumstances, veto the member's participation or specify the duration of the trip. Normally, control would be exercised gingerly; but still responsibility would be institutional.

Benefits that accrue incidentally to the official business of legislators can be tolerated. I see nothing ethically questionable about a legislator enjoying a visit to a resort while conducting or participating in a seminar.

Many professional and business organizations hold their annual and other meetings in more, rather than less, pleasurable environments in order to attract members. This should come as neither a surprise nor a shock to most human beings. What about the danger of a legislator feeling a sense of obligation to a group as a consequence? Take the following case of Legislator Smith: "Six months ago, I spoke at the XYZ company's annual convention held in Ft. Lauderdale. My speech involved the work we were doing in the area of tax policy. My airfare was paid by XYZ, along with lodging and meals for three days, with the total cost probably about $1,000. Now, XYZ has a bill they have asked me to introduce. Should I author, co-author, or even vote on such a bill in committee or on the floor?" I see no reason why any action should be precluded, depending on Legislator Smith's judgment as to the merits of the bill. It is impossible to know how Smith feels toward the XYZ company because of three days in Ft. Lauderdale. But I do believe that the importance of allowing legislative communication with concerned members of the electorate outweighs the slight sense of obligation that might have resulted from the Florida visit.

While incidental benefits can be condoned, direct benefits cannot. A legislator should not be permitted to have a spouse's way paid by the sponsoring organization. Most legislators would agree. The Josephson survey found that while legislators thought taking free trips for official purposes was acceptable, only one third thought it proper for a spouse to be paid for.[17] Moreover, legislators should not receive honoraria for addresses they make by virtue of their being members of a state legislature. Why should they be given extra compensation for performing their legislative duties?

The question of whether a member could accept an honorarium was raised in the state of Washington a few years ago. The house Board of Ethics rendered an opinion that because the existing ethical standards did not expressly deal with the subject, it could not decide the issue. But the board pointed out that the state code of legislative ethics, while not expressly proscribing honoraria, could be construed as an implicit ban. It provides that "a legislator shall not accept any gratuity or compensation for services rendered in connection with legislature employment other than legislative salary."[18]

In a number of states such as Florida and New Mexico, legislators are now prohibited from receiving any honoraria for services they render as legislators. If a legislator is invited to speak as a member of a profession—of law or medicine, for example—that is another matter. As long as the primary focus of the address is not the legislature, legislation, or one's role as a legislator, then an honorarium can be in order. It is interesting that Wisconsin, which has such stringent ethics laws, still permits legislators to receive honoraria for talks on state issues, if the honoraria are "reasonable." That usually means $100 or less, but it depends on the ethics board's determination.

Another kind of legislator travel is of concern here. On a number of occasions legislators have gone on fact-finding trips that were paid for by private interests. The question is whether members should participate in privately funded tours to examine facilities in connection with proposed legislation.

An example from Connecticut makes the point. The state was considering a bill, proposed by the senate majority leader, to legalize casino gambling in a few places. Steve Wynn, the casino entrepreneur, wanted to develop a convention hotel and casino in Hartford. As part of his pitch to the state, in February 1992 he offered members of the legislature an all-expense-paid trip to view the gaming facilities he ran in Las Vegas. When the *Hartford Courant* found out that a number of legislators might accept Wynn's invitation, it editorially called such a trip "ethically improper" (8 March 1992), since legislators should not take a very expensive gift from someone who stood to make a great amount of money from their action. Legislators argued, however, that a field visit to see the workings of a casino would serve a valuable informational function and would help them with their decision on gaming in Connecticut. They did not believe that the state could afford to pay their way, so it would be worthwhile to have a private party do so.

The senate majority leader requested an opinion of the state ethics commission on the propriety of such a trip. The commission's executive director, in his response, indicated that the commission's position was that the state should fund its own operations and activities to avoid actual and apparent conflicts of interest. But the legislature instead had chosen to allow by law "gifts to the state" of "goods or services," which facilitate legislative actions or functions. The reason for such a provision was the budgetary benefits of having private entities fund state activities in tough economic times. This fact-finding trip, the executive director opined, unquestionably served a legitimate state purpose. This was not an endorsement of the trip but rather an interpretation by the ethics commission of the law. As for the ethical question, the executive director went on: "The determination of whether such a trip is appropriate, as opposed to legal, must be made by the potential participants and their colleagues, the news media and, in this case, ultimately by the elected officials' constituents."[19] Most of the 187 members of the Connecticut General Assembly were either frightened off by the press or believed that such a trip was not appropriate. Only four took Wynn up on his offer and went to Las Vegas.

Although it was a working trip, my feeling is that in this instance the large majority of Connecticut legislators made the correct judgment. It might well have been useful, but it was by no means necessary for them to eyeball gaming facilities in Vegas in order to decide whether to legalize casino gambling in Connecticut. They already had a lot of grist for their decisional mill. But the combination of Vegas, casinos, nightlife, together with Wynn's proposal for Connecticut made the trip suspect as far as the press and the public were concerned. An appearance of impropriety weighed heavily against it, while neither responsibility to the legislature nor fairness to legislators weighed in its favor.

There have been proposals made recently to prohibit fact-finding trips taken by legislators but paid for by private interests. I disagree with any blanket prohibition, believing that such excursions should be left to the case-by-case judgment of the legislature. Not all fact-finding trips are as questionable as the one to Vegas. Legislators are invited to tour numerous facilities in connection with matters on their agenda. Members in Connecticut, for example, have toured a nuclear facility in northeastern Massachusetts, visited an energy recycling plant in California, and traveled to Washington DC to observe police detective techniques, all as guests of interested parties. None of these trips, incidentally, stirred negative comments.

Ideally, the state should foot the bill; realistically, this is not apt to happen, not with state budgets as tight as they have been. Legislatures are skittish about using state funds for any kind of travel. We cannot expect legislators to pay their own way, nor should their campaign funds pay, if that is possible. Thus, either a private party pays or legislators forgo whatever legislative benefits may derive from visiting a site. But some people fear that on such an excursion legislators will be unduly influenced by their hosts. It could obviously be made to appear that way. I do not think we have to be concerned that legislators will hear from only one side, no matter who pays for their travels. They are likely to hear from two or more sides, from a variety of lobbyists, experts, and the grass roots as well. A fact-finding trip constitutes another source and another type of information and as such can be fruitful.

Allowing "gifts to the state," as in Connecticut, means that the legislature can choose whether the "gift" is worthwhile. The choice should be with the legislature and can be based on two considerations: first, how useful the fact-finding trip is likely to be; and second, how the trip is likely to be portrayed by the media and perceived by the public. Let the legislature weigh the factors, consider the trade-offs, and determine whether the state has more to gain or more to lose by allowing a legislator to take a trip paid for by a private interest. Sometimes the state will have more to lose, but many times it will have more to gain. Legislators ought to have the intelligence and judgment to figure this out; the responsibility should lie with them.

REGULATION HAS ITS LIMITS

Regulation can be used effectively to control relationships built mainly on lobbyist largess, but it does not serve well to control the development of friendships between lobbyists and legislators. The development of such relationships between lobbyists and legislators is problematic. But law is no remedy.

Romantic relationships, although relatively rare, can create concern. But these relationships can be handled well. Anne MacKenzie is the majority leader of the Florida house, and Walter Law is a lobbyist for an association of small banks. They had been dating, then were engaged for years, and finally were married. Throughout these life changes, they have been free of trouble. Representative MacKenzie has been careful not to help her husband out legislatively, although she does check on the status of bills for him. However, she will not lobby her colleagues on his behalf. She declined an appointment to the commerce committee, which has jurisdiction over banking legislation. When one of Law's bills comes up for a vote, she seeks counsel from colleagues on its merits. It helps, too, that hardly any of Law's bills are controversial when they reach the floor. Compromises have been worked out along the way, so the vote is an easy one. MacKenzie must vote even on banking legislation, since there is no provision for Florida legislators to abstain because of a conflict. She declares her interest and casts a vote. The MacKenzie-Law relationship has worked without outside regulation.

Not all such relationships work so well professionally. It is impossible to generalize about these matters. Much depends on the position of the legislator, the nature of the lobbyist's practice, and just how the two handle their professional interactions.[20] Even if romance does not bloom, friendships inevitably develop over time. Lobbyists are personable and helpful; legislators are gregarious. The two types have much in common.

Friendships are understandable, but the risk of legislators and lobbyists getting too close has to be recognized. It is not easy for legislators who become friends with lobbyists to stay impartial, particularly on obscure bills that are important to the lobbyist but hardly to anyone else. Why offend a friend over a bill that doesn't really matter?

Because relationships have the potential of influencing legislative behavior, some would like to limit them wherever possible. The press casts suspicion on them whenever they develop. For example, the *Boston Globe* on 15 December 1991 ran a story on the fact that several leaders of the Massachusetts house and some of the state's top lobbyists lived in the same enclave on Martha's Vineyard. All the plots had been bought at the same time, and the *Globe* left the reader with the distinct feeling that something was unsavory about the arrangement. The state's director of Common Cause was quoted as expressing concern about the proximity of lobbyists' and legislators' property. "Non-professional relationships between lobbyists and legislators do not engender public confidence," he said.

Despite risks, which can never be eliminated, I see no compelling reason to attempt to restrict relationships further. Regulations in this area are already cumbersome, for lobbyists as well as for legislators. Consider state government relations professionals who are employed by national associations or corporations. Some of them have responsibility for a few states, or even ten or twenty, and some of the unlucky ones have to cover all fifty states. Imagine them trying to keep track of different lobbying regulations from state to state as they visit several places on a two-week trip. For lobbyists with multistate assignments, this area is a mine field. One such lobbyist checks with his company's legal counsel every time he leaves headquarters for a visit to the field.

Given the extent of regulation in this area, it is not surprising that lobbyists here and there misstep as far as disclosure, limitations on entertainment, and reporting deadlines are concerned. Not unusual is the case of the former aide to the chairman of the appropriations committee of the Maryland house. During her first year lobbying, one client contracted with her to amend a bill that had already passed the house in order to have the client included in its coverage. The lobbyist was paid $2,000 for the effort. But the bill was quickly killed, almost before she could get her lobbying under way. Believing that she had not earned the fee, the lobbyist offered to return it. The client would not accept the offer—fortunately for the lobbyist. Otherwise, the lobbyist could have been indicted for working on a contingency fee basis, which is illegal in Maryland.

The Weight of Appearance

Appearance, as a standard, must be given considerable weight in the relationships between legislators and lobbyists. Cozy relationships, based on lobbyist largess, arouse both the media and the public. Many of the practices that go on in many states raise questions that, if unanswered, lead to the further erosion of trust in government. Arguments in favor of fairness to legislators can be made but are not terribly strong. Legislators who claim that they are so underpaid that they are entitled to lobbyist handouts have other recourse—they can raise their legislative compensation, get better jobs on the outside, or leave legislative service entirely. Fairness dictates not that lobbyists continue picking up the check but rather that restrictions be reasonable so that certain exceptions can be permitted.

In the area of legislator-lobbyist relationships, the standard of responsibility does not pull in an opposite direction from that of appearance. Except in some instances (such as that of legislator trips as a result of "gifts to the state"), it is better institutionally to limit the gifts that legislators take. Gifts of any substantial nature may incur obligations on the part of legislators. Such obligations should be minimized, although they cannot be eliminated from the lawmaking process. The more responsible course is to take as little of monetary value as is practically possible. Thus, a no-cup-of-coffee law, with specified exceptions, makes general sense (although it may not apply equally to each and every legislature).

Beyond a certain point, however, the regulation of relationships is of little utility. Indeed, like anything else in political life, if it goes too far it may have perverse consequences. The major purpose of law in this area should be to change legislative cultures so that giving-and-taking is no longer the dominant mode of interaction. Most legislators and lobbyists have already gotten the message.

6

Dilemmas of Campaign Finance

Some of the gravest concerns of legislative ethics are associated with campaigning for office. Although our principal focus in this book is on the legislative arena itself, the principal focus of legislators is on winning reelection. More and more of what they do not only during the fall months before election day in November but year-round is designed to help them stay in office. It is little wonder, then, that the campaign is fraught with ethical dangers. Given the nature of campaign invective today, totally ethical campaigns may be too much to wish for. Realistically, the only attainable objective may be limiting unethical behavior. Political campaigns are designed to achieve power, regardless of ethical values, and despite the criticism and carping, the system overall has worked well. We have competitive politics, with opportunities for substantial participation by citizens. We agree to abide by election results and, thus, enjoy smooth transfers of power from one individual to the next and from one side to the other. Over the years, we have made many changes in the electoral process, but its major features remain intact. We must be wary, therefore, that in trying to enhance campaign ethics we do not do more harm than good. We want to keep the baby but get rid of the bathwater.

Underlying the ethical dilemmas of political campaigns is the fact that candidates and parties have as their principal goal that of winning office. Elections possess the features of games—there are winners, losers, rules, strategies, tactics—and can be analyzed by political scientists in game theoretical terms. But to the principals involved, they are far more than games. For individuals, they mean influence, careers in politics, and personal satisfaction. For parties, they mean majorities in a legislative chamber, positions of leadership, and power over policy. The difference between winning and losing is enormous for both individuals and parties.

The desire on the part of individuals to stay in office and on the part of the legislative parties to win seats makes campaigns and elections moments of ultimate truth. Candidates will do anything—or almost anything—to win. The end—election or reelection, with everything that goes with it—is of utmost value. Because the end involves not only personal but also party fortunes and various policy outcomes, a persuasive case can be made that a broad range of means must be permitted to achieve election or reelection. It would not be right or moral to sacrifice a worthy end to maintain the purity of one's means. This is the rationale that undergirds political campaigns. The drive to win, at whatever the cost, raises many ethical issues. The one that will be discussed here is the influence of money, by way of campaign contributions, in the legislative process.

The Root of Evil

Before state legislatures had come of age, Jesse Unruh, the speaker of the California assembly and inventor of modern-day legislative campaign finance, referred to money as the "mother's milk of politics"—a necessary source of nourishment for a healthy political body. That is still the view of politicians today, although few are willing to say anything positive in public about the part played by money in politics. For the press and the public, money is the root of evil—not all evil, perhaps, but much of it. "The major ethical issue of the next decade," writes ethicist Michael Josephson, "is campaign finance reform."[1]

HOW MUCH DO CAMPAIGNS COST?

No one would deny that political campaigns have to be financed, since it takes money to run a race for legislative office. It requires less in districts that are safe for one party or the other than in those that are highly competitive. It requires less in a state like New Hampshire, where districts are smaller and campaigns are door-to-door, than in a state like California, where state senate districts have a population of 744,000 (and are larger than congressional districts) and state assembly districts 372,000 and where mass media and direct mail are the principal campaign techniques. It requires less in states that have fewer residents, such as Wyoming, North Dakota, and South Dakota, than in states with larger populations, such as Illinois, Michigan, and Pennsylvania.

Depending on the place and circumstances, money will buy the resources needed to run a campaign. Many candidates naturally believe that they cannot get along without the services they purchase, and they acknowledge that these services cost money. In order to reach people with their message, candidates feel compelled to spend. They need television, radio, and direct mail. And they need polls in order to know how to frame their message for different audiences. Yet, despite the calculations of these political clients, the popular belief today is that too much money is spent on campaigns.

People point to California, where Tom Hayden spent a record $2 million on an assembly seat and Cecil Green spent $1.4 million in a special election for a senate seat. In 1992, five senate candidates in California spent over $350,000 in the general elections and ten spent over $250,000 in the primary, while forty-three assembly candidates spent over $225,000 in the general and eighteen spent over $150,000 in the primary.[2] In Washington, five campaigns in 1990 topped the $237,283 record of 1988, and seven other races exceeded $200,000. The 1990 average for forty-seven candidates in the senate races was $111,183. That same year in Oregon, the campaigns of fourteen candidates ran above $120,000.[3] By contrast, campaign costs in states like New Hampshire and Wyoming run only a few thousand dollars for most races. In fact, the highest amount spent on a house race in Vermont in 1992 was $2,262. That same year the top expenditure was $11,880 for a house race in Montana and $21,492 for a house race in Maine. The impression that people have appears to be that even more is being spent than is actually the case. Participants in Minnesota focus groups, for example, thought that contributions were higher than they were and that a state legislator might spend at least $100,000 to $200,000, and sometimes $500,000 to $600,000, in his or her quest for reelection. The highest amount for a house race in Minnesota in 1992 was $42,273.

Alarm is occasioned by the fact that the amount of money being expended has grown markedly over recent years. The trend is unmistakable. In a national survey of 304 veteran state legislators, 79 percent said that campaign fund-raising activity was on the rise.[4] In many places, one can point to the price of tickets for fund-raisers. In Massachusetts, for instance, $100 used to be the ceiling; now tickets go for $125 or $150. Tom Loftus, the former speaker of the Wisconsin assembly, recalls that he spent $11,000 on his first campaign over a decade ago. That was the most expensive race that year. Some of today's campaigns in Wisconsin still are run for that amount, but open seats or competitive races typically cost $50,000 or more. The 1991 New Jersey legislative campaigns totaled $15 million, a 34 percent increase in just four years, with one challenger spending $420,456 and two more exceeding $400,000. Sixteen campaigns cost over $200,000. For the most part, these were New Jersey's competitive seats, targeted by both parties. Toward the lower end of the scale, in Idaho the average cost of running for a senate seat tripled in twelve years, from $4,400 in 1978 to $15,000 in 1990, and in Vermont between 1984 and 1988 costs increased by 52 percent.[5]

Again, critics of campaign finance point to California as a horrible example of out-of-control expenditures. About $1.4 million were spent in legislative contests in 1958. By 1978, the amount had grown to $20 million, and by 1988 it had grown to $68 million. The amount dipped to $54 million in 1990. The drop does not signify a decreased reliance on campaign money in California; rather, it largely results from two factors. First, contribution limits, which were voted in Proposition 73, were in effect in 1990, before the state supreme court reversed them. Second, the gubernatorial race that year was extremely costly and drew funds away from legislative campaigns.[6] Generally speaking, inflation and population growth have something to do with rising expenditures. A study of California found that, after adjusting for these two factors, the amount spent actually decreased from 1980 to 1992.[7] Academics, analyzing the costs of state legislative races, have also noted the nationwide increases. But a recent study that examined data for six houses and four senates (in Idaho, Missouri, Montana, Oregon, Washington, and Wisconsin) found a tremendous variation in campaign-expenditure growth rates.[8] Even where campaign spending is growing, so is spending on everything else, with the U.S. gross domestic product doubling between 1980 and 1992.

Whether or not growth has been consistent, uniform, or dramatic, the absolute amounts spent are deemed to be a threat to democratic politics. The criticisms of the campaign-finance system, as it currently exists in most places, are several. First, the amount of money that is spent is too high. There is simply no need to throw dollar after dollar into political campaigns. Second, the system is unfair because it favors incumbents and discriminates against challengers. Overall, incumbents outspend challengers by roughly two to one, although the disparity is less in the most competitive districts. Third, the system is undemocratic because it is based on inequality. The haves, who can afford to give, wind up with privileged access, while the have-nots are at the rear of the line. Fourth, legislators have to spend too much of their time chasing money when they should be devoting themselves to working on matters of public policy. Fifth, the legislative process itself is distorted, because too much emphasis is placed on what benefits the campaign for reelection and too little on the needs of the state. Sixth, and most important from our perspective, is the corrupting influence of money on individuals engaged in the legislative process.

Elizabeth Drew, in writing about campaign finance at the national level, stresses that it is not the amount of money spent but "what the chasing of money does to the candidates, and to the victors' subsequent behavior."[9] Campaign contributions, according to more extreme views, are quid pro quos—given in return for legislators' votes. One academic critic sees little difference between such contributions and bribes, asserting that politicians and interest groups "engage routinely, not in 'legalized' bribery, as is commonly supposed, but in felonious bribery that goes unprosecuted primarily because the crime is so pervasive."[10]

In my opinion, the case against the present system of campaign finance is wildly exaggerated. This is not to say that money is without moral consequences but rather to assert that its effects are usually more subtle and more buffered than is popularly believed. As Frank Sorauf notes in his book on the subject, the debate over campaign finance has been extremely one-sided. The reformers have enjoyed an overwhelming advantage in publicity and in both moral and political superiority. Despite the fact that the majority of officeholders would prefer to leave things basically as they are, practically no one has defended in public the system as it exists. Sorauf does so, mainly by trying to put the issue of money into proper perspective. I agree with his assessment that money has come to explain too much too easily. The assertion that campaign contributions determine legislators' decisions ignores all of the alternative, competing, and supplementary explanations of behavior. Most important are the effects of legislators' own values, the preferences and needs of their constituents, the influence of party leaders and colleagues, the input from staff, and the merits of the policy arguments. Much more than money is at work in the process. But very few aspects of American politics fit the metaphor of Plato's Cave better than the realities of campaign finance. The reality of the grotesque image, perceived by so many, is "a reality difficult to square with the evidence, but it is just as difficult to ignore."[11]

WHAT DOES MONEY BUY?

Let us focus for the moment on the alleged "corrupting effects" of campaign contributions. Even if other factors play an important role in legislative decisions, it does not mean that money is benign. The important questions to explore are, What do legislators do—if anything—in return for contributions? When? Under what circumstances? Before addressing these questions, however, we shall ask why people contribute. What is their intention; what do they expect in return? By exploring these questions, we will arrive at a more accurate assessment of how money operates in the legislative system; and such an assessment is prerequisite to trying to figure out what to do about money in legislative politics.

"Let's face it," said one of the people in a Minnesota focus group, "you give somebody money, you're not giving them money for nothing." A *Los Angeles Times* poll (3 January 1990) found that by a two-to-one ratio Californians agreed that most state legislators were for sale to their largest campaign contributors. Each contributor wants something in return, even if it is only to feel engaged in the political struggle. The truth is that a variety of motives underlie people's behavior in contributing to legislative campaigns. Often motives are mixed or multiple.

First, people contribute out of self-interest, in the purest sense of the term. The candidate contributes to his or her own campaign. Most candidates invest in themselves, and some invest a lot. At the inexpensive end of the continuum, some arrange to finance their races with practically no help from others. Some manage to pay for a large piece of the campaign action. In 1992, the average personal contribution in California was over $23,000. One was nearly $800,000.[12] It would seem that the use of one's personal wealth has been increasing at the state legislative level, not to mention in U.S. Senate races. Contributions from oneself are not thought to be corrupting, since it is highly unlikely in the normal course of affairs that one would be bought by oneself. Money is not suspect here, although we may not want a wealthy candidate to be able to exceed contribution limits placed on others and outspend an opponent by a large margin. Although we tend to trust the probity of candidates who are wealthy, we still have reservations about their buying their own elections.

Second, people contribute because of friendship. Many of a candidate's contributors are friends and relatives. They give regardless of the candidate's record, stand on policies, or campaign promises. They derive satisfaction from being able to help out. Their relationships usually antedate the candidate's political career and are based largely on nonpolitical considerations. In the smaller states, where campaigns are still rather inexpensive, a sizable proportion of a candidate's war chest may come from friends. But the more expensive the campaign, the less likely it is that personally related contributions will amount to a large proportion of the total. Like contributions from the candidate, contributions that are given out of friendship are not suspect. That is because we assume that contributors want nothing in return that would compromise a legislator's conscience or integrity. No ethical problem attaches to money coming from these sources.

Third, some money is given out of a sense of civic duty or for partisan reasons. Partisan money goes to the candidate because of the party to which he or she belongs. Many Democrats typically contribute to Democratic candidates because they believe that their interests and those of the nation are better off in the hands of Democrats. Such giving may even be habitual, depending less on the qualities of the individual candidate and more on the candidate's party affiliation. Contributors can get returns on their gifts, but they tend to be in the form of general policy positions rather than any specific outcomes. Generally speaking, partisan money is not corrupting, not to a substantial degree. It is still proper in our civic culture for citizens to support the parties and candidates with whom they philosophically agree. When contributions are too large, however, people begin to suspect the motives of the donor. What is he or she getting from the party in return?

Fourth, there is money given by interest groups, the so-called special interest money. These are the funds that we worry about, since we have reason to assume that lobbyists and their principals are contributing in order to get something in return. Much of the money funneled into campaigns comes from special interests—interests that range widely and include labor unions, large corporations and small businesses, professional and occupational associations, sportsmen's groups, and numerous others. In California, for instance, during 1993–94, the largest campaign contributions came from associations of optometrists ($638,802), teachers ($601,250), doctors ($503,742), trial lawyers ($445,364), restaurants ($388,000), dentists ($370,729), and state employees ($335,726).[13]

A large part of the special interest money is channeled through political action committees, or PACs. The percentage of candidates' campaign funds that derive from PACs varies from state to state. But it is not unusual for these committees to account for half of the contributions legislators receive. A review of the campaign-finance literature shows that by the mid-1980s PACs accounted for one third of the funds for legislative candidates in Pennsylvania and Missouri (and a larger proportion of the funds of incumbents). In California and Washington, PACs were responsible for over half the total contributions. In Massachusetts, for example, the *Boston Globe* on 23 May 1993 analyzed over forty thousand contributions during 1991–92. The newspaper found that three fourths of the $8.8 million total was donated by thirty interest groups, with lobbyists and PACs accounting for nearly 30 percent of donations over $50. The *Globe* pointed out that Francis G. Mara, the chairman of the house insurance committee, received more than half his money from PACs and 97.1 percent from special interests who had bought tickets to the legislator's fundraisers. The total, however, was only $34,500, not an outrageous amount.

The fact that special interests do most of the giving should occasion little surprise. Most Americans do not contribute to candidates, and many rank-and-file citizens who do give, give only small amounts. Legislators in states like Illinois, Texas, Michigan, California, New York, Pennsylvania, and Ohio would have to curtail their campaigns were they not able to turn to interest groups and their lobbyists, members, and PACs for the bulk of their funds. Legislators have to rely on special interest money for their campaigns, just as special interests have to rely on legislators for a hearing and help in the process of enacting policies and regulations. Because the two are mutually dependent, we may have cause for concern.

The stage is set for the quid pro quo, an agreement that in exchange for a campaign contribution, a legislator will do such and such for a donor. While the explicit agreement is rare and would legally constitute a bribe, there are all sorts of possibilities on each side of the transaction. Special interests do not give for nothing. The Josephson survey reported that 92 percent of California legislators and legislative staff polled thought that contributors expected special advantages.[14] Giving is instrumental to the accomplishment of group purposes. Clearly, groups would like to be able to influence legislators so that their interest benefits (or, at least, is not harmed) in the legislative process. Dollars are one of the resources that business, labor, professional, and other groups can use to exercise influence. A letter to members from the New Jersey Optometric Association's PAC illustrates the point. The association was trying to pass a bill that would allow optometrists to prescribe eye drops to treat common eye ailments, but the ophthalmologists were strongly opposed. In asking its members to contribute to its PAC, the letter held out a promise: "Hard work and tons of bucks will get us the bill this year." The bottom line for the optometrists was: "If you want it, you have got to pay for it."[15] Naturally, the givers want also to get, but the ethical propriety of their dealings depends on their intentions and on just how close their political contributions come to being bribes.

One intention of campaign contributions is to reelect friends, legislators who are like-minded and vote with the group on the issues. No bribe is intended, none is received. Legislators will defend the system by arguing that money goes to those who are already on the side of the particular interests who give. Money follows votes, not the other way around. To some extent, this formulation may beg the issue. A legislator might have been recruited to a group's cause as a result of campaign contributions at the outset of his or her career. Now, however, the legislator is a friend, possibly a good friend. Democratic legislators receive money from labor and Republicans from business in large part because their philosophies and values coincide. The special interests who give to their friends want to maintain them in office because they serve the interest's purposes or what the interest maintains is the public's purposes. The motivation behind these contributions is a selfish one, but little danger exists that the legislator will be seduced since legislator and lobbyist already are sleeping together.

Another intention of campaign contributions is to get more out of friends. Even if legislators are predisposed in the group direction, they can contribute more or less to a legislative effort. They might be followers or leaders in a group cause. As followers, they can be counted on for their vote, but not much more. As leaders, they will be involved throughout the process and with many of their colleagues. The commitments of time and effort are very different. Campaign contributions may be intended to induce legislators to opt for leadership rather than followership and devote additional time and effort to the cause. Although legislators are not acting contrary to their values or conscience, an ethical issue is posed if contributions induce them to make a greater commitment than they might otherwise make. Along these lines, contributions may also help induce legislators to intervene on a group's behalf with administrative agencies of government, as in the case of the U.S. Senate's Keating Five, who went far out of their way in support of Lincoln Savings and Loan.

Campaign contributions are also given in order to sway the openminded. On many issues, legislators have no record and their constituencies have little or no opinion. Special interest issues, in which each side has narrow concerns, abound in the legislative process but have little currency outside. Many actions are on specifics that may be crucial to the groups involved but to no one else. Money, it is thought, can make some difference with members who have no position generally but may be of use specifically.

While money may also be intended to convert enemies to one's side, this is very unlikely to be the case. Few legislators would consider an about-face in gratitude for a campaign contribution, and few contributors would expect them to do so. More likely is the contribution that aims to soften opposition. Indeed, a good deal of money is channeled with little thought of ideology. How else can we explain contributions to candidates after they are elected when the contributor supported their opponents before the election, or contributions by political action committees that give to both sides? The winners in these instances may not be sympathetic to a group position, but their opposition may be softened. Instead of leading a fight against an interest, they can follow the lead of others. Instead of speaking out forcefully, they can remain silent until called upon to vote.

Instead of trying to persuade colleagues to oppose an interest, they can let their colleagues decide for themselves.

Special interest money is not given without regard to how it can influence recipients. That is the way in which lobbyists, PACS, and state governmental relations executives justify their budgets. Their employers are not charitable institutions. A contribution to the legislator who chairs a committee that has jurisdiction over legislation affecting a group's interests, and especially to a legislator who has opposed the group's legislative program, is designed to exercise influence. It may not succeed, but there can be little question as to its intention.

Campaign contributions are not routed on a one-way street. To some extent they are offered voluntarily, but to some extent also they are offered involuntarily. Special interests give in part to acquire influence but also to avoid losing influence. The solicitation of funds from lobbyists and PACS by legislators has become a high-pressure activity. No special interest contributor is certain of what message legislators are sending when they solicit funds, but most interpret it to mean that giving is the better part of valor. The implication is that those interests that command money have to pay to play. A contribution is like an ante in a poker game —sweetening of the electoral pot is required before one can be dealt a hand.

Michael Josephson, in his survey, found that 67 percent of California lobbyists felt they were coerced into giving.[16] Evidence presented in the trials of several legislators indicated that they indeed were. Many lobbyists feel that they are being shaken down, victimized by a system that has gotten out of control. They do not know what would happen if they stopped giving, and they do not want to find out. In a system where contributions by special interests are a way of life, no interest can afford to behave differently from the others.

Not giving may cost a group standing with legislators who believe that it should be providing financial support to the electoral process. Giving, then, reduces the risk of losing standing in the legislative arena. It not only succeeds defensively, but it also has an impact offensively. Special interest money counts. According to critics of the system, it dominates the process and determines outcomes. According to others (and I include myself here), it plays a much more subtle role and varies by issue, action, and individual.

Money buys influence, no matter what. It is as simple as that, in the view of the press and the public. The print press typically will report on a special interest issue in terms of the votes of members who received contributions from the parties involved. The inference is that the vote follows the money and that money is largely responsible for the legislature's action on the issue. In media accounts, little room is left for doubt, even though the evidence usually is exceedingly weak. People in our focus groups in California, Minnesota, and New Jersey share the media's conviction. They believe that lobbyists approach legislators with promises of campaign contributions if they vote favorably and that legislators, in turn, take the offer of money into account above everything else. (This, of course, would clearly constitute a bribe.) The big contributors, according to focus group participants, are "the ones that get the vote," even though they do not always prevail.

It is difficult, however, to prove what nearly everyone is convinced is true. Although considerable research has been conducted by political scientists on the impact of campaign contributions at the congressional level, the results are inconclusive. Most of the studies have tried to relate money to roll-call votes: some have found a relationship; some only a weak relationship, with party, ideology, and constituency more important; and others no relationship at all. But studies that focus on floor votes fail to take into account many key actions that take place elsewhere or more subtle ones that are difficult to discern and impossible to quantify. Moreover, a statistically significant relationship is not causation. Which came first—the contribution or the disposition to vote a particular way—cannot be demonstrated. A few studies have gone further, examining contributions and the behavior of standing committee members. They found that money mainly bought the marginal time, energy, and legislative resources that were expended in committee work.

The impact of money is not a subject that lends itself to empirical analysis. Roll-call voting data are insufficient indicators of the process and its possibilities. Even committee activity is only the tip of a much larger iceberg. Too many factors shape the behavior of legislators for money to be singled out. There is no way imaginable to hold everything else constant and thus be confident that money is the cause. The only route in exploring the influence of money is to ask legislators themselves. But legislators have mixed views on the subject; furthermore, they are not the most trustworthy of sources when questioned about their own motivations and behavior. Nor are they entirely reliable when asked not about themselves but about the motivations and behavior of their colleagues. Money is too sensitive and too politically charged a subject to speak about or perhaps even to think about candidly.

Despite the fact that empirical evidence linking legislative behavior to campaign contributions leaves much to be desired, I too believe that money talks. Its voice may not usually be loud; its message may not always be clear; but something usually gets through. Except in isolated areas, money's effects normally are indirect and subtle, not direct and blatant. Money may operate subliminally as well as aboveboard. None of this can be proved, statistically or otherwise, but the case is a strong one. It is not one that is conventionally made. Surely, it is not made by those, like Common Cause and the media, who argue the overwhelming and blatant influence of money. Nor is it made by legislators who claim that money is benign because it only flows to the already converted anyway. Nor is it made by lobbyists who admit that money buys access but not much more.

There is widespread agreement that campaign contributions facilitate access. But nearly everyone with standing—which would include group, constituency, or economic status—has, or can have, access. "Access" in politics obviously means more than "admission," "approach," or "entrance," as defined by the dictionary. It means, to some extent, preferential treatment. There is access and there is access, and money buys special attention. If legislators have a pile of pink slips at the end of the day, they will likely put at the top of the pile those from the angels who back them. If legislators are tough to reach during the end-of-the-session crunch, their big contributors still have a good chance of getting in touch with them.

Although legislators and lobbyists acknowledge a relationship between money and access, increasingly such a relationship is being questioned on ethical grounds. Of those legislators and staff members in California surveyed by the Josephson Institute, 70 percent agreed that providing special access to contributors was an ethical violation, while 72 percent of them believed that more than half the legislators did so.[17]

I have argued in a somewhat different context that access is too weak a word to convey how relationships between lobbyists and legislators pay off. A stronger word, I wrote, is "connection," meaning a tie or a bond. In the transactions more is given than even preferred access, and connection serves a broader purpose.[18] Now, I would maintain that prior to either access, connection, or influence a sense of obligation is created by a campaign contribution. If money comes with any strings attached, these strings usually are in the form of obligations that are inevitably felt by recipients. The feeling may be stronger or weaker, but a sense of obligation is there nonetheless. The reasoning underlying such a feeling might run as follows: "Anyone who supports me in my campaign can't be all bad. In fact, they must be somewhat good. Therefore, if I can (that is, if it doesn't conflict with my own values and my constituents' needs), I will help them out."

For former Ohio legislator Dean Conley, contributions create an "attitudinal tendency" on the part of the receiver to be supportive of the contributor: "I'll support you unless I can find or be given a strong reason not to."[19] Senator Fernando Macias of New Mexico echoes the thought, declaring that it is just human nature for legislators to listen more attentively to campaign contributors. "Personally," he stated, "I think it is naive for anyone to suggest that it [contributing to a campaign] doesn't, I won't go so far as to say influence, but it puts you in a special category."[20] Representative Leslie Johnson of Arizona described how she came to feel a sense of obligation: "I had a lobbyist host a fund-raiser. After that I realized I felt differently about him. I regarded him as a friend. That made me uncomfortable."[21] Not everyone, however, realizes just what is going on and acknowledges being softened up, as Representative Johnson did.

Bill Lockyer, president pro tem of the California senate, is one who does. He is unusually candid in commenting on the "indelible impressions of who supported you and who opposed you," especially the first time a legislator runs. "It sometimes takes years to be able to sever that sense of connectedness, responsibility, obligation, whatever you might call it." Conversely, Lockyer remembered that the largest contributor against him in his first race was the realtors. "It took a while for me to look at a bill sponsored by the realtors fairly," he recalled. "I'd try, but I'd have this little feeling that they were my enemies."[22]

The sense of obligation that develops with respect to campaign contributions operates either at a conscious or less than fully conscious level. Legislators who are aware of incurring obligations rarely are involved in an explicit exchange of contribution for a specific action or inaction. That behavior is beyond the pale. More likely, the exchange is implicit, with legislators adjusting their behavior to the need for money. They understand what they are doing and justify it by consequentialist reasoning. The ends—their election—justify the means—occasional cooperation with the interests that fuel their campaigns.

Jesse Unruh of California was a skilled practitioner of this mode of legislative politics. Unruh raised money from the interests long before it became commonplace for legislative leaders to do so. He felt it was necessary to fund Democratic assembly campaigns, elect majorities, and enact legislation he believed to be of benefit to the people of California. Along the way, however, the speaker had to give the groups who fueled his fund-raising something in return. He did so but felt he was providing them with relatively little compared to what the Democrats and the state were gaining. Fleshing out policies and programs that benefited California, in Unruh's view, justified the bones thrown to the special interests.

I believe that legislators often reason this way. Their election depends on reaching the voters, which depends on financing a media campaign, which in turn depends on special interest contributions. If they lose to their opponent, the reasoning of legislators goes, the people in their districts will suffer. That is because their opponent (1) cannot be trusted, (2) is not competent, (3) has the wrong values, (4) supports misguided policies, and so on. Moreover, there is the danger that the other party will gain control, or greater control, and this will undermine the well-being of state and district. It would be irresponsible of them not to do what is required—up to some undefined point—in order to win reelection. If that means going along on unimportant issues or in marginal respects to help a contributor, so be it. Reciprocity is the name of the game in elective politics.

Such justification is not beyond the pale. The legislative process is driven by the engines of negotiation, bargaining, compromise, and trade-off. The campaign, after all, is part of the process. The problem with such reasoning is that it can be applied quite indiscriminately. It can justify almost any behavior on the part of legislators. Whatever they do, then, becomes morally, as well as politically, necessary if they are to win and, thus, govern.

A number of legislators do very little to compromise their principles, some because they have few to compromise, but most because they may not be engaged in particular issues or specific behaviors. There are those who are in denial, believing that campaign contributions have no effect on them. Whatever they believe, contributions do have some effect. I suspect that legislators become more inclined to listen attentively to a group's substantive arguments if that group has contributed to their campaign (or has been friendly and supportive in other ways). Much of the policy that is proposed by various groups affords considerable leeway for legislative decision making. In today's world, lobbyists and the interests they represent make arguments on the merits. In more and more places, lobbying is becoming merit- and substance-based. Whatever goes into the decisions that legislators make, they have to be prepared to defend these decisions on the merits. Thus, legislators need not simply repay favors from their contributors. All they have to do is see the merits of a contributing group's position. Merits normally can be found on both sides. The optometrists have a good case, but so do the ophthalmologists. The insurance companies argue persuasively for tort reform, and trial lawyers make a compelling argument against it. When the cases are reasonably balanced and other factors—such as one's principles, record, or constituency—do not intervene, the legislator has to decide whom to go with and how far to go. The nudge of a generous campaign contribution can cause legislators to look at the information furnished by that group much more positively than the information furnished by the opposition. As a consequence, legislators' actions are based on policy, not on money—although the money helped them to conceive of the policy arguments differently than otherwise would have been the case.

Whether the process they employ is one of justification or of rationalization, the overwhelming majority of legislators are limited in what they will do to fulfill obligations. Campaign contributions do matter, but less than most of us assume. The more important an issue, the less they matter. The effects of money appear at the margins or when other things are equal. Incurred obligations usually are fulfilled on narrower issues, more specific items, and peripheral behaviors, few of which are highly visible or have a clear public interest connotation. Obligations are less likely to be fulfilled where legislators are constrained by commitments, beliefs, constituency pressures, or strong partisan considerations.

The influence of money, political scientists believe, is in inverse proportion to the importance of an issue. Frank Sorauf has pointed out that the influence of PAC contributions tends to be strongest on "the narrower less visible issues before the Congress," which are referred to inside the Beltway as "free votes."[23] The same applies at the state legislative level, where the large majority of issues fit this mold. Among them are many "special interest" issues that have only indirect relevance to statewide policy. They primarily affect the pocketbooks of various business and professional groups. These interests try to manipulate the regulatory environment, gain ground at the expense of rivals, or try to put competitors out of business by seeking state intervention favorable to their cause. For every group looking for some advantage, some other group is resisting being taken advantage of.[24]

Take, for example, the "Car Wars," fought out between Hertz and Avis on one side and Alamo and smaller firms on the other. The main issue in this battle waged throughout the states was the collision damage waiver (CDW), a contract provision in which the rent-a-car company waives its right to recover damages against the renter. Alamo and the smaller companies, which rent primarily to individuals, profited from the fees for such waivers, while Hertz and Avis, which deal primarily with self-insured companies, had less of an investment in the practice. It was in the interest of Hertz and Avis to have CDWs prohibited or restricted by legislation, since they would put their competitors at a major disadvantage. Both sides, of course, argued the merits of their position in public policy terms. It was a complicated issue on which few legislators had a position and in which few constituencies had an interest. The role of lobbyists and campaign contributions might well have made a difference here. Another example is provided by the struggle over ankle injuries between orthopedic surgeons and podiatrists. The issue is whether or not podiatrists should be permitted to work on ankles, an issue that hinges on the definition in law of where the foot stops and the ankle begins.[25] It is difficult to imagine that many legislators had deeply held beliefs on this issue or that many of their constituents would be seriously concerned. Legislators could adopt either argument; they might go either way. On an issue like this, money might make a difference as to whose argument received greater weight and ultimately how legislators lined up. Alternatively, money might make for a contest that neither side wins. The result is a draw, no decision or gridlock, and a chance later on to raise more money from the two sides, who again wage battle.

Campaign contributions might have an effect on broader, more visible issues, but probably not on their fundamental dimensions. The effect is more likely to be on specific items. Take the tort reform battle, which encompasses insurance, product liability, and workers compensation legislation. In this nationwide contest, the trial lawyers and consumer advocates line up on one side and insurance, business, and doctors line up on the other. Many legislators have staked out positions on this contentious matter, but they still have considerable elbow room on the details of the legislation. Whichever side they are fundamentally on, they can tilt in the other direction on specific provisions. In legislation, the specifics are where it's at anyway. Tax policy offers another example of the importance of the interstices of legislation. Certified public accountants are generally opposed to a sales tax on services; but should there be one, they want to be exempted as a small business. A legislator who favors such a tax could still serve the interests of the CPAs, and a generous campaign contribution might stimulate a thought process that leads to such service. When legislators raise taxes, they frequently turn to tobacco, since "sin taxes" are the least painful of all. The amount of additional taxes that might be imposed on cigarettes ranges considerably. How much legislators decide to levy will depend on a number of factors, one of which may be campaign contributions from the tobacco industry.

Money counts far more at the periphery than at the core, and that includes the peripheral behavior of legislators. Campaign contributions are not likely to affect legislators' roll-call voting behavior or their decisional behavior as members of a standing committee. It is more likely to affect the way legislators relate to the lobbyists who are responsible for the contributions. Legislators will provide lobbyist supporters with valuable information, pointing out that the lobbyist has a problem with legislator A or legislator B, alerting them in advance that something is about to happen, warning them that they are heading for trouble. Legislators will also favor their funders by introducing them to other members, opening doors, vouching for their integrity. Most important, legislators may ensure that lobbyists and clients who have contributed get a seat at the table, meaning that they are invited in on critical negotiations among the contestant groups in efforts to reach a compromise.[26]

As mentioned earlier, campaign contributions may be intended to modify the behavior of legislators, making them a little less vehement than they might otherwise have been. John Vasconcellos, a veteran member of the California assembly, described the temporizing effects of money: "When you know that the next day you've got to ask for a thousand dollars or five thousand dollars for your campaign from some group, it is more difficult to be explicitly 'anti' their position. You may speak against them, but you speak more softly rather than rant and rave."[27] If a legislator speaks out forcefully, he may persuade several colleagues and bring over some votes that otherwise might have supported the measure. If a campaign contribution can help accomplish that, it would have served the contributor's purpose.

Campaign contributions are made with the intention of advancing the donor's interests in some manner. Donors may not know what effect the contribution will have, if any, but they do not want to take the chance associated with not giving. Many of us take a dose of vitamins daily, not knowing whether they are effective. The evidence that they do help is inconclusive. But if we can afford the vitamins, why run the risk of not taking them? Campaign contributions are a better bet, even though the givers may not get a big bang for their bucks.

Those on the receiving end tend to feel obliged, and their obligations are translated by processes of justification and rationalization into actions at the margins, actions, however, that extend beyond access. Obligations are a normal part of political life. Money is by no means the only thing that creates obligations on the parts of legislators, or anyone else for that matter. Working in a campaign, supporting the legislator on issues, being a friend of the legislator—all tend to oblige legislators in some way.

Obligations that legislators feel cannot be eliminated from the legislative process, nor should they be. But campaign contributions differ from friendships, political support, and so forth. It is not that they appeal to the legislator's self-interest and therefore are corrupting. Whatever contributes to a legislator's reelection serves the legislator's self-interest and cannot in this respect be distinguished from money. For legislators, the political and personal are intertwined. Winning reelection is in both their personal and political interest. They would claim, moreover, that it also is in the public interest. Money is distinctive, because its distribution in society is not based on democratic principles as are votes or popular support; its distribution, moreover, is extremely unequal.

How Money Can Buy Less

Money in politics has an unsavory appearance. Even though appearance as a standard should not dominate, we ignore it at our peril. When legislators act in the interests of groups that have contributed to their campaigns, the question of influence is raised in the public mind. Many observers believe that when an official accepts large contributions from interest groups, whether or not the official's judgment is actually influenced, citizens are morally justified in suspecting that the official's judgment has been influenced. We are compelled to deal with the problem of money, if only for the sake of appearance.

But more than appearance is involved. The obligations that campaign contributions engender ought to be reduced. John Saxon writes that the harm flows not from money itself but from the likelihood that the influence is disproportionate to that which it should have. He also maintains that while other forces may also have disproportionate influence, "the *least defensible* influence which can compromise autonomous legislative judgment is money."[28] I would agree that money is distinctive, because legislators' principal obligations should be to their own values, their districts, their supporters, their colleagues, and the institutions in which they serve. They should not be to the funders of their reelection drives. In this way, the ethical standard of responsibility will be furthered. So will that of fairness, since there is no good reason why monied interests should have marked advantages. The number of people, the merits of the case, dedication, resourcefulness, and the like ought to have free play in a democratic system. Money also is a form of participation, but its play ought to be limited.

Reducing the obligations stemming from campaign contributions is not as simple as reformers make out. In part, that is because our campaign finance systems are by no means simple. They have multiple purposes, including encouraging challengers to run; leveling the playing field; permitting candidates to get their message across; enabling legislators to raise funds without spending inordinate time and effort doing so; keeping down the total amount spent on campaigns; and trying to ensure that special interest money does not corrupt recipients. These purposes are not subscribed to by everyone, but each is held by an important segment of the public. Nor are these purposes consistent. For example, permitting candidates to get their message across and keeping down the total amount spent on campaigns work against one another. When the media are the primary communicators and repetition is required if an audience is to be informed, it is hard to see how a message can be delivered at low cost.

A number of recommendations have been offered to reform campaign finance in the states. We shall examine several of them in terms of their likely effect on legislators' sense of obligation. Some recommendations would have little or no effect but are intended to accomplish something else entirely. We have to keep that in mind in assessing a recommendation's merits as far as obligations are concerned. We have to recognize also that we are intervening in a larger system than that related to obligations and that changing one element may have effects on others. It is advisable to try to anticipate those effects and decide whether the trade-offs are worthwhile. We may decide that reducing obligations is not worth adversely affecting competition or making fund-raising a more time consuming activity for legislators.

Legislators, on their part, generally tend to be satisfied with the arrangements under which they won, and have continued to win, their offices. Yet, they will act contrary to their own interests when under pressure. Legislators do not agree on what the solution might be.

Citizens, on their part, believe that the current system is corrupt and corrupting, but they are far from agreed on what should be done to improve it. They have not come out in droves to support public financing or any reform, for that matter. A recent exercise, part of the Democracy Agenda Project, made the point beautifully. The exercise gave 222 midwesterners, broken up into 19 groups, several hours to inform themselves about the problem of congressional campaign finance and possible solutions. People read a paper that described the system and its problems and gave the arguments in favor of and opposed to various solutions. Then the people in the groups discussed campaign finance and voted on their preferences. This "attentive public," which was critical of elements of the system, still could not reach consensus on proposed solutions.[29]

The record of campaign finance reform, moreover, does not offer much hope for success. That is because past efforts have led to consequences that were neither anticipated nor welcome. Reformers have not been able to achieve their major goal—damming the flow of money. Their attempts have only caused money to flow into other channels, whether as direct contributions, indirect expenditures, soft money, independent expenditures, or bundled donations.[30] This is not a counsel of despair; it is not an argument against trying. But we must recognize that it is unlikely that we can compose a perfect system. If we did, it would be watered down in translation. While we are at the business of reform, moreover, it is important that we do not make things worse. We have to determine in the present discussion whether obligations can be reduced without adversely affecting other elements of the system. If they cannot, then how much is the reduction worth in terms of costs?

EXPENDITURE CEILINGS AND PUBLIC FINANCING

Many of those who advocate reform in this area agree on the need for spending limits. The arguments supporting spending limits are that they curb the demand for money and free candidates from the heavy burdens of fund-raising; create a level playing field for candidates; and reduce the dependence of candidates on private money. Expenditure limits, however, are contingent upon public financing or candidates' voluntary acceptance of these arrangements. That is because the U.S. Supreme Court in *Buckley v. Valeo* ruled that limiting expenditures would be a restraint of speech and unconstitutional, unless accompanied by grants of assistance.

Despite the support for expenditure limits and public financing among reformers and ethicists, the public has yet to rally to the banner. Public opinion polls show different patterns of response, depending upon how the question is asked. In 1988, two campaign finance initiatives were on the ballot in California. Proposition 68, which provided for public funding and expenditure limits, got 53 percent of the vote, but Proposition 73, which banned public funding, got 58 percent and prevailed. Two years later, Proposition 131, which provided for both term limitations and public funding, lost by a two-to-one vote.

Limiting expenditures might help to reduce the obligations legislators feel to contributors. This assumes that contributions from any single group will be lower, which would undoubtedly be the case, if public financing were involved. Legislators, of course, could feel under obligation for lesser as well as for greater amounts. But if less money has to be raised from the same pool of contributors, it would tend to moderate the sense of obligation. Therefore, this proposal is a promising one from a legislative ethics point of view.

Public financing is also supposed to be fairer, in that it provides a base of support for individuals who want to challenge incumbents. Without public financing and spending limits, incumbents have significant advantages in fund-raising. However, restricting expenditures will hurt challengers and help incumbents. Indeed, several political scientists have found that any restrictions on the flow of campaign money benefit incumbents.[31] Public financing and spending limits tend to be of benefit to those challengers who have little chance of winning anyway, partly because their opponents have the advantages of office and name recognition and partly because the districts they run in are dominated by voters that identify with their opponents' party. But public financing and spending limits are of much less benefit to challengers, who may have to spend more than incumbents in order to be elected in relatively competitive districts.

The concept of public financing is an appealing one, but what has been the practice? Has public financing proven to be workable? The record is mixed. At the gubernatorial level, it is employed in twelve states and has worked well in a few of them. New Jersey's public financing of gubernatorial general and primary election campaigns has been quite successful. At the legislative level, public financing has been less than a clear success. Although four states have enacted public financing for legislative elections, only Minnesota and Wisconsin have provided adequate financial support for state legislative campaigns. Minnesota's system has received good grades; Wisconsin's failing ones.

In Wisconsin, public financing has been available for campaigns for all 132 seats in the legislature. If candidates agree to spending limits of $34,500 for the senate and $17,250 for the assembly, they receive 45 percent of the totals in public funds. The system has not worked, partly because the expenditure limits have been kept too low. Candidates in tough races, where seats are targeted by one or both parties, turn down public funding when they can raise on their own more than the expenditure limit. The parties still use public monies, but mainly to fund "nuisance challengers" to harass incumbents. Meanwhile, independent expenditures by the teachers union, prolife groups, dummy fronts, and other groups have been increasing. While participation in the Minnesota system is high, candidates in the critical, competitive races tend to pass up public funding because of the spending limits that accompany it. These candidates do not want to take a chance on limiting their expenditures. In contrast, an incumbent who appears relatively safe can afford to accept public funding, in addition to the advantage of incumbency, and a challenger in a hopeless race has nothing to lose and funds to gain.[32]

New Hampshire recently instituted expenditure limits, but without public funding. Those legislators who agree to accept the limits have their fees for filing and petitions waived. Then, they have to abide by a $15,000 cap for senate primary and general elections and a limit of $.25 per registered voter for house elections. During the 1990 election, only 5 of 1,430 candidates declined to accept the limits. Six senate candidates, who had agreed to the cap, exceeded the amount allowed for the general election and were assessed fines.[33]

While expenditure limits with public financing may have some positive consequences in reducing legislators' obligations to monied interests, there are negatives as well. Unless special adjustments are made, such a system may tilt the playing field even more toward incumbency rather than leveling it for challengers. Public financing, as a floor and not a ceiling, may have more beneficial consequences, but reducing the obligations incurred by campaign contributions is not a principal one.

We have little confirmatory evidence that legislators will buy into such a system, that it will even be funded, and that it will work as the designers planned.

CONTRIBUTION LIMITS

The most popular vehicle in this field is contribution limits, which are in effect in thirty-four states. The amounts vary, depending upon the size of the state. In 1988, California voters approved Proposition 73 to limit contributions to $1,000 from individuals for each fiscal year.[34] New Jersey's 1993 campaign finance law capped contributions for individuals at $1,500. While reformers criticized the amount as being too high, the senate president explained that the goal was to "create a balance" so that legislators could run competitive campaigns in expensive media markets while eliminating any appearance of impropriety between individual legislators and contributors.[35]

Contribution limits are a modest, but nevertheless important, step in an effort to reduce legislator obligations. With a cap of $1,000 or $1,500 for a campaign that may run into hundreds of thousands of dollars, the legislator need not feel indebted to any individual donor. The assumption is that a diversification of the supply of money will dilute its influence. But extremely low limits will make it difficult for candidates to raise funds and will require them to spend more of their time soliciting contributions. In Missouri, for instance, a statewide initiative limited contributions to $200 for candidates for the state senate and $100 for candidates for the state house, thus forcing candidates to work even harder at fundraising.

Although contribution limits are a sine qua non, there are ways of getting around these restrictions. Candidates themselves are not limited in how much of their own money they can spend. "Soft money," which is given to the political parties for party-building and voter registration activities, also evades the limits. Even more serious are independent campaigns run by groups on behalf of a candidate but without the candidate's involvement. Such campaigns can be unrestrained, since the candidate cannot be held accountable. From the point of view of democratic accountability, it is preferable by far that money go to candidates or to political parties and not to other entities.

The danger of evasion is greater if the contribution limit is substantially lower than the traffic will bear. For example, in 1990, when California temporarily had contribution limits, independent expenditures grew markedly. In 1991–92, after Proposition 73 had been struck down by a federal court, independent expenditures decreased.[36]

Despite instances of evasion, most contributors and most campaigns adhere to the specified limits. Many contributors welcome caps. They feel that they are being asked for more and more, and they find it difficult to refuse. To them, campaign finance has become something of a shakedown. The lower the limits, the more time legislators have to spend fundraising and the greater the advantage candidates with personal wealth have. Moreover, lower limits benefit incumbents. As long as the limits are not unreasonably low, limits work. Candidates may have to spend somewhat more time fund-raising, but not an enormous amount. They still should be able to expend enough to reach voters with their message. Contribution limits have to strike a balance between the goal of restricting dollar amounts and enabling both incumbents and challengers to raise money and compete.

POLITICAL ACTION COMMITTEES

Just as individuals are limited in how much they can contribute, in more than half the states so are PACs. A legacy of the campaign-finance reform of the 1970s, PACs are a means of replacing corporate and large individual contributions with funds from organizations of like interests that are visible and accountable. The argument for limiting PAC contributions in order to constrain obligations is the same as that for limiting individual contributions. But while individual contributions are acknowledged as legitimate by virtually everyone, many critics of current campaign-finance systems want to abolish PACs or place severe limits on what they can donate to candidates.

The press and the public oppose PACs because they represent special interests and supposedly exercise too much influence in the legislative process. Reformers and ethicists are critical of these organizations, too, and also of those who take their money. Cody and Lynn articulate a commonly held view: "A politician's willingness to take money from PACs is one of the clearest indicators of his or her sense of ethics."[37] Take California's PACs, for instance. There are over sixteen hundred such organizations, and they give overwhelmingly to incumbents. Given the cost of campaigns, legislators have come to rely on PACs, leading them to cultivate a "twin constituency"—an electoral one and a financial one.[38] A number of proposals have been made to ban PACs at the national level,[39] but PACs continue to fund federal election campaigns.

Recently, an attempt was made to rid Kentucky of PACs, even though they were limited to donations to candidates of $500 per election. After a task force had been organized to come up with an ethics package, the governor pressured members to do away with PACs. By a vote of nine to seven, the task force recommended a ban on PAC contributions. The battle began with the *Lexington Herald-Leader* condemning PACs and legislators who received a large percentage of their funds from them. The newspaper identified twelve members of the house who had received large percentages in a twenty-one-month period before the 1992 elections. But the total amounts from PACs ranged from $10,000 to $41,000, with most at the low end. Editorially, the paper accused Senator Walter Baker, who ran unopposed in 1992, of getting all his money from PACs. Actually, all his money amounted to only $1,950.[40] Baker, according to his account, did not solicit any funds, but he used almost half the money he received to buy a new copier for his very low cost campaign. He believed that legislators should do some campaigning at election time, even though they were running unopposed. The governor and the *Herald-Leader* did not succeed in having PACs prohibited, but the bill that was enacted did limit the contributions received by legislative candidates to $5,000 or 35 percent of the total from PACs in an election cycle.

The speaker of the Kentucky house referred to the PAC issue as "kind of a phony issue." Doing away with PACs, according to him, would not remove special interest money from the legislative races.[41] Even when PAC contributions are severely capped, special interest money flows to the candidates by alternate routes. In Arizona, for example, the PAC run by U.S. West Corporation gave its maximum contributions, but they were very low. With half the money it had raised left over, the U.S. West PAC mounted independent campaigns in a number of key races.[42] Wisconsin law limits PACs to $500 for assembly candidates, with each candidate able to take only about $8,000 from all PACs. Yet, the special interest money still gets through by means of independent expenditures and bundling (whereby individuals with similar interests are solicited and represented through the same channel).[43]

As long as contributions by PACs are limited to reasonable amounts, they serve a proper purpose in our system. According to Curtis B. Gans, director of the Committee for the Study of the American Electorate, interests represented by PACs are neither "evil" nor "special" but are part of American pluralism. "The right to collectively organize and contribute is something that should be encouraged and not discouraged," according to him.[44]

PACs represent individuals who see eye to eye on particular interests, who donate voluntarily to their coffers, and who prefer to express their interest collectively rather than individually. PACs are aboveboard; the public knows who is giving, and it can infer that the contributions are intended to further a particular position. If this source of funding is eliminated or markedly curtailed, money will flow anyway. It will be much more difficult, if not impossible, for the public to connect the givers with a position. But the connection will still be made for the legislators. Little, therefore, will be accomplished, while the disclosure of information will be impeded.

SECRECY AND DISCLOSURE

If legislators do not know who gives, they cannot feel obligated to any individual or group. One suggestion is that campaign contributions be given anonymously. That surely would depress special interest giving, and probably other giving as well. Moreover, those who donated would let it be known, and perhaps even those who did not donate would make claims. This, indeed, would be playing Russian roulette with campaign finance, except that five chambers, rather than one, would be loaded.

Another suggestion is that the legislator be removed from fund-raising entirely, so that he or she has no information about the process. The analog is that of a blind trust for public officials with holdings that might lead to a conflict of interest. But in the area of fund-raising, a blindfold can never be securely fastened. Even the most removed legislators will hear about who contributed how much to their campaigns. Their information may be incomplete, even distorted, but the word will get through. In any case, I believe that the donee's donor is owed thanks. Of course, professional fund-raisers or campaign staff may express thanks on behalf of a legislator, without the latter being involved in the transaction. But I do not think that this is an appropriate way to respond to a show of support. Morally, the legislator has to be at least minimally involved in the thanks.

Keeping the source and amount of contributions secret from legislators is both philosophically and practically out of the question in a system that rests on full disclosure. Virtually everyone, critics and defenders alike, believes that public knowledge of who gives how much to whom is vital, no matter how strictly campaign finance is regulated. But like anything else, disclosure is no panacea. The information that is disclosed is more often used improperly than properly. It is reported out of context, used inferentially, exaggerated, and distorted. Both the press and candidates are culpable in this regard. Important information may not be disclosed in a timely manner and not be available until after the election has been held. Special interest money may purposely be held back until just before the election so that it does not have to be filed until afterward.

Meanwhile, candidates can spend, taking out loans earlier with the knowledge that the money will be coming later.[45]

Finally, implementation and enforcement of disclosure requirements are spotty. Election law enforcement agencies tend to be overtaxed in terms of the scope of their responsibility but underbudgeted in terms of their ability to do the job. One unfortunate result is that information on contributions cannot be presented in user-friendly form, nor can the information be analyzed by the agency compiling it. In California, for instance, despite disclosure requirements passed as part of the Political Reform Act of 1974, the last comprehensive study of the sources of campaign contributions was conducted in 1985. Because of budget constraints, neither the secretary of state nor the Fair Political Practices Commission (FPPC) has been able to issue reports.[46]

Disclosure is imperfect, but it serves our ethical purposes as well as the broader purposes of the state. With a good system of disclosure, even if legislators feel obliged to generous contributors, they will try to hold their obligations in check to prevent their opposition from getting more grist for the campaign mill. Giving by special interest groups might be held to lower levels than would occur if the amount of contributions could be kept secret. While disclosure is not an ideal answer, it may be the best one we have.

FUND-RAISING GROUPS AND PRACTICES

Barry Keene, the former majority leader of the California senate, recalled that in his freshman year he found a check for $1,000 on his desk the day before a vote on an agriculture bill. "I sure needed the $1,000," he went on, "but it was so obvious that I returned the money." That was the first ethical challenge he faced, but it was "so clear an issue that I could make an easy decision." Incidents such as this do not fit into a customary pattern, but they occur nonetheless.

So does the solicitation by influential legislators from groups over whose bills they have some control. It is by no means unheard-of to have the chair and members of a committee solicit funds from the group sponsoring a bill that has been referred to their committee. It is not unheard-of for such a solicitation to take place a day or so before the committee is scheduled to vote on the bill. Lobbyists regard this as irresistible pressure to which they must respond positively or else risk the consequences. Legislators, as well as lobbyists, question the practice. Michael Josephson, for example, found that two out of three California legislators and staffers responding to his survey felt that it was improper for committee chairs to solicit contributions from lobbyists who were regularly involved with their committees.[47]

California fund-raisers used to be held in the house districts of members. Now nearly all of them are held in Sacramento. They tend to be scheduled at the peak of the legislative workload, when special interests have a lot riding on members' decisions. Full-time legislatures like California's cannot avoid fund-raising during the legislative session. But the majority of legislatures whose sessions are limited in length can restrict the times in which legislators can solicit and receive funds. Eighteen of them have placed restrictions on contributions during the session.

Barring contributions during the session does not eliminate the possibility of money exerting influence, but it may reduce it. Ways exist to avoid such bans, but the likelihood is that the large majority of givers and takers will abide by the rules. At the very least, appearances will be served if contribution and action are separated by a period of time, which is not to say that connections that are distant are necessarily any more ethical than those that are proximate and explicit. Realistically, however, under the circumstances quid pro quos will be more diffuse than otherwise.

Legislatures are also beginning to prohibit lobbyists themselves from making contributions to campaigns. As of 1994, twelve states had banned lobbyists from contributing to campaigns. They could continue, of course, to advise their clients on contributions, and that is where they can exercise considerable clout. Recognizing this, California Common Cause is trying to get members of the legislature to pledge that they would not ask lobbyists to solicit contributions for them from their clients. Instead of using lobbyists, legislators would solicit the clients directly. The location and timing of fund-raising and the role of lobbyists are not the only relevant matters. Who raises money for legislators also counts. In the smaller states, where campaigns are much less expensive, there are few options. Legislators have no personal staff. They cannot afford professional fund-raisers, and they really do not need them. In the larger states, however, the question of who raises the money is an open one. California has had the most experience in the field of campaign finance. More and more members are no longer relying on themselves and their staffs; instead, they contract with professional fund-raisers to do the job for them. This is not only an efficient method but it distances legislators somewhat from the money-grubbing process. It also distances their staffs. All this tends to depersonalize the process and cut down on legislative obligations to contributors. It is a worthwhile advance in the business of campaign finance.

One of the outstanding campaign-finance controversies revolves around legislative party committees, party leadership committees, or leadership PACS. As Democratic speaker of the California assembly, Jesse Unruh established the practice of raising money from the special interests and dividing it up among Democratic assembly candidates. Democratic and Republican leaders of California followed in Unruh's footsteps, with Speaker Willie Brown surpassing all other state legislators in his ability to raise large war chests for his candidates, exceeding $5 million for the 1992 elections and over $4 million for the 1994 elections. Since Unruh's time, legislative parties in forty of the nation's states have developed some form of leadership committee to act in a similar capacity. In some places, such as California, the fastest-growing source of campaign financing has been transfers from legislative leaders and party caucuses to legislative candidates rather than the direct funding of candidates themselves.

One justification for leadership committees is that they strengthen the political party system. Contributions to these committees assign to the speaker and minority leader in the house and the president and minority leader in the senate, sometimes along with a group of their colleagues, the job of allocating campaign funds to members. Leaders can channel the funds where they are most needed—to the most competitive districts, where races have been targeted. Thus, supporters of the system argue, the legislative party's resources are distributed as intelligently as possible. The legislative party benefits from this approach, and to some extent so does party government in the states.

In 1990, New Jersey's Ad Hoc Commission on Legislative Ethics and Campaign Finance, which I chaired, gave its support to legislative leadership committees. It recommended that contributions made to these committees should be limited to $25,000 (the same as the state party committee), whereas those to candidates be limited to $1,500 from individuals and $5,000 from PACs. The commission based its recommendation on the belief "that the role of the party in legislative elections should be strengthened and that increased party unity and centralization is desirable."[48]

While leadership committees are now part of the process in New Jersey and many other places, they are being challenged from a number of quarters.[49] Reformers, lobbyists, and legislators themselves are all uneasy with the new tools given to leaders. One New Jersey senator has referred to legislative leaders as the "syndicate managers" for the flow of political money. Critics maintain that the ability to tap into special interest money gives legislative leaders too much power over legislative party members. If members do not go along with them on issues and, more important, do not back their bids for reelection to leadership, they will be denied funds crucial for their survival.

No doubt, some leaders at times make use of their fund-raising and fund-allocating powers in such ways. For the most part, however, leaders are constrained in what they do, although a recent study by two political scientists indicated that leadership PACs tend to benefit leaders, at least somewhat.[50] They have less leeway than might be thought, because members expect that the money will flow to those who are in the toughest races. Generally it does. If it did not, the leader would surely be called to task. As New Jersey's senate president, Donald DiFrancesco, explained: "I can assure you that I would not last long as Senate President if I distributed party funds in anything but an equitable manner."[51] While the possible abuse of power by leaders cannot be dismissed, other factors are more important in assessing the merits of this aspect of campaign finance.

Legislators generally are not enthusiastic about a system that hinders their own fund-raising efforts. Leadership PACs do just that. They exert a stronger pull on potential contributors, thus taking money that would otherwise have gone directly to the campaigns of rank-and-file members, including members who are not in great need. The most junior and least influential legislators suffer most as a consequence, particularly if they are from relatively safe districts that are not targeted in the election. With leaders pressing for money, contributors find less of a reason to give to members. Except for the relatively few from highly competitive districts who are the beneficiaries of leadership muscle, legislators generally would rather be able to raise and spend their own money. Often, when they depend on leaders for campaign finance, strings are attached. They have to spend it in certain ways or receive the services of consultants chosen by legislative party leadership. Legislators can make a case from their individual and selfish points of view, but as far as the probable electoral success of their party is concerned, leadership PACs do the job they are supposed to do.

Lobbyists and the special interests that fund a large part of the campaign-finance system would prefer to see leadership PACs abolished. They cannot, however, publicly advocate their position without risk of alienating legislative leaders. These critics make two principal points regarding their powerlessness vis-à-vis legislative leaders. First, they cannot resist leadership requests for contributions without putting their legislative agendas in some jeopardy. Leaders can kill anything they want, and lobbyists and special interests cannot be sure whether they will or they won't. Second, their contributions can be used by leadership to support legislators who oppose the cause of those who contribute, which is not what givers intend.

These arguments are potent ones. Leaders, primarily those of the majority party, are in a position to shake down groups for contributions. Assembly Democratic leaders in New Jersey, for example, were accused by a lobbyist several years ago of explicitly threatening her client's legislative program if she did not contribute generously to their party's campaign. A state investigation produced no evidence to confirm the accusation, but any lobbyist naturally will feel pressured when asked for a contribution by top legislative leaders. Explicit or not, the pressure is there, and it is much more difficult to refuse the requests of leaders than those of individual members. I do not believe that all pressure can or should be eliminated from fund-raising by people in public office, but at some point it becomes excessive. Leaders are more likely to reach that point than are members.

If we assume that special interests have little choice when solicited by leadership, then we must also assume that they have little choice as to where their monies go. The leaders themselves direct the funds. When contributors give to individual legislators, they generally fund those with whom they agree or those who hold key positions, whether they agree or not. Rarely do they contribute to out-and-out enemies. Leaders, however, can take their money and forward it to people who will vote against them every time. This type of system is not fair, at least not fair to those who give in order to support like-minded candidates. Contributions made to leaders are less likely to be made because of philosophical and programmatic agreement and more likely because of a sense of practical necessity.

The leadership PAC system, I believe, suffers ethically on these interconnected grounds: it is intimidating to those who are expected to give and it denies them the choice they should have in participating in the electoral process.

One of the ethical advantages of leadership PACs relates to the matter of obligations. Leaders serve as a buffer between special interests and legislators. While legislative party members may feel a sense of obligation to leaders who raise monies for them, they do not have to feel obliged to the interests that contribute. They do not know the source of their funds, so they have no way of knowing whom they owe. Thus, leadership PACs accomplish one of the purposes that should be served in reforming campaign finance: the obligations of legislators are reduced. Yet, there is a price to be paid.

While members are relieved of obligations, leaders take them on. But the obligations become diluted in the transfer. Because of a sense of entitlement that derives from their power, leaders, on the one hand, feel less of a sense of obligation. But they have the ability, on the other hand, to deliver more in return for what they get. While members can be helpful to the interests that back them, leaders are able to be helpful plus, especially when it comes to defensive tactics. They can refer bills to hostile committees, have them killed in a standing committee, or get them passed over by a rules or calendaring committee. Or they can put out the word that they endorse this or that bill. Either way, they are in a position to pay back. The question is, How much do they pay back? There is no precise answer, for such payback varies from state to state, from leader to leader, and from one issue to the next.

A system that operates in this way raises ethical questions. Rank and filers may feel a sense of obligation and may translate that sense into behavior. But there is just so much they individually can do. Leaders, while feeling less obliged, can do much more. With the reelection of members their responsibility, they may be inclined to do whatever has to be done to raise the requisite funds. They surely can rationalize that their ends justify helping out here or helping out there, particularly on esoteric matters that do not affect the public interest writ large. While the incidence of unethical behavior may not be great, its implications may be substantial. Despite having opted, as a member of the New Jersey commission, in favor of leadership PACs only a few years ago, I am very uncomfortable with a system that facilitates such payoffs.

Because they are so active in fund-raising, legislative leaders may also be putting themselves in very precarious positions. They are the ones who are most exposed to investigation and to undercover stings. Art Hamilton, the Democratic minority leader in the Arizona house, was a primary target for investigators in AzScam. He believes those in leadership positions were targeted because they were raising money for their parties. "That's what we were about," said Hamilton. But Hamilton was suspicious of the undercover agent being used by the authorities and turned down three opportunities to meet with him.[52]

To add to all of this, leadership PACs have played an important role in the increasing politicization of the legislature. Leaders took on responsibilities for the management of campaigns, with fund-raising a principal element. Nowadays, legislative leaders spend a good deal of their time and energy on the upcoming campaign, with campaigning a never-ending activity within, as well as outside, the legislature. Thanks to the preoccupation with the campaign, many issues now are raised for partisan purposes—to put members of the other party on record, to embarrass them, to put them in an impossible political situation. The legislature today is awash in partisan campaign politics, to the detriment of the legislative institution and the legislative process. Legislative leaders are turning into campaign managers and, as a consequence, are neglecting their institutional duties. None of this serves the legislature well. Thus, from the perspective of responsibility to the legislature as an institution, the elimination of leadership PACs would probably be a gain rather than a loss. This would not remove legislative leaders from campaign politics. They would still help members raise funds and would still involve themselves in upcoming legislative campaigns. But their campaign role would probably diminish, at least to some degree.

However I personally started out on this issue, I have come—albeit regretfully—to the conclusion that, on both ethical and institutional grounds, leadership PACs ought to be curtailed—at least in a number of states, if not in all of them. They should either be abolished or the contribution limits to such groups ought to be lower. Let members assume the burden of obligations, thus relieving leaders of the need, however rare the occasion, to deliver. This is what is beginning to happen. In recent years, transfers from leadership PACs have been prohibited in Arizona, Connecticut, Iowa, Kansas, Kentucky, Michigan, and South Carolina.

Drawing on Campaign Accounts

In their quest for reelection, legislators establish campaign funds into which they deposit the monies they raise. Campaign expenses are drawn on these funds. No one would argue about the costs of consultants, managers, direct mail, and television and radio advertising being legitimately related to campaign purposes. But what about expenses that are less directly tied to the campaign? How far should legislators be allowed to go in drawing on their campaign accounts?

In recent years, legislators have turned to their campaign funds to supplement the costs they incur living in the state capital during legislative sessions and traveling to out-of-state conferences. They have good reason to do this. First, in many states, their salaries are low, and their per diem allowances barely cover the minimal expenses they incur when away from home during legislative sessions. Second, they used to be able to supplement their official compensation with food, beverage, and other gifts furnished by lobbyists. They can no longer do so, since they are limited in what they can accept and are subject to disclosure requirements that can prove politically harmful. Third, with state and legislative budgets tight, legislators cannot travel to conferences and conventions as they once could.

Where no clear limits have been imposed on how campaign funds should be spent, legislators have interpreted campaign-related expenses broadly. Texas legislators, for instance, used to draw on their accounts for practically all the costs associated with living in Austin. In California, campaign funds pay for dining, travel, car phones, and whatever appears to be related to getting elected. In Kentucky, campaign funds were reported to have been used to buy box seats at the Kentucky Derby and tickets to University of Kentucky basketball games. They paid for a legislator's membership in the National Rifle Association and for a legislator's donation to the National Organization of Women. One member charged

$4,100 for a car phone, $500 for pager bills, and another $500 for a subscription to the *New York Times*.[53] Massachusetts legislators were also reported to have made liberal use of campaign accounts—for car leases and car loan payments, cellular phones, club dues, designer clothes, charitable donations, and tickets to Boston College games for constituents. When Charles Flaherty, speaker of the house, was fined by the state ethics commission in 1990 for taking tickets to a Celtics basketball game from a lobbyist, he paid his legal bills from his campaign fund.[54]

Both legislative and election law enforcement commissions have begun to clamp down on the use of campaign accounts. In its new campaign reporting act, New Mexico specified narrow limits, prohibiting using the funds for personal or legislative session living expenses. This was done despite the fact that New Mexico's legislators received only $75 per diem in Santa Fe and no salary. No longer could members count on their campaign funds for living expenses. In Massachusetts, legislators have not been reimbursed by the state for travel (to conferences and such) for years. Instead, they have paid for such travel and other expenses out of their campaign funds. But the Massachusetts Office of Campaign and Political Finance ruled that a number of legislators had violated the law by using their accounts to travel to Puerto Rico in December 1992. The legislators ostensibly went to attend a conference sponsored by the Council of State Governments but spent their time elsewhere, golfing and partying with lobbyists.[55]

Those who administer the law, the regulators, have considerable discretion in deciding what is permissible and what is not. In California, campaign funds can be used only for legislative or governmental purposes. This allows for meals with constituents and trips that can be interpreted as being related to campaigning or legislating. From a legislator's point of view, practically everything qualified. "There's very little I do in life," said one senator, "that's not connected with my reelection." The FPPC, and not legislators themselves, has the authority to decide what is "personal" and what is "political." The FPPC maintains that any expenditure over $100 should be directly related, while smaller expenditures can be less directly related. It maintains also that these expenditures have a "reasonable" relationship to political or governmental purposes. But establishing operational standards is difficult indeed, and the FPPC and the legislature acknowledge that this sorting-out process can be a minefield. Still, California has succeeded in formulating specific prohibitions on expenditures for personal use.

Minefield or not, standards have to be established and legislators have to observe them. People who contribute to candidates do so in the belief that their contributions will be spent on the campaign or on campaign-related activities. For legislators to do otherwise would be to ignore the intention of their supporters, indeed to deceive them. That is neither right nor prudent, no matter how underpaid legislators are or how restricted they are by meager state budgets. Clearly, campaign accounts should not be used to augment a legislator's income or life-style. Nor, in my opinion, is it appropriate for funds to be spent on objectives related to government or public office, such as legislative travel. These expenses ought to be paid by government itself out of public funds and by means of budgetary allocations. How can we conceive of government paying for political campaigns, through public financing, without expecting it to pay for the everyday operations of government? Campaign funds ought to be reserved for campaign purposes, which can be broadly interpreted, but not without reasonable limits. Legislators and regulators cannot avoid taking on the job of managing campaign funds so that they are faithful to the purposes intended by contributors. It is not an easy job.

Intervening on Behalf of Contributors

The corrupting influence of campaign contributions extends beyond the realm of legislation to that of casework, in which a legislator tries to help out a constituent by intervening with an administrative agency. The case of the Keating Five, members of the U.S. Senate, sensitized us to the issues involved in the advocacy of a constituent's interests. The constituent, Charles Keating, had contributed to the senators' campaigns. The Senate ethics committee, after investigating, found that the senators had gone farther than they should have.[56] The committee went on to lay down guidelines for constituent representation, two of which related to campaign finance. It recommended that senators pay attention to the size and history of the campaign contributions and the proximity in time of the contribution to the action.

This presents problems for legislators who are called upon by constituents who have backed them financially. What about the propriety of a legislator's behavior in the following rather typical situation? An article in the *San Francisco Examiner* on 13 July 1992 detailed the case of California senator Quentin Kopp, inferring that he acted unethically in intervening for a constituent. The article leads off with, "It pays to have friends in the right places when you need a political favor." The occasion was the disqualification by the Port of San Francisco of a construction company's low bid for a six-million-dollar contract to build a container terminal at Pier 80. The article went on: "Using his official Senate stationery, lawyer Kopp fired off a two-page letter of protest, in which he demanded further consideration. He also threatened to inform the mayor's office and media of the waste of taxpayer money, since the bid was $300,000 below the nearest competitor." The article concluded that the construction company had contributed $500 to Kopp's 1991 campaign committee and that the company's two attorneys were Kopp's "old buddies." In the last paragraph of the piece, Kopp was described as maintaining there was nothing improper in what he did. "I'd do it for any goddamn constituent," he was quoted as saying.

Should a campaign contribution disqualify a constituent from his or her legislator's help? If the answer to that question is yes, then we have to conclude that legislators should not be able to help a major bloc of their supporters. Constituents would then have an incentive *not* to contribute to their campaign.

Barring total public financing of political campaigns, legislators will continue to have to raise funds in order to win reelection. It is absurd to think that they will not be able to provide their contributors with the same representation they provide other constituents. It is not fair to deny even large contributors (which may mean different things in different contexts), whatever the appearance may be. Yet, according to Michael Josephson, a number of legislators would be willing to do so. While legislators surveyed by Josephson do not see intervening on behalf of constituents as a matter of ethics, 35 percent feel it is improper to contact a department about issuing a license for a constituent's company if the constituent had made a substantial contribution to that legislator.[57]

What is ethical, in my judgment, is not to deny the large contributor services others may receive but rather not to deny others the same services afforded the large contributor. This would mean no greater intervention by a legislator on behalf of a contributor than on behalf of someone else. The level of intervention should not depend on a constituent's campaign support; it should depend instead on the merits of the particular case, including the impact of its resolution on the constituency.

If appearance proves to be a dominant consideration, then it will be much safer for legislators to do as little as possible. Intervention beyond mere inquiry may entail greater risk than a legislator wants to run. If legislators follow the prescription that they ought not to intervene seriously, unless they are persuaded of the merits and importance of the case, intervention will be reduced. But we must be careful that the constituency service and casework functions are not adversely affected by a chilling atmosphere. For these are among the critical tasks—along with lawmaking, budgeting, and oversight—that legislatures are expected to perform.

Money in Perspective

Our focus, in examining the subject of campaign finance, has been on the ethics of giving and receiving, with greater emphasis on the latter. We might also have discussed the ethics of campaigning, but that is another can of worms. From an ethical perspective, campaign-finance arrangements should serve to reduce, not eliminate altogether, the sense of obligation that candidates feel in return for monetary contributions. This does not mean that money should be removed as a form of participation in elections but only that money should buy less from the candidates.

In order to accomplish such a goal, contributions can be limited, public financing can be provided, expenditures can be capped. Obligations can be reduced and, thus, the autonomy of legislators (at least as far as money is concerned) can be enhanced. Presumably, citizens would have fewer grounds for suspicion and might come to trust their political institutions more. If nothing else, the appearance standard would dictate that we try to exorcise money.

Were eliminating the corrosive effects of campaign contributions on officeholders the one and only goal of campaign-finance reform, prescription would be relatively simple. But it isn't. The goals are multiple, and they tend to come into conflict with one another. If we want to level the playing field, making it possible for challengers to compete effectively, we ought to think hard before imposing expenditure limits. If we desire to lighten the fund-raising load of officeholders, we should be wary of making contribution ceilings too low. If we believe that candidates should have the ability to get their message across, we have to allow them enough money to do it. Do we want individual candidates with personal wealth to be unlimited in what they can give to their own campaigns, while their opponents have to abide by strict contribution limits?

We have to keep in mind the several goals to be pursued, and not only one. According to the standard of responsibility, a legislator ought to adopt a systemic perspective and try to balance several goods and the means of achieving them. This calls for deliberation, caution, and incremental action. Indeed, this has been the general pattern of campaign-finance reform in state legislatures: a record of change and even some progress but without remarkable results.

The complexity of the system must also be recognized, if reforms are to meet a standard of responsibility. It is one thing to fail to anticipate consequences that might arise when campaign-finance law is changed. It is another thing entirely to ignore consequences that are not intended but would appear likely anyway. It should occasion little surprise, for example, when lowering a contribution limit is followed by a rise in independent expenditures. Nor should anyone be surprised by the fact that, given the budgetary constraints on funding election law enforcement agencies, disclosure requirements work differently in practice than is implied by theory.

It is deceptively simple, in my opinion, to bow to appearances and rush to a judgment that takes only that standard into account. However, fairness to candidates and responsibility for the electoral process and the legislature generally require further deliberation, leading to less obvious answers and a careful balancing of goals involving the ethics of law-makers with those involving related features of the system.

7

The Management of Legislative Life

In 1968, political scientist Nelson W. Polsby described the U.S. House of Representatives as an institutional body with boundaries between it and the outside environment. As a political institution, the House determined its own rules and managed its own affairs.[1] State houses and senates, while less bounded than the Congress, followed a similar pattern. Legislators were masters of their own houses. No longer; now management is imposed on the legislature from outside the institution itself. Boundaries between the legislature, on the one hand, and the environment, on the other, hardly exist anymore.

Master of the House

Issues that relate to ethics, in particular the growing importance of appearance, have served as a lever for the legislature to be pried open and directed from outside. To a greater or lesser extent, this is happening everywhere. But the case of the Minnesota House of Representatives provides a telling example of how the media and the public are rewriting the rules of the game and how legislators are trying to adapt to them. Representative Dee Long, the first woman speaker in the state, also became the first prominent victim of the new "ethics of internal management."

Although its culture is progressive and moralistic and its politics have been squeaky clean, Minnesota has not been a stranger to scandal of late.

A Republican candidate for governor and a U.S. senator have helped change the political atmosphere from one that was essentially trusting to one that has become much more cynical.

Speaker Long's case is different from the others, however. Institutional scandals brought her down. One of them has been dubbed "Phonegate" by the state media; three others I shall take the liberty of labeling, in the same spirit of overkill, "Duluthgate," "Skigate," and "San Diegogate." These scandals, and the way she handled them, led to Dee Long's resignation as speaker on 4 August 1993, less than two years after her election to the top position in the house. Although she cited "personal reasons" for stepping down, her Democrat-Farmer-Labor (DFL) colleagues had pressured her to resign because of the bad publicity the majority party in the house was receiving. The day after giving up the speakership, Long apologized to the people of Minnesota "for any perception of wrongdoing or embarrassment" she may have brought to her office and to the house.[2] Later on, she admitted her culpability in the series of affairs. "I will not deny," she said, "that I should have been far more careful about appearances."[3]

Appearances, it is true, had a lot to do with Long's demise. In this section we will look at what occurred at each step along the way. What did the speaker do and what were her options? We will pay special attention to the ethical standard of appearance, especially as it came into conflict with those of responsibility and fairness, and try to determine which standards should have weighed heavier.

Phonegate

On 17 March 1993, Dave Smith and Dennis McGrath of the *Minneapolis Star Tribune* broke a story about what soon became known as the Phonegate scandal in Minnesota. They reported then that $50,000 of unauthorized long-distance telephone charges had been discovered on the account of House Majority Leader Alan Welle during the fall of 1991. The next day, Speaker Dee Long wrote to the state attorney general asking him to investigate the house's handling of the incident.

Actually, the unauthorized use of Welle's phone had been discovered in the legislature over a year earlier, in November 1991. Hundreds of calls had been flooding the house's telephone system, indicating that something was wrong. At that time, Dee Long was speaker-designate, waiting to take over the office when her predecessor, Robert Vanasek, left. It was determined then that toll fraud had been committed, using Welle's access number to the WATS systems. Immediately upon discovery, the WATS line was shut down temporarily and calls were routed through operators. Several months later, the system was made more secure by being changed to one that required personal credit cards. Welle insisted throughout that he had no idea how his access number had gotten out or who had committed the fraud. An internal probe was launched, and within a short time the telephone company, MCI, began its own investigation. By January 1992, however, neither investigation had succeeded in getting to the source of the fraud.

What had happened, which was not revealed until over a year later, was that Welle had given his son the access code, to be used in case of emergency. Welle's wife was very ill and his teenage son was on his own at home. It was not unusual, moreover, for legislators to routinely give members of their families their telephone access codes so that they could be reached at work in case of an emergency. Welle's son thought his father was presenting him with a "free thing." He shared the code with a cousin, and then the two of them shared it with their friends. Soon the code number had found its way onto electronic mail bulletin boards across the country and had become a boon for a number of college students. The resulting fraud amounted to approximately $90,000.

One criticism that arises at the outset involves the management of the house. Why weren't phone bills properly monitored so the overrun would be discovered more quickly? The fact is that individual legislators received copies of the house bill, one huge bill, and not itemized accounts for each member. It would have been very time-consuming for them to pick out their own calls. With all their other responsibilities, legislators were less than diligent about such administrative details. Moreover, the house administrative staff was not monitoring the system. Detecting fraud was not high on its agenda either. Finally, it is by no means clear which house leader had responsibility in late 1991. The outgoing speaker had not been an assiduous administrator. His predecessors had run a much tighter ship, while Speaker Vanasek had given the staff much leeway and little direction. Long had been selected by the DFL caucus to be speaker, but she would not assume authority until Vanasek actually departed and she officially filled the position. By late 1991, Vanasek had stopped functioning as speaker, but there had still been no formal transfer of power. Long was not yet in charge.

It is not fair to fault Long for administrative oversight of the house during the period before she actually assumed office. Although she had some authority as majority leader, she had to tread gingerly lest she step on the speaker's toes. Legislative management, moreover, tends to be sloppily conducted, even in the best of places and at the best of times. Indeed, many legislators refer to the term "legislative management" as an oxymoron. Members are preoccupied with their lawmaking, constituent service, and campaigns rather than with keeping accurate accounts. Staff is overwhelmed with all kinds of higher-priority tasks. No one is looking for fraud, except the legislative auditors who focus on executive agencies.

There is a question as to whether we can reasonably expect legislatures to be as scrupulously administered as the media and the public might feel to be desirable. There is also a question as to whether such oversight is worth the amount of time and expense it would require. The WATS system that the house had in place was saving the state over $500,000 in annual operating costs; but the WATS system was not as secure from fraud as credit cards. With a switch-over to private credit cards and reimbursement for legitimate expenses, legislators could be held more accountable for their expenditures. But the cost to the state, and to the taxpayers, would be considerably higher. It is doubtful that the amount of money saved by tighter control of fraud will come near to matching the amount expended on the credit-card system.

Although members of the legislature knew what was going on during this early period, the public had not been informed. Without pressure from outside, Long took action to change the system, even if it meant a higher cost to the state. Her intent was to prevent something similar from happening again. On this point, Long could not be criticized for poorly managing the house. She took into account both potential appearance and her responsibility to the institution in deciding on the course she did. And, certainly, she could not be faulted for any ethical lapses, at least not with respect to the administrative practices reviewed here.

One major question concerns the decision to pursue the telephone-cost matter internally rather than making it public. There is emerging agreement, in hindsight, that Long should have gone public as soon as she learned about the overrun on Welle's telephone bill. Given what transpired, in retrospect we can appreciate that going public might have been the prudent course. But at the time, a telephone bill believed to be in the range of $50,000 did not appear to be anything that would cause a scandal. Moreover, it was the job of the house, and of the speaker as principal administrative agent, to manage internal matters. House expenditures, even extraordinary ones, were an internal matter. The administrative job was not to make an issue of the telephone bill or escalate its significance, but rather to try to find out how it happened and prevent it from happening again. Making the information public would not have accomplished anything administratively. Nor did the public have any particular need to know. It was Dee Long's responsibility as leader to deal with the problem as expeditiously as possible, recognizing that the main business of the legislature was making laws and appropriating funds for the state. In the context of the legislature's functions, the telephone bill was a relatively minor matter.

Even if the public was not informed, law enforcement authorities should have been notified, critics contend. Here, too, agreement in hindsight seems easy to reach. Outside law enforcement authorities were not notified until March 1993, only after the fraud had been reported in the press. Why not immediately? Probably because house administration did not seriously conceive of fraud at an early stage. The telephone overrun was first discovered by the Department of Administration in November 1991. It informed David Kienitz, the director of house administrative services, who called on MCI to pursue the investigation. One consideration here was whether the telephone company had responsibility and thus would foot all or part of the bill for the excessive costs. When investigators reported that they were not able to get beyond a certain point, Kienitz concluded that further investigation would not be fruitful in finding culprits; even if they were identified, successful criminal prosecution or civil recovery was unlikely, and the house was liable for payment of the bill.

The situation was reported to Speaker Vanasek and Speaker-Designate Long, but nothing was communicated beyond the house itself. The attorney general's report on the affair was critical of the house action, stating that its reporting to law enforcement authorities "leaves something to be desired." It went on to note, however, that neither law nor the administrative system imposes clear standards and procedures for the investigation of incidents of fraud or for their timely reporting to proper authorities.[4]

If the house's primary concern had been to track down the guilty parties, then it might have contacted law enforcement immediately. But at this early stage, the thought was not of fraud but rather of mishap or inadvertence. Long had in mind her responsibility for managing the house, which, among other things, meant bringing the issue to closure and devoting herself to the principal business of the body. It also meant shielding members, and particularly members of her caucus, from needless damage. The MCI investigation had apparently gone as far as it could. Little would be served by further investigation, while valuable time and energy would be lost.

In retrospect, Dee Long made an unwise decision politically. Reporting possible fraud to the authorities would have taken her off the hook, absolving her of responsibility. Is that what the speaker should have done, in view of her administrative role in the house? No, not according to the traditional notion that the legislature devises its own rules. To Long's knowledge no crime had been committed; rather, an access number had gotten loose. The administrative solution consisted of solving the problem, not establishing guilt. Given her role in the house, the speaker pursued an administrative solution.

With a new telephone system in place, the house moved on with its business. The matter seemed to be laid to rest, or "covered up," as the press later put it. Then, in March 1993, two reporters with the *Star Tribune,* apparently tipped off by a member of the DFL caucus that Alan Welle's number had been used for unauthorized calls, began an investigation. The reporters asked Speaker Long for the house telephone records. Long refused, on the grounds that it would be illegal to hand them over. Although there is a presumption, under an open records law, that all data are public in Minnesota, the legislature's telephone records are an exception. According to twelve words inserted by a conference committee and buried in a 1989 appropriations act, "notwithstanding any law to the contrary, legislators' telephone records are private data."[5] The story broke, the telephone overrun became public, and the press insisted that the speaker turn over the records. She held fast, refusing to surrender the records because it would have been illegal. As she explained, "I didn't become speaker to break the law."

It would seem that Long had little choice but to do what she did—uphold the law—and she was supported by a majority of members of her caucus. This, however, infuriated the press. She did, however, make the records available to law enforcement authorities. Long requested that the records be subpoenaed by the Ramsey County attorney, which they were; she then surrendered them. She also wrote to all house members asking that they cooperate with the attorney general's investigation. Finally, Long began a process by which the legislative records would be made available to the press and the public. She initiated a review of the 1989 privacy law by the legislature, and shortly thereafter the house unanimously passed a bill opening up the phone records to the public. The issue was resolved. Meanwhile, the 1989 law had been challenged in court, with the ruling that the provision protecting telephone records violated the single subject clause required by the Minnesota constitution and thus was unconstitutional. The issue was again resolved.

The press got the records they desired and began to look for instances of other misdeeds. They came up with several members who had used the state WATS line for personal calls: one who had used his access code beyond his term in office, and a senator who had made his access code available to a lobbyist friend, who used it for calls to South Africa. As for Long herself, the press uncovered a few calls to Italy on her office number, but they were not hers. The press inquired into calls she made from Florida, but they turned out to be on legislative business and not of a personal nature.

By this time the speaker had lost all control of how the affair was being communicated to the public. The press was accusing the speaker of "stonewalling," despite the fact that the records had been released, both to law enforcement and the press, the privacy law had been repealed, and the house was cooperating with the investigation. Now, too, the talk shows were making hay of the issue. The public's perception of all this was that the house had tried to cover up. Once this view formed, it did not change. As one legislator noted, "The public is not forgiving."

In defying the demand by the press for the telephone records, Speaker Long had probably given up any chance of a fair hearing. The *Saint Paul Pioneer Press* called for her resignation. Long was no match for the media. She might have been able, as some members later suggested, to resolve the issue and end the story at an earlier point, rather than letting it run on and on. All this may be true, for in the new environment in which legislators live and work, not having the press at the top of one's agenda may have been a mistake.

Some also believe that being a woman was of no help to her and may have been a liability. As a woman leader, Dee Long was treated differently by house members. They tried to shield her more than they would have tried to shield a man. A press conference in March 1993, following a DFL caucus, is indicative. After a few questions, Long appeared to be besieged by reporters. Her colleagues thereupon surrounded her and swept her out of the room, putting file folders and hands between her and the cameras. The speaker looked as if she were a defendant being led out of a courtroom.[6] That picture had an impact. Moreover, as a woman leader, Long was especially newsworthy. Men had fallen from grace before; they had had ample opportunity. But women in power were few and far between; they were latecomers to the scene. Given the criteria for newsworthiness, the first woman speaker of the house under fire had all the makings of an excellent story. Vigorous pursuit was inevitable.

Not handling the press well is hardly an ethical failing. The most serious ethical charge against Dee Long was that she tried to cover up a mess and protect her majority leader, Alan Welle. In March, just after the rumor began circulating that Welle knew more than he had told, the majority leader stepped forward to acknowledge his involvement in the fraud. At a tearful press conference, he admitted that his teenage son had spread the number. When he was informed that his line had been overused, Welle initially had no idea of what had happened. After talking to his wife and son, he learned that his son had used the number himself and had given it to his cousin and two junior high school friends. In order to protect his family, and because of his wife's illness with cancer, Welle said nothing. According to the attorney general's report: "At no point during the investigation of the toll fraud, or while the decision to pay the bill was pending, did Welle disclose that he knew the source of the fraud."[7]

The question, however, is, What did Dee Long know and when did she know it? She has been accused of knowing about the telephone scandal fifteen months before it all came out but covering up in order to shield her caucus from political embarrassment.[8] She denies any knowledge of Welle's involvement until the rumors began in 1993. And although she proceeded with an internal investigation, no effort was made to cover up. It was just that nothing was done to bring in the press or the public. Had Long tried to protect her party, she would have tried to keep the overrun from the opposition caucus of Independent Republicans (IRS). But they were informed by May 1992, and no IR legislators seemed to regard it as a big deal. Moreover, no Republicans tried to use the issue for partisan purposes, as they could have.

Welle's involvement may have gone farther than he acknowledged, however. There is evidence that the director of house administrative services in December 1991 requested that the MCI investigation not be pursued further. Kienitz, the director, claims to have no recollection of that. There is speculation that Welle, then majority leader–elect, told Kienitz to terminate the probe. Welle denies that.[9] In any case, no evidence has been produced that Long knew about or was involved in these matters.

The speaker's culpability covers a much shorter time span—from the time she heard that Welle had been lying until she demanded his resignation as majority leader. Although it is acknowledged that Long did not know about the Welle family involvement until shortly before he acknowledged it publicly, the press is critical of her delay in denouncing him. According to her, the day after the newspaper article reporting rumors of Welle's cover-up appeared, she asked the attorney general to investigate. It took a while longer for her to ask for his resignation, however. The DFL caucus itself was conflicted. At first, his colleagues wanted to support Welle, sympathizing with his family troubles. But with public criticism and talk-radio sentiment overwhelmingly against him, the caucus quickly shifted. On her part, Long was responding to caucus feelings and trying to give Welle a chance to come forward and own up. She had been told of Welle's involvement a few days before the story broke, but she failed to speak out publicly until he had made his statement and the attorney general had reported. From then on, she was way behind the curve on Phonegate.[10]

The speaker was off in her timing but not in her ethical reasoning. Some declare that she should never have believed Welle in the first place. Early on, when it was discovered that the huge expenditures were on his number, she should have suspected he was to blame. But Welle told the speaker and others that he had no idea how it happened.[11] Long had no reason to disbelieve him. He was a colleague, chosen by the DFL caucus to be majority leader, and he had never lied to her before. Is one blameworthy for trusting the word of a fellow legislator? Or is being trusting a fair way to treat a colleague who has given no reason for doing otherwise?

Later on, as the rumors circulated, the speaker was guided by standards of fairness and responsibility rather than appearance. She could not publicly accuse Welle on the basis of rumors. That would hardly have been fair to him or responsible behavior on the part of a legislative leader. And she felt that it would be best for him and his family if he came forward on his own. So she waited for him to do so. But once his guilt was established, punishment was swift and certain. Welle had to step down as majority leader. That did not save him from indictment, however. The result, within a year, was Welle's resignation from the house as part of a plea agreement which allowed him to plead guilty to a gross misdemeanor instead of being prosecuted on a felony charge. By this time, however, the speaker had been forced to resign from her leadership position as well.

Miniscandals

Although Phonegate was the major scandal affecting Dee Long's administration of the house, other incidents also played a part in her demise. They were hardly full-fledged scandals but were used by the media to criticize the speaker, the legislature, legislators, and legislative ways. They added to the public's perception of legislators as far removed from the citizenry they were supposed to represent. They also challenged the way the house was being managed, implying a need for new standards. Two of these incidents occurred before the telephone overrun had become public knowledge. One occurred afterward and proved to be the straw that broke the speaker's back.

The first issue that led to criticism was what the *Minneapolis Star Tribune* on 5 August 1993 referred to as the "annual ski junket to Duluth." Since the early 1960s the Duluth Chamber of Commerce had invited all the members of the legislature to visit the city and participate in some of its activities. The idea, of course, was to impress lawmakers with Duluth's needs and hope that they would be sympathetic when it came to legislation and local aid. Business interests paid the legislators' expenses. Until 1993, the biennial trip had not been considered improper, but then it became a bigger issue. Reporters went; legislators were interviewed; and the names of all those who made the trip were listed in the press. Not every legislator went skiing on the Duluth trip, but a number did and may even have enjoyed themselves. Skiing became the principal target of critics.

The speaker, who did not go on the trip, was asked why she didn't stop it. Should she have done so? Could she have? It is hard to imagine her telling (or even requesting) the Duluth chamber to call it off. It is not at all easy to conceive of her counseling legislators to stay home. Neither the speaker nor members saw any ethical reasons for them not to respond to the Duluth invitation. Visiting Minnesota's communities was a legitimate part of a legislator's job. There was nothing wrong with a legislator going beyond his or her district. Being lobbied by businesses, by municipalities, and by citizens was also part of the job. Legislators' expenses had been paid, but these expenses were not high. No one in the legislature entertained the idea that complimentary meals or entertainment would affect legislative judgment. Moreover, little had been made of the Duluth trip in the past, so there was no reason to believe that anything was wrong with it.

What legislators came to realize was that the political climate had changed. Members were becoming more concerned about the trips they took and how their opponents would use them in the next election campaign. They were also becoming concerned about what people would think—if they were skiing when other people were at work and if they were enjoying themselves at their jobs when others had to endure pain. Legislators may have been doing their jobs properly, learning about Duluth and its needs, but that would not be how it appeared to citizens of the state. When the time came due, legislators would suffer for their sins.

Skiing was at the heart of another controversy that arose only a month or so later. In February, the speaker called a legislative recess and then took a customary ski trip with a circle of political female friends, known as the "Hot Flashes." IR leaders criticized the trip because it took place before any progress had been made on the state budget.[12] The press joined in with cartoons and editorials, and references were made to the "snow bunnies.'' Television and talk-show radio gave the women's trip nasty coverage.

Dee Long's ski trips with friends dated back to 1987. They were scheduled during breaks in the long session. The 1993 trip had been planned in November and December of the previous year. The speaker and the senate majority leader agreed, as was customary, on dates for the legislative recess. It was not decided on unilaterally. The recess made for a long weekend, canceling work on Thursday, on which day committees normally met, but not affecting Friday, since early in the session legislators spent Fridays in their districts.

The break did not interfere with the legislative process, despite partisan criticism to the contrary. It was scheduled early in the session when little was going on. Legislative staff was reviewing the budget that was being proposed by the governor. Until the staff had done its work, legislators could not do theirs. They could spend their time more profitably back in their districts and would actually be saving the state money by not drawing per diem expenses while in St. Paul. The issue was certainly not that the legislature came to a grinding halt to convenience the speaker.

Long and her friends went skiing on their own, not at the expense of or accompanied by a bevy of lobbyists. But they did go skiing, and skiing is perceived as an elitist sport. No one would take a long weekend to go bowling. Moreover, Long was taking her vacation when most other Minnesotans had to be at work. The public could well be envious of these political women, whose life-style was different from their own. To make matters worse, the Hot Flashes wound up skiing in Canada. They had originally intended to go to Colorado but decided against it because of their disagreement with the state's position on gay rights. By the time they had altered their plans, the only place they could go was British Columbia. So they went, at what turned out to be some political risk. Why didn't Long and her friends ski in Minnesota, why not near Duluth! The media and the public may not have been questioning the speaker's ethics, but they were in fact establishing new guidelines for legislators' life-styles.

Life-style was again the issue that August, when Long and a number of her legislative colleagues attended the annual convention of the National Conference of State Legislatures (NCSL) held in San Diego. NCSL included as members the fifty state legislatures and represented legislators and legislative staff throughout the nation. Its annual meetings normally were well attended and even better attended when they were held in attractive locations like San Diego. NCSL's meetings did not escape the attention of the press, including Minnesota's.

As a legislative leader, Dee Long would be expected to participate in the convention. Several of her DFL colleagues, however, advised her not to go because of the media frenzy in the state. She continued to refuse to have her agenda dictated by the press, feeling a sense of responsibility to her professional association. When interviewed by a reporter about her pending trip, she commented that it would be a working trip and not a pleasure trip. Her words soon came back to haunt her.

KSTP-TV, Channel 5 in the Twin Cities, followed Long and the Minnesota delegation to the San Diego convention. Struggling to survive in a competitive media market, Channel 5 was looking for whatever scandal it could find. A legislative junket promised to provide one. In order to sneak unnoticed into the convention, a KSTP producer pretended he was from the *Saint Paul Pioneer Press*. That got him press credentials. A hidden camcorder stalked legislators and managed to film Long and a few of her colleagues in compromising positions. Channel 5 showed its audience Dee Long riding in a golf cart, playing golf in a tournament sponsored by RJR-Nabisco. It also had footage of her arriving late for a working meeting and additional footage of another Minnesota representative going to an X-rated movie house and a Minnesota senator taking his wife and two children to Tijuana.[13]

Minnesota citizens were led to believe that their legislators were irresponsible—having a good time at taxpayers' expense. The television coverage surely struck a responsive chord. The truth in the case of the speaker is much different, however. Long traveled to San Diego on a Saturday, before the NCSL convention really got under way. By doing so, her airfare round trip from Minneapolis/St. Paul was about $250 instead of the $1,200 it would have been without a Saturday-night stay. She, and not the state, paid for her room for Saturday and Sunday nights and also for the Friday night before she left the following week.

Dee Long arrived at the hotel where she was staying at 1:30 P.M. on Saturday. That afternoon she played seven holes of golf, paying her own way. The next day she played in an RJR-Nabisco tournament, missing an afternoon meeting that she was considering attending. However, she did attend meetings all Monday and some on Tuesday, for which the state was not paying hotel expenses. She spent all of Wednesday and Thursday at the convention. One could say that the weekend was hers to spend as she wished. She played golf and did a little work, but not at state expense. During the week, she participated in a number of official functions. But KSTP did not have film of her making a presentation at a meeting or sitting in on other sessions; nor did it mention that she organized a group of legislative leaders from flood-stricken states. Nor was there a note of the fact that she had a good reason for being late to a meeting with Carol Browner, the administrator of the U.S. Environmental Protection Agency. She was late because she had been in her hotel room on the telephone to her capitol office, working on Minnesota state business.

Consequences for the House

The most immediate consequence of Phonegate and assorted scandals was the resignation of the majority leader, followed by that of the speaker. Welle surely had to go, but Long might have survived. That she did not is attributable in part to the media, with the KSTP-TV report the knockout blow, but also to her own caucus in the house. For a variety of reasons, Long's colleagues wanted her to go, and they asked her to resign.

A number were upset with her because, in organizing the house as the new speaker, she deprived them of some of their power. She shook up the committee structure, putting fiscal responsibilities in the policy committees and moving veteran members around. Junior members gained, while some seniors lost out. The latter did not forget. A much larger number of her DFL colleagues would have stuck by her, but they were running scared, fearful of losing the 1994 elections. In their view, the speaker would be a lightning rod that would cost the DFL its majority and some of them their seats. Long herself understood that DFLers regarded her as an albatross. Especially concerned were the freshman members, an unusually large crop, who were most sensitive to the public's discontent with politics and were alarmed by Ross Perot's showing in the state. Long felt pressure from her caucus for her resignation. Some of Long's good friends, feeling that it was best for her to get out of the line of fire, also thought she should go. On their part, the Republicans could hold back, feeling that they would gain in partisan terms either way. If the speaker stayed or if she left, they would have an election issue.[14]

Other consequences had to do with the administration of the house. The telephone system was changed, ensuring greater accountability but also greater costs. The telephone records of individual members were opened up to public scrutiny, giving the press more grist for its mill and making abuse potentially very expensive politically. Other ways to tighten administrative control were also considered, having been recommended by a bipartisan committee appointed by Long. A management audit of the house would be done by an independent consultant, commissioned by the committee. For a time, at least, management improvement was high on the agenda. It was the natural response of a legislative body to scandal.

Of even greater significance are some other consequences that can be tied, in part, to Phonegate and the travel scandals. Legislators have been intimidated. Most are afraid to travel; some will not go anywhere at state expense. A few will simply pay their own way to the NCSL conventions and similar events. A number will not travel at all, even with their own funds. They know that "too many trips" can be made an issue by their opponents in the next campaign; they may have made it an issue in their own campaign running against an incumbent earlier. A large group of DFLers, thirty or so, went so far as to sign a "no perks" pledge, forswearing gifts of any kind, to demonstrate their purity.

The governor, Arne Carlson, adopted legislative reform as his top priority in 1994. In response, the house DFL caucus, trying to keep the wolves at bay, put together a package of ethics legislation, which passed the legislature in 1994. They had something to run on in their quest to retain the majority.

Perks and Prerogatives

Dee Long's fall, according to the *Minneapolis Star Tribune*, which helped bring her down, "speaks volumes about the current public mood of intolerance for perks and privileges and business-as-usual in the political establishment" (5 August 1993). Citizens perceive the life-style of legislators as grandiose, replete with an assortment of perquisites that are by no means available to ordinary people. Minnesota's legislators, according to members of one of our focus groups, are not only offered favors, but they ask for them, and if they are powerful enough, they demand them. Californians express resentment about their representatives: "They began to feel that it's their due. . . . They feel that they have been elected God, not just to represent the people, but to have the power and the perks." New Jerseyans in our focus groups also have perceptions of legislators awash in privileges: "They have their own state car and some of them get a chauffeur to drive them around. They take trips and jaunts. They get tickets to special events. They have special license plates so that they can park wherever they want. They have offices in which they conduct personal business."

People tend to exaggerate the fringe benefits of legislative office, probably because of recent revelations about the U.S. House of Representatives and intermittent stories about the U.S. Senate. Federally subsidized haircuts, cafeterias and dining rooms, stationery stores, and gymnasiums; a bank for house members; special parking privileges for representatives at National Airport; and large allowances for offices and staff are among the benefits of life on Capitol Hill. But few state legislatures come close to matching Congress in member salaries, staff, or other resources. California is one state where the resources available to individual members had been abundant. But with voter initiatives and budget cuts, the California legislature has retrenched, and some of the former perks are gone.

Except in a handful of states, the perquisites of legislative office are few and far between. Nevertheless, they do raise ethical problems for those who use them. The perks that accompany positions of power can be abused, and instances of such abuse will always be found. But today, because of pressures from the media and the public, the reins are tightening and the risks of exposure are rising.

The public today is being informed of the pettiest details of legislative life, and legislators have had to become more conscious of just what they can and cannot do. It is now becoming clear that they should not bill personal or business long-distance telephone calls to the state. If they do, they risk having their actions made public, through legislative audits or an aggressive press. If they inadvertently charge a personal or business call, they are just as liable to criticism.

However, there are many questionable situations. Take the case of a New Mexico legislator who has a business in Albuquerque. He assumes that when serving in the legislature in Santa Fe he can use the state WATS line to call his business office. After all, he is not receiving compensation, only per diem, for the time he spends in the legislature. Under emerging standards, however, such calls would not be allowed, no matter how low legislators' compensation. Take the case of the same legislator, calling his family long distance to notify them he will not be home until very late. As a personal call, should it properly be charged to the state?

More and more legislators, in states where ethics have become front-page news, are erring on the side of caution. They would rather not have to explain and justify. Moreover, in some places legislative guidelines explicitly prohibit legislators from using public resources for private purposes. Washington's ethics guide, for example, specifies that personal long-distance calls should not be billed to the state but rather should be billed to credit cards. Wisconsin is among the strictest of states. It prohibits legislators from using phones for private purposes, even if they intend to reimburse the state. Wisconsin legislators must have personal calling cards if they are going to use their office phones for private calls. By the same logic, a Wisconsin legislator could not use a postage meter to send out a private letter, even if the legislator intended to reimburse the state with stamps the next day. The idea is that state resources should not be used for private purposes, with "use" meant to include borrowing.

The Minnesota case showed how the media could intrude into the affairs of the legislature, opening up the details of administration to outside scrutiny. It showed also the dangers associated with legislative travel, whether at the invitation of a civic association, on one's own, or on legislative business. Among the so-called perquisites of legislators, none seem to attract as much attention as trips, or junkets as they are called in the media.

Legislators' travel is reported in the press, so legislators fear that their opponents will try to make something of it. Members who are active in legislative organizations, such as NCSL, take a number of trips each year, and they receive special mention. Colorado's Paul Schauer, an active participant in NCSL activities, was given the "Frequent Flyer" award by the media as the house member who traveled most. Interviewed on television, Schauer defended his travel and argued that the state got its money's worth when he met with legislators from other states or with Colorado's congressional delegation.

As happens elsewhere, Denver's press played "gotcha" with Schauer, trying to catch him double dipping, taking per diem payments, or doing private business while on a state trip. On one journey, he cost-shared travel from Denver to Washington DC for the legislature and then to New York City on business. The state paid for part and his company paid for part. But the press maintained that Schauer should have returned to Denver from Washington DC and then taken a separately billed trip. Separate billing might have been cleaner, but it would have been a major inconvenience for a legislator who still had to earn a living on the outside. Had Schauer traveled to New York City for his company and let the state pay, then he would have been culpable. But he cannot be criticized if he shared costs equitably. Suppose, however, that he had company business in

Washington DC, where he was attending the legislative meeting. Then would it have been permissible to let the state pay full freight? Probably not, particularly if he was spending time on company business that otherwise should have been devoted to the conference. But if he had free time, why shouldn't he spend it on business? He could otherwise have used it for reading or for recreation. Assume, also, that his company has made it possible for him to take time off to do legislative work. Then it seems fair that the legislature return the favor, at least in small part. Schauer's obligations are complex, and the correct ethical course depends on particular circumstances. Deciding what is proper, rather than politically sound, is a matter of ethical judgment.

Dee Long's jaunt to San Diego to attend the National Conference of State Legislatures convention in the summer of 1993 had unfortunate repercussions for her. Traveling to San Diego also affected legislators from all over the country. The critical press was by no means confined to Minnesota. The convention was a principal feature of coverage by the press in many other places. Even balanced reporting gave citizens back home the impression that their legislators were up to no good. Take, for instance, an article written by Mary Hynes, a reporter for the *Las Vegas Review-Journal*:

> The crowd sways to soul music and munches on heart-attack food at the famous Hotel del Coronado. . . . Some of the evening's party goers wander from the brightly lighted tennis courts, where the band is playing, to the beach. . . . Earlier in the week, the legislators and their families were feted to the tune of $300,000 at Balboa Park. . . . On other evenings, legislators could choose from among the myriad dinner and reception invitations from special interest groups. (8 August 1993)

The article, which ran on a Sunday, points out that the Nevada legislators, along with those from across the country, were at a vacation destination, staying in luxury hotels, on an excursion beyond the budgets of many of their constituents. The outing, which was made to look like an excuse for a family vacation, cost Nevada taxpayers about $52,000.

The *Las Vegas Review-Journal* account did not stop there but went on to grant forthrightly that appearance might only have been skin deep. It mentioned that legislators did pay for their families, some even paid their own way, and a number had lost wages from their jobs while attending. It noted the attendance of legislators at convention meetings and also at parties given by corporations. Despite the admission that legislative work was being done, the opening paragraphs and the overall flavor of the Las Vegas newspaper article could only feed public suspicions.

Editorial criticism accompanied reportorial accounts. Maine's speaker of the house, John Martin, was chastised for taking nearly two dozen (out of a membership of 251) representatives with him to San Diego for NCSL. It was wrong, according to the press, for the legislators to spend thousands of tax dollars for travel in a state whose budget had been so hard hit. Exceptional is the editorial that appeared in the *Clarion Ledger* of Jackson, Mississippi, on 26 July 1993. It approved of the trip that forty-five Mississippi legislators and key staff members took to San Diego, even though the state had to pay a bill of $24,000. Rejecting the charge that it was a tax-paid vacation, the editorial indicated that it was valuable for Mississippi lawmakers to have discussions with and gain ideas from legislators representing other states.

This is definitely a minority point of view, however. People think of travel as fun, and most of them do not get to travel as part of their jobs. They are envious of those who do, particularly when the beneficiaries are paying for their trips with the people's money. Given the opportunity, they express their indignation. When Bud Burke, president of the senate in Kansas, is back in his district, constituents come up to him and say that they do not want to see their legislators traveling at public expense. Because of feelings such as these in Kansas and elsewhere, "travel terror" reigns throughout the states. In many places, money for travel is severely restricted anyway, and few members can attend their national organization's meetings. Others are reluctant to go anywhere and thereby run an unnecessary risk. A growing number of those who do go are paying their own way or dipping into their campaign accounts to cover the costs.

There is no doubt in my mind as to the value of legislators getting together and meeting with one another. During the normal course of legislative affairs, they have little time to talk with their colleagues. Out-of-state legislative conferences afford them the opportunity to strengthen the relationships they have with one another, which, in turn, facilitates the process when they return home. Much of their free time at such conferences is spent informally with colleagues from their own chamber. Additional time is spent with legislators from other states, trading ideas on legislative solutions to pressing problems and, of course, discussing politics. Even if legislators failed to attend a single plenary session, panel, or workshop, they could benefit overall from their informal exchanges. But most do attend, and many participate in the legislative organization's formal program—on education, criminal justice, welfare, health, budget and taxes, legislative structure and procedure, and a myriad of other subjects. They have an intense interest in subjects that they have to address in their states and a need to meet legislative and outside experts in these fields. Conferences and conventions make all of this possible.

It is true that some legislators use such meetings as occasions for play and family vacations. I do not know just how many are out solely for a good time, but my guess is that it is a very small proportion of the total. These legislators spend most of their time, from arrival to departure, on the golf course or tennis court or sightseeing during the day and somewhere off campus at night. They are an aberrant few. The large majority of legislators attending one of these meetings are serious about the work. They return to their states with new ideas and new contacts and can and do contribute more to the legislative process as a result.

It is understandable that legislators also want to enjoy themselves when they have a chance to get away from the statehouse, and conventions and conferences make such enjoyment possible. Conventioneers do take time out to recreate, but such recreation—whether on the golf course or at the swimming pool—normally includes discussion with one's colleagues about matters of the public's business. Legislators talk business wherever they are because they are preoccupied with it. Most are workaholics. In the evenings, legislators partake of receptions and dinners, hosted by various groups, and entertainment, organized by the sponsor of the conference. There is much food and drink to be had and colleagues with whom to share company. Like members of other professions who attend annual meetings of their association, legislators manage to have a good time. Some bring their spouse and some their children, at their own expense, in order to be able to share the time with their families (whom they neglect almost entirely when the legislature is meeting).

The press feeds on legislative conventions and the public reacts indignantly. With regard to how one's travel to a legislative meeting appears, it is better not to go. From the point of view of the legislative process and the member's responsibility to a profession, it is better to go. One issue, it seems to me, is whether it constitutes unethical conduct for a legislator to engage in personal activities while in a location to which he or she has traveled in order to engage in official legislative activities. In my opinion it does not, not if one's personal activities do not interfere with the legislative business to be conducted and do not result in an increase in the costs of the trip to the state. I would argue that for most legislators, some personal activities actually promote the legislative business that has to be done. There is no reason why having a good time should be considered unethical. It may be for a few who take advantage of the system, but for most it certainly is not.

Yet, today, if legislators are enjoying themselves, they are suspect. Ordinary citizens have been undergoing economic uncertainty, which leads to anxiety, pain, and suffering. They want their legislators to share such feelings with them in what may be a new requirement for democratic representation. But legislators in convention are too happy a lot for the people they represent. Were they to meet in unpleasant places, bear inclement weather, and have no time at all for play (in other words, were they to suffer more), they could better withstand challenge on ethical grounds.

This is not to say that there are no ethical issues involved in legislators' attending their associations' meetings. What can be done about those legislators who abuse the privilege? If the legislature does not want the press to dictate what is acceptable conduct, then the legislature itself should bear the responsibility. We shall return to this proposition in chapter 8. For now, we can say that it is up to the senate and house, through their leadership, to determine who travels where at state expense. For the most part, legislative leaders have not made tough decisions. Rarely do they deny travel funds to those members who do not use them appropriately. That is what they should do, and will have to do.

There is, however, a major issue associated with the conventions and conferences that legislators attend. It pertains to the role of the private sector in bankrolling the social events, receptions, and dinners at legislative meetings. Take as an example the 1993 annual meeting of the National Conference of State Legislatures, held in San Diego from July 24 to July 29. The principal social events were an opening reception at Balboa Park, with a performance by the vocal artist Dionne Warwick, and a closing dinner at the Hotel del Coronado. These events had to be paid for, as did luncheons, special sessions, shuttle buses, and so forth. Some of the costs of the convention were borne by registration fees for individual legislators, lobbyists, and other attendees. But a large amount, especially the costs for the social events, had to be raised from the private sector. Among the larger contributors were ARCO, Bank of America, Food 4 Less Supermarkets, Philip Morris U.S.A., San Diego Gas & Electric, Disney, Ameritech, GTECH, and Xerox. The money was raised by a California host committee that included California's speaker of the assembly and president pro tem of the senate as honorary cochairs and the assembly and senate Republican leaders as honorary vice-chairs. The executive committee included eight members of the legislature and four executives from large contributors, and the host committee had as members forty-four more California legislators. This was surely a group with fund-raising ability, one whose entreaties would be difficult for California businesses to resist. The social events of other NCSL meetings and the meetings of other associations, such as the Council of State Governments, are funded in a similar way.

In the case of NCSL, the states where conventions have been held have competed with one another in providing spectacular social events. This has led to something resembling an arms race, with each host committee trying to outdo its predecessors in fund-raising. In addition to the organized events that are part of the official program, countless receptions are held for legislators and legislative staff sponsored by individual states, who have raised monies from the private sector, or by business groups of various sorts, who are digging into their public affairs budgets. Finally, of course, the convention sessions, hotels, and events are teeming with lobbyists of every type, representing corporations, unions, advocacy groups, and associations, as well as those who are independent contractors. Their goal is to socialize with as many legislators as possible. At legislative meetings, therefore, low-key lobbying is part and parcel of the legislator learning process.

How appropriate is all of this from an ethical standpoint? Essentially, these meetings and the incidental activities are quite legitimate, but things can get out of hand. Some people have proposed that legislative meetings be funded solely by legislative associations and member fees and that the private sector–sponsored social events be eliminated, along with the fund-raising by the host committees. There is considerable merit in such a proposal. One wonders about the obligations incurred when legislators on a host committee raise money for a function. I suspect that they are few and have little weight or bearing on legislation. That is because the private sector is expected to donate, and businesses have budgeted for this as they have for campaign contributions. It buys them little, except perhaps good will, which they already have.

Even if private sector financing of the meeting were eliminated, groups could still sponsor social events completely on their own. The receptions would undoubtedly continue and, unless state laws prohibited members from such entertainment or required them to disclose it, legislators would keep on attending. (Even those states with the strictest ethics laws allow members to attend out-of-state receptions.) Not much would change. The fewer the receptions, the more likely individual lobbyists would substitute for these occasions by entertaining legislators one on one or in small groups. If the transmission of influence is thought to be a danger, then the larger functions are healthier than the smaller ones. The interactions that take place in a big crowd are a lot more diffuse.

I believe that one need not be concerned about legislators being influenced or obligated by attending social functions at legislative meetings. But I do believe that the entertainment can be, and is being, overdone. It is enjoyable, yet excessive. While the functions that are offered outside of the formal convention cannot be controlled, those that are part of the official program can and should be. They serve an important purpose in that they bring legislators together informally but as members of a national group. Thus, it would be a disservice to eliminate them. NCSL or CSG, as the national membership organizations, should take greater responsibility than they do now. They should raise the funds, instead of having different host committees compete each year. In that way, the competition among the states where the meeting is held would be curtailed. Expenditures could be controlled and held to a reasonable amount. Excess funds could be channeled to the foundations of NCSL and CSG and be used for projects that might help legislative institutions.

Strong national legislative organizations, and the meetings they hold, are worthwhile. They should be fostered, not inhibited. To ensure that legislators are not influenced or obligated, it would be necessary to virtually abolish meetings. That hardly would be worth the price. Whenever legislators get together, there are risks of their being contaminated by lobbyist influence. For important ends to be accomplished, these rather minor risks have to be run.

Management from Outside

When it comes to questions of management and life-style, the standards that we have been using come into the sharpest conflict. Appearance, as it is conveyed by the media and perceived by the public, dictates an entirely different approach than do the standards of fairness and responsibility. The Dee Long case suggests that whatever looks bad, or can be made to look bad, will get legislators into trouble. In her behavior throughout Phonegate and the miniscandals, Speaker Long was trying to be fair to her colleagues and responsible in terms of managing and protecting the institution. She did not cave in to appearance, and she paid an unexpected price.

Unfortunately, from my perspective, legislators are learning from this and similar experiences that retreat is the better part of valor. They are becoming less and less likely to buck appearance for the sake of the rights of colleagues or the well-being of the institution. The penalties are simply too great.

A major shift is under way. Legislatures are not only permeable on matters of policy, but they are also up for grabs on matters of management. Not too long ago, state legislatures had the freedom to manage their own affairs, including the determination of their own ethical standards. As far as its inner life and working habits were concerned, the institution enjoyed considerable autonomy. Not anymore.

Today's legislature is fully exposed and highly dependent. Pursued by relentless media, the legislature can no longer manage itself. If it does not thoroughly consider its appearance, as communicated by television and radio and in print, it risks encouraging even greater cynicism and scorn by the public. Twenty-five years ago state legislatures were modernizing and strengthening themselves on their way to becoming proud institutions. Since then, however, the drumbeat of criticism and the perpetual bashing have taken a high toll. Legislatures no longer can manage their own affairs, including the ethics of members and the processes by which they fulfill their legislative responsibilities—enacting laws, passing a budget, and overseeing the conduct of state government.[15]

8

Toward More Ethical Legislative Bodies

"If I'd been more of a person willing to draw lines, to stay carefully away from the edge, then I'd be getting on a plane for Sacramento on Monday instead of getting into a car to drive to Lompoc." With this comment, Alan Robbins, the California senator convicted in Shrimpgate, was about to leave for the minimum security prison where he was to serve his sentence.[1] Robbins, by his own admission, did not know where to draw the line. And whether they acknowledge it or not, many other legislators in California and elsewhere are not entirely sure where to draw it either.

Sure or not, the responsibility is theirs—as individuals, as well as in their roles as legislators. It is a personal responsibility, not only a professional one.[2] Knowing where responsibility resides is one thing; knowing just how to exercise it is another. Ethics assumes that there is a distinction between right and wrong, and individuals have a moral obligation to do their best to do the right thing. On that we can all agree, legislators no less so than anybody else. At the extremes, it is easy to distinguish acts of good from those of bad. But in the real world of politicians and politics, the shadings of gray far outnumber those of black and white. It is in the indeterminate gray zone that legislators have to choose. It is here that they need guidance. For many of them, the arbiter of ethical choice is their conscience. "It's a personal thing," says one legislator. "You have to rely on people's common sense and decency," says another. Yet, people of common sense and decency can and do disagree as to what is ethical and what is not. If we want to narrow the range, more than internal guidance is necessary.

The Role and Limits of Law

Even though ethics begins with the individual, law has become a principal means of guiding and disciplining state legislatures. In recent years, legislatures have been making a large body of law relating to legislative ethics. As a consequence, we have today more state laws and rules designed to regulate the conduct of legislators, enhance legislative ethics, and control the amounts and flow of money in legislative elections.

Law establishes a general framework, one that varies (and should vary) from state to state, depending on the nature of the legislature. What is more appropriate in full-time professional bodies may be less appropriate in part-time citizen bodies. What is enacted in the wake of a scandal is quite different from what is enacted without such an impetus. Despite variations, in earlier chapters I have indicated that a number of ethics laws and rules are worthy of consideration and adoption by state legislatures.

Conflict of Interests

• Prohibition on exercising influence where one's personal interest is in conflict with the proper discharge of one's duties.

• Ban on accepting compensation other than one's legislative salary for services rendered in connection with one's legislative duties.

• Provision for disclosure of financial interests, particularly sources of income.

• Limitations on lawyer-legislators representing clients before state agencies involved in licensing, permitting, contracting, and rate making.

• Provision that a legislator can disclose a personal interest and then participate in decision making on an issue.

Gifts and Travel

• Ban on gifts from lobbyists and their principals to legislators (or, in some states, limits with disclosure), making exceptions for receptions and small unsolicited gifts.

• Limits on trips taken at the initiation of groups, with out-of-state travel channeled through the legislature.
• Support by state for travel by legislators to professional meetings and for site visits in connection with legislative issues.

Campaign Finance

• Setting of contribution limits, with amounts varying by state.
• Full and timely disclosure of contributors and reporting by individuals and PACs.
• Restrictions as to the times during which legislators can solicit or receive funds.
• Prohibition of contributions by lobbyists.
• Curtailment of leadership PACs or reduction in the size of contributions leadership PACs can receive.
• Rules on the uses of campaign accounts, by defining electoral purposes and eliminating expenditures for personal or office needs.

Laws and rules such as those mentioned above have had positive effects on legislatures. They have sensitized members to conflict of interest problems and provided guidelines that are understandable, if not specific. They have brought about greater disclosure of legislators' financial interests, campaign contributions, and lobbyist expenditures, so that the public has information to make its own determination on legislators' conduct in office. New laws have also made some progress in reducing the obligations that legislators may feel toward those who can afford to entertain them or contribute to their campaigns. Most important, new laws and rules have succeeded in reshaping capital cultures in a number of states where things had gotten out of hand. Tallahassee is not the same place that it used to be, when legislators traveled at will, accepted gifts of every sort, and expected that the lobby would always be there to pay the tab. Columbia and Frankfort are far different from the way they were before Operation Lost Trust and Boptrot led to ethics reform. The cultures have changed, and legislators are no longer encouraged to behave with the ethical abandon that they once did.

But law has its limits. It cannot succeed in reforming campaign finance unless we reach some agreement on what we want such a system to achieve, recognizing that a number of the objectives that we presently have in mind may be contradictory. Nor can law prove effective if legislators themselves are not supportive of it. To really succeed, ethical rules should be rooted in an underlying ethical consensus among members of the legislature. It does not serve us well for everyone to try to out-ethic everyone else in law as part of an arms war with an ethics arsenal. Moreover, too much law, without foundations of support, lends itself to evasion. Systems based on prohibitions and negative sanctions, as Jane Mansbridge writes, are likely to foster the search for loopholes as part of an overall resistance to regulation. When loopholes are discovered and exploited, more specific rules are promulgated to plug them up.[3]

Law, moreover, can be too restrictive, too inhibiting. Excessive ethics regulation may have a chilling effect on the process. The *Seattle Weekly,* reacting against the Washington media's vendetta against the legislature, expressed second thoughts about what should be done: "The over-regulation of political life, too eagerly abetted by journalists, has reached the point where we are trying to take the politics out of politicians, like puritans rooting out sin" (8 July 1992). We have to allow for mistakes in a political process, and ethics regulation cannot allow for such "immorality." With the stakes so high, the attention of legislators is diverted from trying to solve the problems of the state to protecting themselves from possible (and inadvertent) wrongdoing.

Law tends to beget law. The more statutes we have on the books, the more we need. Ambiguities and inconsistencies are discovered; questions arise; clarity and consistency are sought. State ethics commissions, which have jurisdiction over legislatures in a number of states, issue advisory opinions and bring enforcement action. The legislature responds with amendatory law. The momentum is toward ever greater specificity in order to eliminate doubt.

Law also leads to violations, which result in prosecutions (and, hence, the demand for more law). As a Kentucky legislator commented on the enactment of the ethics reform package in early 1993, "People will be found guilty of ethical misconduct, almost overnight."[4] Ethicist Michael Josephson also recognizes the dangers of a growing body of new laws and rules creating new offices. Each one poses a possible trap for the unwary legislator.[5] In making too much law, legislators feel they are setting themselves up for possible prosecution. In view of the political ambitions of prosecutors and the economic motivations of the media, they fear that they are sitting ducks, with each law on the books ammunition for the firing squad. Once criminal penalties are provided by statute, they are there to stay—even though the punishment may be in excess of the crime. In today's climate, it is not possible to reduce or eliminate criminal penalties without running serious political risk. On the other hand, if prohibitions were not on the books, criminal penalties could not exist. Misjudgment on the part of a legislator might lead to criticism and, conceivably, censure, but not prison.

For legislators the risk is even greater when the law changes rapidly, as has been happening of late. They cannot keep up with rules of the game that are in rapid flux. Just as they are becoming familiar with one set of rules, under pressure from outside they enact a new set. The earlier rules are revised while they are still being tested and learned by legislators. The result of all of this is uncertainty and confusion, and danger.

That is why former congressman Bill Frenzel of Minnesota concludes, "When we create these laws, we are subtracting value from the system."[6] But legislators feel compelled to pass laws because of the climate of accusation that is now sweeping the nation and states. The belief that corrupt and unethical officials monopolize public office leads to greater and greater efforts to root them out and reform the system. Suzanne Garment likens the situation to that of trawling for fish. "We act as if there were huge fishlike schools of offenses, those that are crimes and those that deserve to be, swimming out there in the turgid sea of business and politics. The better our enforcement of laws and regulations, the more of these fish we will catch." The presumption is that just about any fish is worth catching—the legislator whose interests come into conflict as well as the legislator who extorts money from a lobbyist. According to Garment, we do not want any fish to get away—we feel that we have to catch the small fry as well as the whoppers. "If we are not snaring these little fish," she writes, "we must simply shrink the size of the net's holes."[7] With more law, nothing will get through our nets (although some big fish will swim around them).

Today's legislators are demoralized, not only by the laws they feel forced to pass but by the hostile climate which has infected their own institution and their process. Legislators are apologetic for their own behavior, not only that of errant colleagues. They don hairshirts and flagellate themselves in order to curry favor with the public and get reelected. Although they should be minding the store, they are willing to give it away in order to preserve themselves and their majorities. Many legislators feel badly about what they have to do in order to survive, and some decide that the costs are too high. Still a distinct minority, these legislators opt to exit from office. A number of those who leave voluntarily tend to be the ones whom we would like to see remain in office.

Legislators are used to making law to deal with whatever problem confronts them, including ethics. They are their own worst enemies, particularly when coerced. But law has its limits. It will not apply perfectly or universally. It will never be a panacea, and it will always be subject to evasion. As Meg Greenfield writes, while moral upgrading is worthwhile, it cannot be micromanaged. "There almost certainly will be some cheating, some diversion, some hanky-panky. If the law is good, it will do its broad job and most people will stay within its general rules. Some breathing room must be left for human judgment and dignity and discretion to come into play."[8] Additional laws and rules and stricter enforcement may appease the media's and the public's appetite, buying respite for public officials in the short run. Or it may have the opposite effect, demonstrating to citizens that what they suspected was true, that the motives of legislators cannot be trusted, and thereby further undermining confidence in government.

Law and regulations, moreover, require diligent but sensitive administration, which does not come easily. Legislative ethics committees, which operate in most legislatures, have little credibility with the press or the public. They are buffeted by pressures of various sorts. Procedural and due process requirements conflict with the need to settle a case. On one side, colleagues want to be treated fairly and have their actions assessed in a broader context. On the other side, the media want guilt established and punishment dispensed. Insofar as rank-and-file citizens become involved, they approach the matter from the media's viewpoint. For legislators, serving on a legislative ethics committee is a no-win situation; it is time consuming and painful and virtually without reward or even appreciation. It hardly comes as a surprise, therefore, that legislators are reluctant to serve on such bodies.

The alternative to the administration of ethics from within is the administration of ethics from outside the legislature. In California, Connecticut, Florida, Kentucky, Rhode Island, and several other states, independent commissions have broad enforcement powers—launching investigations of violations in response to complaints or on its own, issuing advisory opinions to legislators, promulgating regulations to implement the ethics code, monitoring filings, and so forth. The tendency for an ethics commission is to regard legislators not as clients who need help but as people who are too easily tempted unless restrained by regulations. Relationships between legislatures and ethics commissions are at best strained and at worst hostile. An adversarial "us-versus-them" atmosphere is almost inescapable.[9]

Given the penalties they face, legislators naturally concentrate on the rules and regulations they are required to follow. What must they disclose? Who must disclose it? Are they members of a "class" that may benefit by their actions? This necessary preoccupation with a myriad of rules, many of which still leave room for interpretation, leaves legislators little time for thinking about ethics—and little incentive, also. Compliance with ethics law may indeed be undermining consideration of questions of ethical conduct—of what is right and wrong under what circumstances.

In the longer run, the constant resort to regulation is enervating, demoralizing, and dysfunctional. Moreover, externally imposed standards and procedures will never be entirely effective. Legislators have to take ethics seriously. Pressures from the outside help them to do so.[10] The enactment of law is one way to proceed, but the assumption of responsibility by the legislative community is another. While the former method is widely used, the latter has been largely neglected.

A Responsible Legislative Community

The Hastings Center realizes that we cannot rely on the discretion of individual legislators, or the law, or the judgments of constituents. "Legislatures must assume a collective, institutional role in the regulation of ethical conduct in order to protect themselves, and the vast majority of their members who are ethically conscientious, from the damage done by the unscrupulous few."[11] To put it another way, legislatures have to try to prevent their apples from rotting, in order to keep the whole orchard from being torched.

Members of the legislature collectively share responsibility for the ethical behavior of the institution and its individual members. They are guardians of the institution in which they serve, obliged to keep it a healthy agent of representative democracy. When a member crosses the line or a scandal erupts, the legislature as an institution inevitably suffers damage. The more damage suffered, the more difficult the task of repair, the more disabled the institution.

Legislators cannot meet their institutional responsibility simply by the enactment of ethics law or by the promulgation of a code of ethics. They have to work at the ethics business continuously, developing a consensus on what is appropriate and what is not, training themselves in ethical reasoning, and educating the public as to what representative democracy is about. In the legislative system, the more law and sanctions can be kept in the background and the more regulation can be transacted through moral suasion, the more effective they will be.[12]

Moral suasion requires the involvement of a strong legislative community. The irony is that as the need for legislative community has grown, legislative norms and customs have become weaker. No longer do members agree, as they once did, on the importance of reciprocity, institutional loyalty, and courtesy. No longer do individuals in the senate and the house trust one another as they used to. Colleagues are more likely to go back on their word when it is in their interests to do so. Partisan competition has also weakened institutional ties. More and more issues are being raised and played out for partisan purposes to promote the electoral prospects of one party at the expense of those of the other. It is difficult for members whose careers are threatened by a determined opposition to join with their electoral opponents on matters of institutional concern.

The legislative parties, which are currently campaign organizations as well as agencies of governance, fragment the senate, the house, and the legislature as a whole. Other subcultures also tend to be divisive when it comes to institutional concerns. Gender, race, and ethnicity split legislators into caucuses and groups which can work at cross-purposes with the institution as a whole. Add to all this the extreme individualism of members in the contemporary legislature and it is little wonder that legislative systems have tilted toward the ambitions and interests of individuals and factions at the expense of collective responsibilities. Under current circumstances, it is a wonder that legislatures can get much done at all. Yet, they manage reasonably well.

Even if the institution were more of a piece than it is presently, the hurdles in transmitting common values to each succeeding generation of legislators would be formidable anyway. The tenure of legislative leaders is not likely to be as long as in the recent past, as rank-and-file members insist on opening up the top positions to them. In those states—twenty-one at the latest count—that have imposed term limits on members, high turnover will prevent the institution from assimilating new members. The socialization process will be markedly retarded.

With the legislature as institutionally weak as it is, dealing with the ethics of members will truly test its capability. Yet, there is no alternative, except to cede completely moral authority to people who have little understanding of, commitment to, or responsibility for the legislature and the legislative process. The legislative community, as diffuse as it may be, still exists and has the potential to establish ethical standards for members and help in their enforcement. Indeed, the challenge of taking on ethics can be one that will reinforce among members a sense of shared values and a community in common. If the institution is to maintain itself and repair damage that has been done to it, ethics offers it an opportunity.

The success of this enterprise will depend greatly on legislative leadership, as well as on the willingness of members to follow their leaders. Leaders will have to set an example in their behavior. They will also have to encourage their members in working toward consensus on ethical practices. It is up to them also to help steer members in their behavior, so that those who cross the line, or come too close, are cautioned or even sanctioned if necessary. Finally, both leaders and members must take on the job of civic education, taking seriously the enormous job of explaining to people what the legislature is all about and what they can reasonably expect and not expect of this political institution.

EXEMPLARS

Legislative leaders, according to the Hastings Center, influence ethical behavior by the example they set for members. "If they so choose," Hastings maintains, "they can elevate the level of political discourse, set the standard for interaction with special interests, and affect the overall moral tone of the assembly."[13] Tom Loftus, the former speaker of the Wisconsin assembly, took his role as exemplar quite seriously, acknowledging that Democratic members might imitate his behavior. He was conscious of trying to be a good example. In doing this, Loftus was especially sensitive regarding his relationships with lobbyists: "A leader who is real chummy with lobbyists should realize that it is noticed. The appearance is wrong, and some legislators will conclude that this is the way the big boys act."[14] Other leaders also ought to take on responsibility for setting the tone and performing as role models of ethical behavior.[15] However, most legislative leaders probably give little thought to this aspect of their jobs; they have so many other leadership tasks to occupy them. Some legislative leaders may, indeed, set wrong examples in one way or another.

Willie Brown, speaker of the assembly in California, has demonstrated an outstanding ability to raise huge sums of money for his legislative party's campaigns. His preoccupation with and success at fundraising, almost to the neglect of policy, sends a message to other members of the legislative community. Campaign finance in California has been pushed to the limits, and the ethical climate probably has suffered as a consequence.[16] Had Speaker Brown chosen to focus his formidable talents otherwise, the California legislature might be a different place today.

Gib Lewis, the former speaker of the Texas house, set the tone in Austin. A good speaker by all accounts (nonpartisan, fair, and protective of members), Lewis stepped over the ethical line. He committed violations of ethical conduct, some illegal and some not, on several occasions. Journalist Molly Ivins described Lewis as "ethically challenged" and once observed that he had the ethical sensitivity of a walnut. He traveled on the tab of racing lobbyists, failed to report business interests held jointly with lobbyists, and had to reimburse his political campaign fund for the mistaken use of $25,000.[17] That is not the example that leaders in Texas, or anywhere else, should set.

Don Blandford, who as speaker of the house was convicted in the Boptrot sting in Kentucky, set one kind of example. Well liked and respected by his colleagues, Blandford was considered to be an able leader—but he was a product of, and contributor to, Kentucky's old political culture. His successor as speaker, Joe Clarke, in his ethical demeanor was quite the opposite. Before his selection as speaker, Clarke had served for two decades and had acquired the reputation among his colleagues of being one of the most ethical members of the legislature. He had little time for entertainment and little taste for perks. Other legislators had no reservations whatsoever about accepting complimentary basketball tickets from the University of Kentucky, but Clarke had insisted on paying for them.

Upon arriving in Frankfort, freshmen members of the house were advised, "If you want to vote like a statesman, vote the way Joe Clarke votes. And if you want to vote like a politician, vote like ------ votes."

After Blandford was indicted on bribery and racketeering charges and had abandoned his campaign for reelection to the speakership, Clarke declared his candidacy and was chosen by his colleagues to be speaker. He was an ideal choice for the position, particularly at this time in the history of the general assembly. Even the *Lexington Herald-Leader*, which was so condemnatory of the legislature, waxed enthusiastic in an editorial: "He is the perfect antidote to the revelations of Boptrot, representing as he does the decent core of the state legislature" (29 November 1992).

Upon taking office, the new speaker saw the need for leadership to set a very different example. When a colleague noted that the walls in the speaker's office were bare, in contrast with the memorabilia that hung in the office under previous speakers, Clarke replied, "This is where we work" and "bare's the way we're going to operate."[18] To reinforce the message of the decor, Clarke quickly changed the relationship between leadership and the lobby. His predecessor used to have space reserved for lobbyists in his suite, with a secretary assigned to serve their receptionist needs. Clarke cleared his office of the lobbyists, exiling them to a small office in the Annex. The other members of the house leadership soon followed his example, barring lobbyists from using the telephones in their offices. The appearance of the house underwent a substantial change.

Another signal was conveyed to the house membership with Speaker Clarke's changes in his outer office. Under Speaker Blandford, lobbyists contributed trays of goodies—cold cuts, bread, and fruit—which were set up for legislators and others to enjoy. Speaker Clarke dispensed with the lobbyists' food. Instead, he personally bought broccoli, cauliflower, and carrots and brought them to the office for members to share. The *Louisville Courier-Journal* headline gave the matter just the interpretation that was intended: "Speaker Clarke's lean cuisine signals emphasis on clean" (2 February 1993).

TRAINING

The Hastings Center, among other authorities, recommends that legislatures do more to encourage discussions of ethical issues among their members. This should be the business of orientation sessions that legislatures routinely hold for new members, as well as of training programs conducted by universities and legislative organizations like the National Conference of State Legislatures. Ethics seminars, in the view of Hastings, ought to be established in all legislatures on a regular basis.[19]

If externally imposed standards cannot be fully effective, internally developed standards are called for. This necessitates members getting together, discussing ethical issues, and trying to reach some agreement on where ethical lines should be drawn and what behavior should be discouraged. The major task is that of establishing a sense of what is permissible and what is not. "Ethics training," as it is called, is now offered to legislators in several states. New Mexico and Kentucky instituted such training most recently. California and Connecticut have had it for a while, albeit with mixed results.

The Connecticut Humanities Council and the Connecticut State Ethics Commission held a conference on ethics, apparently convincing the leadership of the legislature that the education of members on these issues had to be an ongoing effort. When a revised ethics code was passed later in the legislative session, the council and commission were mandated to conduct sessions on a biennial basis. The first biennial program, a one-day session in the Legislative Office Building, was held in January 1993. Although there were a number of lobbyists and legislative staff in attendance, only twenty to thirty legislators were present at any time to hear several speakers and a panel discussion on ethics.

In Connecticut, legislation mandated that ethics training be provided, but it did not require legislators to attend. In California, since Proposition 112 passed in 1990, triggering implementing legislation, the law also requires that ethics training be provided, but it goes further by requiring every legislator, lobbyist, and member of the professional legislative staff to take ethics training once each biennium. The attendance of legislators at the sessions held in 1991 and 1993 was far better than that in Connecticut; and those who were absent were given a chance to attend training at another time during the year. The type of training is not specified by law, and the California assembly and senate have approached the subject differently. In the first round the assembly relied on a review of law and regulation by legal staff, while the senate brought in ethicist Michael Josephson from outside to go beyond the formalities and engage in a discussion with members of what they thought was right and what they thought was wrong.

In neither Connecticut nor California have legislative leaders given much more than formal endorsement to ethics training. They have provided little in the way of presence or support and have thereby communicated to members that, although the training may be required, it is not very important. In Connecticut, Senate President John Larson made welcoming remarks but did not stay for most of what followed. Legislative leaders stressed to the press that they were not responsible for ensuring attendance and explained that bad weather and legislative business might have had an effect. House Speaker Thomas D. Ritter thought the deadlines for submitting bills for the session and for organizing committees might have interfered with attendance. Moreover, he added, since the conference proceedings were shown on video monitors throughout the capitol, it was possible that legislators other than those who were physically present had tuned in.[20] In California, President Pro Tem David Roberti made a token appearance at the mandated ethics training for senators and then left to conduct other business. Even the chair of the ethics committee, who had jurisdiction over the training, was dubious. A number of senators had complained to him about having to attend the session on ethics, leading him to consider modification of the program.

Ordinarily, you can lead a horse to water, but you can't make him drink. In this case, while it is tough to lead a legislator to ethics training, it is easier to get him to drink. By that I mean that once legislators embark upon a discussion of ethical issues, they take the subject seriously and make headway. This is the impression I got in conducting the training for the California senate in 1993. At a panel session that was open to the press, Ed Davis, a former member of the senate, stated the typical legislator view that members learned their ethics long before they came to the legislature. Yet, he admitted that he did learn something from the training conducted by Michael Josephson two years before. The ethicist had confronted members with the case of a member who called a lobbyist to get a campaign contribution. "Isn't this pressure?" Josephson asked. Davis admitted that he was forced to agree and decided thereafter to stop making fund-raising calls.

The most productive part of the California training, in my opinion, occurred behind closed doors, where the senators could be relatively candid. If legislators are to talk openly with one another and work toward the development of an ethics consensus, the press has to be barred from these sessions. Otherwise, members will be compelled to protect themselves politically and posture for public consumption. Nothing would be achieved. The closed-session discussion in California, which I facilitated, did accomplish something. Although questions with regard to fund-raising and the role of money led to defensiveness and finger pointing on the parts of senators, a discussion of the case of the Keating Five resulted in the communication of different views on how far legislators should go in representing constituents, including constituents who were also contributors to legislators' campaigns. I believe that this relatively brief conversation in which members compared practices may have affected the subsequent thinking and behavior of some of them.

This type of conversation should be longer, more frequent, and more ongoing rather than merely a biennial occasion. It is not enough to have an ethics committee or commission hold one of its orientation sessions, where legislators are walked through the code, registration forms, and advisory opinions. Such meetings, which familiarize legislators with law and process, are requisite but not sufficient. Legislators also have to slog through the gray areas of ethics, making a commitment of time and energy and bringing to the endeavor a sense of purpose.

The objectives of such sessions should go well beyond what we normally think of as "training." First, such discussions can raise the ethical consciousness of legislators. Many of them have had little occasion to think about the ethical implications of their behavior, particularly since they are overwhelmed by the political ones. Awareness is an important initial step. Second, structured conversations will give legislators an opportunity to compare notes with colleagues on what they did and what they believed to be proper and improper under various circumstances. The range in practice and judgment is likely to be considerable, but, whatever the spread, members can see just where their colleagues stand.

Third, the very engagement in the discussion of ethics may bring legislators closer to a consensus on certain issues. Right now, there are differences in beliefs and in practices—by gender, by race, by seniority, and by individual. The lack of agreement and understanding is hidden by general codes of ethics, which legislatures pass without internalizing. An honest discussion would reveal differences and work, wherever possible, toward bridging them. At least, the gap could be identified and even narrowed. Fourth, in time legislators may increase their ethical competence, that is, their ability to reason morally. As Gutmann and Thompson write, "Without a trained capacity for moral deliberation, legislators will be ruled only by habit and tradition."[21] And, most important, by politics.

I realize that this is a heavy agenda for legislators, who have so much else on their minds. Still, I believe that lawmakers can reflect more on ethics without overburdening either themselves or the system. Legislators, however, are not likely to sacrifice more immediate concerns for an ongoing exercise in ethics. A move in this direction will require the leadership of people who appreciate the increasing connection between ethics and the health of their institution.

Training in ethics may focus on particular problems, as well as range more broadly. Take, for example, the unfair campaigning engaged in by legislators, specifically the irresponsible trashing of the political system and the legislative institution. Unfair campaigns to win election or reelection are not ethical, but still many legislative candidates make allegations that are untrue, defamatory, misleading, or irrelevant to the legitimate qualifications for the office sought or to issues about which the electorate is legitimately concerned.[22]

Many observers of the electoral system note that campaigns are becoming increasingly confrontational, negative, and unfair. Moreover, the legislative process itself is being used as a staging area for such battles, with each legislative party introducing bills to prevent flag burning or get tough on crime that are brought forth mainly so that combatants can send out negative mailings in the districts of those voting against popular positions. Today's legislature, through its political parties, is a major participant in "hit piece" wars. Candidates and their parties explain that they have to do what they are doing; otherwise, they risk losing the election. Excuses of the type "If I don't do this, someone else will" try to shift moral responsibility to the wider system, but it cannot be shifted. Furthermore, campaigns of this nature have corrosive effects on the legislative community, making bipartisan cooperation even tougher. A former Wisconsin legislator who now works as a lobbyist in the state of Washington believes that an ethical environment requires civility and courtesy: "I think it is quite hard to maintain professional courtesy and civility when the person you may sit next to in committee through long committee sessions for two years, share anecdotes with and feel close to, is on the radio essentially telling lies about you in your district at campaign time. These things not only change the public's view of us, but also change our ability to get along with each other."[23]

The campaign-related charges made against Democrats by Republicans and vice versa damage relationships within a legislative body. The campaign-related charges made against the legislature and its practices damage the institution in the eyes of the public. The campaigns of challengers frequently charge that incumbents are abusing their offices by taking trips to legislative conferences at state expense and enjoying too many perquisites of legislative life. The campaigns of challengers (but even the campaigns of incumbents, particularly those in the minority party) accuse the legislative system of not working for the good of the state and of being responsible for all of society's ills. It is in the interest of each state legislator, moreover, to blame just about everything on the legislature in general and other members in particular. "The institution is rotten, the other members are rotten, my opponent is rotten—but I'm OK, indeed, better than OK." That is the rhetoric one hears today.

Legislatures ought to confront the issue of campaigns and their impact on the institution. In each legislative chamber, members should meet together—first along partisan lines and then on a bipartisan basis—to try to reach agreement on what is unethical in campaigning. They surely ought to be able to agree, as incumbents, not to attack their institution and, as legislative party members, to try to dissuade challengers from doing so. The two parties need to enter into a truce that places institution bashing off limits. This will be easier for the majority than the minority, but the institutional obligations of each certainly ought to be one focus of ethics training.

All this, I admit, is much easier said than done. The legislative parties do not trust one another. Each party, moreover, is apt to be composed of several factions. Leaders do not want an issue used against them by the other party or someone in their own camp. They are not willing to call on members to stop grandstanding on certain issues, such as pay and perquisites. It will take strong and persevering leadership to overcome these hurdles. Perhaps this is too much to expect in a future that promises less permanent and weaker leadership.

COUNSELING

Legislative leaders will get little credit—either with members or the public—for coming to grips with ethics. But if they fail to do so, their institutions surely will suffer. Setting an example is requisite but not sufficient. They must go further, providing counseling and guidance and establishing standards and expectations. It is up to them to initiate such behavior and not just wait for members to come to them for advice or for scandals to erupt.

Leaders are understandably reluctant to intervene on moral matters. They are politicians, not ministers or therapists. Tom Loftus, for one, does not think that legislative leaders can be expected to police their colleagues, although he does acknowledge that they can set an ethical tone for the institution.[24] Leaders can indicate what is expected of legislators when they attend meetings of legislative and other groups at state expense. They should be expected to participate seriously, with work the principal focus and pleasure the by-product, rather than vice versa. Even if they are reluctant to intervene forcefully, they can try to discourage unethical behavior. In Maryland, for instance, a legislator asked a lobbyist for the use of her credit card. The lobbyist appealed to the speaker, who spoke to the legislator. "I think she misunderstood you," said the speaker, avoiding any hint of reprimand but making his position clear. Although oblique, the message got across—leadership expects members to refrain from shaking down lobbyists.

More proactive policing by leaders rarely takes place. The reluctance of leaders to take on members who are straying from the straight and narrow path is easily explained. Most often leaders, and members alike, are not sure who is straying, who the rogues are. Legislators are less close-knit as a community than they used to be, so their colleagues, including their leaders, are not often conscious of what they are doing. Paul "Bud" Burke, the president of the Kansas senate, for example, indicated that he had no idea at all which of his thirty-nine colleagues might have been too close to the line. Twenty-one were new, and the rest he just didn't know about. According to Burke, knowledge is usually lacking and suspicions are seldom called for.[25] More often than not, when a member gets into trouble on ethical grounds, it comes as a surprise. Of those legislators convicted in the Boptrot sting in Kentucky, for example, only two might have been suspected by colleagues. No one would have imagined that several would have gotten into such trouble, and a few others were considered to be not very bright.[26]

Even suspicions have not been enough to prompt leadership intervention. Certain members may have a reputation of being too sharp, treading too near the edge. Loftus writes about Dick Shoemaker, who ran into ethical difficulty in Wisconsin. He might have been suspect because of the issues he took on and the interests he supported, which involved drinking, smoking, and gambling. Furthermore, he hung around with lobbyists, and it might have appeared that he was on the take.[27] But while Loftus and others in the Wisconsin assembly may have had their suspicions, they had no evidence. Rarely, if ever, do leaders have evidence. If they got involved, they would have to proceed on the basis of perception and hunch rather than grounded reality.

Leaders are not philosophically, temperamentally, or politically inclined to call members to account for questionable (albeit not illegal) behavior. In the legislature members generally subscribe to the belief that they are not there to make moral judgments on colleagues. As a member of the Kentucky legislature stated, "It's too much to expect legislators to confront one of their own and pass judgment."[28] They pass such responsibility on to other agencies, such as the constituency. "If they want to send him up here, it's their fault," is the rationale they employ.

The fragile nature of leadership is another reason for nonintervention. The case of California and the behavior of senate leader David Roberti illustrate the point. Roberti, like many other leaders, was disinclined to confront colleagues with questions about their probity. It was not the way to build or maintain consensus in the Democratic caucus. Like other senators, Roberti probably had doubts about the conduct of Joseph Montoya, Paul Carpenter, and Alan Robbins. All three had reputations for heavy-handed fund-raising and questionable back-room deals long before the FBI caught up with them. But Roberti was not about to sacrifice support and votes in order to try (and perhaps not even succeed) bringing them into line. According to Roberti, "You police somebody on Monday, and on Tuesday, you're asking for his vote."[29] "There are only so many people you can treat as pariahs," he said. "If you don't get their votes and can't put majorities together, that gets heavy criticism, too—or the loss of my job."[30] Roberti not only neglected calling his members on the carpet, but he also took no action to limit their power. Indeed, he had provided Robbins the chairmanship of a major "juice" committee (that is, a committee that, because of its subject matter, can be expected to generate more than the normal amount of campaign contributions for its members). When Roberti became president pro tem, he split up the banking and insurance committee and gave insurance to Robbins, and he kept Montoya on as chair of the business and professions committee long after it was widely suspected that Montoya was using his position for personal gain.[31]

Anyone with an appreciation of the job of legislative leadership can empathize with Roberti. He did not want to jeopardize the support he already had and could summon in the future just to provide moral guidance to colleagues. Moreover, how effective would intervention be? Roberti acknowledged that on one occasion, he did have a conversation with one of the senators over the lawmaker's "reputation." He raised the issue of "heavy-handedness" with the senator, albeit in a vague way. Still, "I got my head chopped off."[32] Had he really confronted the suspect senators, it might have caused a rift in the caucus. While some members would have said, "It's about time," others would have said, "It's their own business." Inevitably, the accusation would have leaked to the press and become public.[33] Arguably, Roberti's action might have had some deterring effect, but it surely would have required the expenditure of substantial political capital.

Powerful forces militate against leadership intervention in offering moral guidance to members. But it can be done, it has been done, and it has proven effective. When there are members on the edge, "they could be jerked back," is the way Jane Hull, the former speaker of the Arizona house, put it. When a charge or instance of unethical conduct comes to the attention of a legislative leader, he or she has no excuse not to intervene. In Ohio, for example, a house member of dubious reputation tried to shake down some lobbyists for large contributions to his campaign. The lobbyists complained to Vern Riffe, the speaker, who called the representative in and read him the riot act. (Riffe was about to hold a fundraiser and was concerned that his effort would suffer because of his colleague's behavior.) The speaker did not take away the representative's committee chairmanship or punish him in any other way, but his words had the intended effect; the member pulled back.[34]

Other leaders have counseled members when they felt they were too close to the edge. In doing so they have paid a political price, jeopardizing their power base. But, given the ethical problems that legislative bodies face today, they can afford to do no less. They must do whatever they can to deter members who might discredit their institution. Once a legislature's reputation has been damaged, it is too late for full recovery.

EDUCATING THE PUBLIC

In a democracy, the public also has responsibility for the ethical integrity of its elected representatives and of the legislatures in which they serve.[35] The public, I submit, is not fulfilling its responsibility. Voters expect legislators to do certain things in a certain way, and they expect certain things from their government, but their understanding of the legislative institution and the legislative process is very limited. The contemporary role of the public was well expressed by a frustrated member of New Mexico's house, Blake Curtis, who said, "People are demanding what they think they want in something they don't understand. They don't know where we're at or what we're doing."[36] Like state legislators everywhere, Curtis pointed out that when he is not home in the district, some of his constituents think he is in Washington. They confuse their legislators with their congressmen and cannot distinguish the state legislature from the U.S. Congress.

The public today is a highly participant one, despite the fact that turnout for elections has declined over the years. More people today are involved through interest group activities and grass-roots lobbying efforts than ever before. Their opinions are being communicated through public opinion polls, talk radio shows, and letters sent directly to their representatives. These participants are still a small proportion of the entire electorate but a vigorous and influential one.

The negative orientations that people now hold toward their legislatures, as well as toward other political institutions, are in large part a function of what they see and hear in the media and in political campaigns. Both the media and campaigns are driven by the pressures of competition for an audience. Given popular taste, the negative and accusatory works better than the positive and explanatory. This unrelenting bombardment is doing damage to political institutions and constitutes a significant danger to representative democracy in the United States. If other channels of information existed and the public were better informed, it could address the problems of its institutions in a responsible rather than visceral manner.

The focus groups we conducted in California, Minnesota, and New Jersey indicated that a little knowledge can go a long way. Several participants admitted their deficiencies as citizens. "I really don't know who's doing what or where, who's representing me, or whatever," said one New Jerseyan. "I would like to be more informed, but it's really hard to do," said another. Participants in the Minnesota groups had a greater knowledge of their legislature than did those in California and New Jersey, but they too had misperceptions about the nature of the legislative process.

During the course of the focus group sessions, each of which lasted less than two hours, the discussion itself contributed to the civic education of participants and seemed to have some impact on their attitudes. Whereas New Jerseyans and Minnesotans, in particular, started out more cynical and angry, as they engaged in discussion their positions softened. They began to appreciate the pressures that public officials experience, the difficulties they face in trying to please their constituents, and the ethical dilemmas they encounter. Participants recognized that different people and groups have different interests ("everyone has his own particular ax to grind"); compromise is an essential part of the democratic process; legislators have an extremely hard job satisfying people; people cannot expect to get their way all the time and their expectations have to be lowered; and the public does not have enough of an idea of how government works and, thus, may expect too much.

A New Jerseyan concluded that politics was not as bad as it might otherwise seem, if one gave it some thought:

> I didn't even want to think about it—get it out of my face. But when you start talking about it and thinking about it, it's not as threatening as thinking about this whole corrupt system. It's easy to think that, because that's what we get a lot—this politician did that. And when you sit down and talk about it, it's not as threatening. We are this government, and that's kind of a realization.

At the conclusion of one of the sessions in Minnesota, several of the participants vowed to pay more attention to the legislature. One admitted responsibility: "I can't just sit in the background like I have been." Others said they would read more and try to get briefed about the legislature.

The question is how "the people" can become a responsible public, a deliberative body of informed citizens rather than a mass of individuals.[37] Obviously, the best educational method is that of involvement, so that individuals can learn about the legislature first hand, without the mediation of a press intent on gaining an audience or political candidates intent on winning votes. One Minnesotan, for instance, mentioned to others in the focus group that he had become interested in the legislature five years before when he started his own business. He commented that he used to be cynical, but since he became more involved he developed greater regard for legislators, "who are trying to do the right thing." The familiarity that one gains through involvement may well breed empathy for elected public officials.

The legislature cannot rely on citizens becoming involved in such a way that they develop understanding. But it can begin to face up to the responsibility it has for helping to educate the public with regard to the institution and the process. Legislators must take on as principal functions of the bodies in which they serve not only making policy, determining the budget, exercising oversight of government, and representing and servicing constituents. They must also take on the function of educating the citizenry. This goes beyond the task of explaining the issues in all their complexity and the reasons for one's choices.[38] It relates to the very nature of the democratic process and the role of representative assemblies. It includes addressing questions of values, interests, and due process. It includes also exploration of conflict, compromise, and consensus building in democratic politics. Public education, moreover, has to enhance people's understanding of the ethical dilemmas and difficulties of holding legislative office and the way in which such problems can be addressed.

The type of education visualized by public officials and that I suggest here may not be the type of education that citizens always appreciate. But there is no substitute if the public is to play a responsible role in shaping its political institutions. It is easier for the public to become educated with regard to issues as its initial impressions develop into more stable and coherent judgments. But it should also be possible for the public, through a deliberative process, to achieve a better notion of what legislatures are about.

One purpose of civic education, to use a popular political cliché, is to attempt to level the playing field. Legislatures do not deserve the trashing they are receiving at the hands of the press and from members and challengers running for election. They do not deserve the opprobrium in which the public now holds them because of the corruption, greed, and stupidity of a relatively few members. Although there is considerable room for improvement in their demeanor and performance, legislatures in the states deserve far more support than they are currently getting.

Legislatures need public support in order to function at all effectively in a fragmented society undergoing economic and social strain. If legislatures are to redress the imbalance between citizen cynicism, on the one hand, and citizen confidence, on the other, they will have to do the job themselves. They cannot leave it to the press or hope that the press will behave differently. "The press is what it is because of news values and imperatives," and any appeals can only have marginal influence.[39] Nor can legislatures depend on the high schools or colleges to make state government a meaningful part of the lives of student-citizens. The schools have more than enough to do now, and the disciplines represented in higher education can hardly be counted on. As a legislator from Iowa put it, "Nobody's going to explain us to the public, but us."[40]

State legislatures, as well as the U.S. Congress, have to take a more active role in informing the public and shaping opinion about their institution. Individual members of these bodies share responsibility for educating the public about the essential nature of a legislative body.[41] This will involve an ongoing conversation about representative democracy, including the topic of legislative ethics, among legislators, educators, commentators, and the citizenry as a whole.[42] It will require that the legislature take the lead in presenting the institution and the process to people who may be far removed from it. This is not the place to detail a communications strategy, but such a strategy will have to make use of technologies that can capture an audience's attention in the modern age. Films and video tapes of the legislature in action and C-Span-type coverage or evening wrap-ups of the day in the legislature are among the vehicles for presenting the legislature to the public. Legislators on visits to schools and clubs in their districts should devote some of their talks to the legislature and the process, in addition to promoting their policy causes and, of course, themselves.

Educating the public as to the values and ways of representative democracy is an enormous task. But it cannot be undertaken or accomplished unless legislators themselves come into agreement on the virtues of their own institutions. Most of them probably still feel some sense of belongingness and loyalty, but in recent years centrifugal forces have overcome centripetal ones. Division and conflict tend to weaken institutional pulls. If the legislature is to raise itself out of a downward spiral, leaders and members will have to accord institutional concerns a much higher level on their agendas. The incentives to do this are not great. The reelection prospects of legislators will not be enhanced; their constituents will not be made happier; their substantive programs will not be furthered. But their responsibility to the institution in which they serve will be met. That would be a big step toward more ethical legislative bodies.

Notes

1. Introduction

1. See the argument presented in my "The Legislature: Unraveling of Institutional Fabric," in *The State of the States,* 3rd ed., ed. Carl Van Horn (Washington DC: CQ Press, forthcoming).

2. *Louisville Courier-Journal,* 4 October 1992.

3. Interview with Senator Jean Lloyd-Jones, Iowa, 10 May 1993.

4. *Minneapolis Star-Tribune,* 8 March 1994.

5. Tom Loftus, "Legislative Ethics: The Rules of the Game," *Spectrum* (winter 1993): 29.

6. Christopher Schwarz, "Remodeling the Lobby," *State Government News* (May 1994): 28.

7. Hastings Center, *The Ethics of Legislative Life* (Hastings-on-Hudson NY, 1985), 27.

8. Michael Malbin, "Legislative Ethics," in *Encyclopedia of the American Legislative System,* ed. Joel Sibley (New York: Charles Scribner's Sons, 1994), 2:1155.

9. Quoted in Garry Boulard, "Pluperfect Purity," *State Legislatures* (January 1995): 31.

10. Dennis F. Thompson, *Ethics in Congress: From Individual to Institutional Corruption* (Washington DC: Brookings Institution, 1995), 48.

11. Don Harris, "It Will Never Be behind Us," *State Legislatures* (July 1991):

39; also Rob Gurwitt, "Deadly Stings—Wounded Legislatures," *Governing* (June 1991): 25–31.

12. Remarks of Representative Art Hamilton, Arizona, at "Hard Lessons in Ethics," conference sponsored by the Eagleton Institute of Politics, Rutgers University, Phoenix, Arizona, 23–24 October 1993.

13. Thompson, *Ethics in Congress,* 10–25.

14. Bruce Jennings distinguishes between "ethical reasoning" and "ethical judgment." The former pertains to the identification of general governing principles or rules appropriate to a given circumstance. The latter pertains to the capacity to discriminate among available courses of action "on the basis of an interpretive understanding of shared values embedded in an ongoing institutional practice and in a broader form of communal life." See his "Taking Ethics Seriously in Administrative Life," in *Ethical Frontiers in Public Management,* ed. James S. Bowman (San Francisco: Jossey-Bass, 1991), 67–68.

2. What's the Beef?

1. Suzanne Garment, *Scandal: The Crisis of Mistrust in American Politics* (New York: Times Books, 1991), 5, 114.

2. Representative Blake Curtis, New Mexico, at "Hard Lessons in Ethics," conference sponsored by the Eagleton Institute of Politics, Rutgers University, Phoenix, Arizona, 23–24 October 1993.

3. Arthur Maass, "Bad Federal Policy on Local Corruption," *Spectrum* (winter 1993): 19.

4. Robert N. Roberts and Marion T. Doss Jr., "The Federalization of 'Grass Roots' Corruption," *Spectrum* (winter 1993): 9, 11.

5. Elaine Stuart, "Trial of Smears," *State Government News* (May 1994): 23.

6. Sissela Bok, *Secrets* (New York: Pantheon, 1982), 268.

7. Tom Loftus and Al Cross, "Lies, Bribes and Videotape," *State Legislatures* (July 1993): 43.

8. "Givers and Takers," *Lexington Herald-Leader,* special report, January 1993.

9. Bayless Manning, "The Purity Potlatch: Conflict of Interests and Moral Escalation," in *Political Corruption,* ed. Arnold J. Heidenheimer (New Brunswick NJ: Transaction Books, 1970), 309.

10. Manning, "The Purity Potlatch," 309.

11. William Schneider, "Coarsening of Public Life Continues," *National Journal,* 21 May 1994, 1218.

12. *Albuquerque Journal,* 14 February 1993.

13. *Los Angeles Daily News,* 14 June 1992.

14. Senator Joe Carraro, New Mexico, at "Hard Lessons in Ethics," conference sponsored by the Eagleton Institute of Politics, Rutgers University, Phoenix, Arizona, 23–24 October 1993.

15. Senator Chuck Blanchard, Arizona, at "Hard Lessons in Ethics," conference sponsored by the Eagleton Institute of Politics, Rutgers University, Phoenix, Arizona, 23–24 October 1993.

16. See Eric M. Uslaner, *The Declining Comity in Congress* (Ann Arbor: University of Michigan Press, 1993).

17. Garment, *Scandal,* 7.

18. Loftus, "Legislative Ethics," 28.

19. *Times Mirror* survey, released 16 March 1994, 1, 2, 11, 55.

20. Interview with Representative Rick Trumbley, New Hampshire, 12 November 1992.

21. Josephson Institute of Ethics, *Actual and Apparent Impropriety: A Report on Ethical Norms and Attitudes in State Legislatures* (Marina del Rey CA, January 1992), 8–9.

22. Gary Moncrief, Joel A. Thompson, and Karl T. Kurtz, "The Old Statehouse Ain't What It Used to Be: Veteran State Legislators' Perceptions of Institutional Change" (paper prepared for the annual meeting of the American Political Science Association, Washington DC, 2–5 September 1993).

23. *Times Mirror* survey, 1, 61.

24. Peter A. Brown, "Gotcha Journalism," *State Legislatures* (May 1994): 22–25.

25. *National Journal,* 27 November 1993, 2864.

26. Senator Joseph Carraro, New Mexico, at "Hard Lessons in Ethics," conference sponsored by the Eagleton Institute of Politics, Rutgers University, Phoenix, Arizona, 23–24 October 1993.

27. Representative H. John Underwood, New Mexico, at "Hard Lessons in Ethics," conference sponsored by the Eagleton Institute of Politics, Rutgers University, Phoenix, Arizona, 23–24 October 1993.

28. "Freedom of the Press," *New York Times,* 24 December 1993.

29. "Public Cheated of Truth in Health Care Debate," *Star-Ledger,* 23 February 1994.

30. See Doris A. Graber, *Mass Media and American Politics,* 4th ed. (Washington DC: CQ Press, 1993), 173.

31. Thomas E. Patterson, *Out of Order* (New York: Knopf, 1993), 135, 203.

32. Moncrief, Thompson, and Kurtz, "The Old Statehouse."

33. Patterson, *Out of Order,* 8, 17, 19.

34. Jack Coffman, at the annual meeting of the Council on Governmental Ethics Laws, Minneapolis, 21 September 1993.

35. Jeff Freye, KGGM-TV, Albuquerque, 21 September 1993.

36. *Lexington Herald-Leader,* 8 May 1992.

37. *Lexington Herald-Leader,* 3 February 1993.

38. "Hyper-Journalism vs. the Public Interest," *Louisville Courier-Journal,* 21 February 1992.

39. Brown, "Gotcha Journalism," 25.

40. Jay Johnson, KIRO-TV, *Proceedings of the Washington House of Representatives,* Session on Legislative Ethics, 23 January 1992, 30.

41. Harwood Group, *Citizens and Politics* (Dayton OH: Kettering Foundation, 1991), 5, 19.

42. Much of the information reported below is from these six focus groups, which were conducted for the author by the Center for Public Interest Polling of the Eagleton Institute of Politics, Rutgers University. They were held in New Jersey on 30 March and 1 April 1993, in California on 19 April 1993, and in Minnesota on 3 May 1993.

43. *USA Today,* 29 July 1993.

44. *Salt Lake Tribune* poll, reported in *State Capitols Report,* 20 May 1993.

45. University of New Mexico Institute for Public Policy, Survey Research Center Report, *Quarterly Profile of New Mexico Citizens* (winter–spring 1989): 3.

46. These questions were commissioned by the author and administered by the Center for Public Interest Polling of the Eagleton Institute of Politics, Rutgers University. The survey of 801 New Jerseyans was conducted 10–16 February 1994.

47. On a similar item, New Mexico citizens graded their legislators as follows: 3 percent, A; 10 percent, B; 33 percent, C; 36 percent, D or F. *Albuquerque Journal,* 19 April 1992.

48. University of New Mexico Institute for Public Policy, Survey Research Center Report, *Quarterly Profile of New Mexico Citizens* (winter–spring 1991).

49. Garment, *Scandal,* 287.

50. John D. Saxon, *Hearings on Reforming Congressional Ethics Disciplinary Procedures,* Joint Committee on the Organization of Congress, Washington DC, 25 February 1993.

51. Manning, "The Purity Potlatch," 311.

52. Garment, *Scandal,* 2.

53. Saxon, *Hearings.*

3. The Quest for Standards

1. Amy Gutmann and Dennis Thompson, "The Theory of Legislative Ethics," in *Representation and Responsibility: Exploring Legislative Ethics,* ed. Bruce Jennings and Daniel Callahan (New York: Plenum Press, 1985), 168.

2. Vanessa Merton, "Legislative Ethics and Professional Responsibility," in *Representation and Responsibility,* ed. Jennings and Callahan, 313.

3. Bruce Jennings, "Legislative Ethics and Moral Minimalism," in *Representation and Responsibility,* ed. Jennings and Callahan, 157.

4. See William H. Simon, "Ethical Discretion in Lawyering," *Harvard Law Review* 101 (April 1988): 114.

5. Gary C. Jacobson, "Political Action Committees, Electoral Politics, and Congressional Ethics," in *Representation and Responsibility,* ed. Jennings and Callahan, 52.

6. Daniel H. Lowenstein, "Political Bribery and the Intermediate Theory of Politics," *UCLA Law Review* 32 (1985): 796–98, 801.

7. Michael Josephson, "The Best of Times, the Worst of Times," *Spectrum* (fall 1992): 41.

8. Commission on Federal Ethics Law Reform, *Report* (Washington DC, March 1989), 1.

9. Hastings Center, *The Ethics of Legislative Life,* 10.

10. Daniel Callahan, "Legislative Codes of Ethics," in *Representation and Responsibility,* ed. Jennings and Callahan, 223–25.

11. U.S. Senate Select Committee on Ethics, *Hearings on Revising the Senate Code of Official Conduct Pursuant to Senate Resolution 1-09* (Washington DC, 1981), 85–87.

12. Mark H. Moore, "Realms of Obligation and Virtue," in *Public Duties: The Moral Obligation of Government Officials,* ed. Joel L. Fleishman, Lance Liebman, and Mark H. Moore (Cambridge MA: Harvard University Press, 1981), 8.

13. John D. Saxon, "The Scope of Legislative Ethics," in *Representation and Responsibility,* ed. Jennings and Callahan, 206–7.

14. *New York Times,* 24 November 1991.

15. Thomas Sinclair and Charles Wise, "Substantive and Procedural Dilemmas in Congressional Ethics," *Annals* 537 (January 1995): 46.

16. Dennis F. Thompson, *Hearings on Reform of Congressional Disciplinary Procedures,* Joint Committee on the Organization of Congress, Washington DC, 25 February 1993.

17. One analog is that of a lawyer representing a corporation. Here, too, the client is not an individual but rather a CEO, board of directors, shareholders, employees, and so on. Whose interests best define those of the corporation? Another analog is that of a lawyer who brings a class action suit that represents a number of people whose condition and interests vary. To whom is the lawyer obligated?

18. Monroe H. Freedman, *Understanding Lawyers' Ethics* (New York: Matthew Bender & Co., 1990), 87.

19. Joseph S. Ellin, "Special Professional Morality and the Duty of Veracity," in *Ethical Issues in Professional Life,* ed. Joan C. Callahan (New York: Oxford University Press, 1988), 135.

20. Callahan, "Legislative Codes of Ethics," 224; Freedman, *Understanding Lawyers' Ethics,* 4–5.

21. Congressional Quarterly, *Congressional Ethics* (Washington DC: Congressional Quarterly, 1992), 145–51.

22. The sixth, seventh, eighth, and tenth standards need not be mentioned here.

23. Peter G. Brown, "Assessing Officials," in *Public Duties,* ed. Fleishman, Liebman, and Moore, 291.

24. Barbara Ley Toffler, *Tough Choices* (New York: John Wiley & Sons, 1986), 22–23.

25. Dennis F. Thompson, *Political Ethics and Public Office* (Cambridge MA: Harvard University Press, 1987), 103.

26. Saxon, "The Scope of Legislative Ethics," 200.

27. Thompson, *Political Ethics,* 7.

28. Hastings Center, *The Ethics of Legislative Life,* 35.

29. Gutmann and Thompson, "The Theory of Legislative Ethics," 174–75.

30. Gutmann and Thompson, "The Theory of Legislative Ethics," 174–75.

31. Hastings Center, *The Ethics of Legislative Life,* 34–36.

32. Bok, *Secrets,* 258.

33. Since Pompeia's behavior (she allowed Clodius to visit her in Caesar's house) resembled guilty behavior, it was deemed wrong and she was blamed. See Julia Driver, "Caesar's Wife: On the Moral Significance of Appearing Good," *Journal of Philosophy* 89 (July 1992): 331–43.

34. *Politics, Power and Ethics* (Marina del Rey CA: Josephson Institute for the Advancement of Ethics, 1988), 37.

35. Josephson Institute of Ethics, *Actual and Apparent Impropriety.*

36. Dennis F. Thompson, "Paradoxes of Government Ethics," *Public Administration Review* 52 (May–June 1992): 257; Jacobson, "Political Action Committees," 49.

37. Thompson, "Paradoxes of Government Ethics," 257.

38. Josephson, "The Best of Times," 36; Carol W. Lewis, *The Ethics Challenge of Public Service* (San Francisco: Jossey-Bass, 1991), 52.

39. Gutmann and Thompson, "The Theory of Legislative Ethics," 178–79.

4. Interests Are Always in Conflict

1. W. J. Michael Cody and Lynn R. Richardson, *Honest Government: An Ethics Guide for Public Service* (Westport CT: Praeger, 1992), 49–50.

2. Hastings Center, *The Ethics of Legislative Life,* 34–35.

3. Saxon, "The Scope of Legislative Ethics," 206.

4. Data provided by the National Conference of State Legislatures.

5. Washington State Legislature, *Common Sense Guide to Legislative Ethics* (Joint Board of Legislative Ethics, January 1991).

6. *Santa Fe Journal,* 20 January 1993.

7. Adapted from Joel L. Fleishman, "Self-Interest and Political Integrity," in *Public Duties,* ed. Fleishman, Liebman, and Moore, 63–64.

8. Tom Loftus, *The Art of Legislative Politics* (Washington DC: CQ Press, 1994), 144.

9. Thompson, *Political Ethics,* 128.

10. Alan Rosenthal, "Political Protocol," *State Government News* (January 1993): 35.

11. Joseph Zimmerman, *Curbing Unethical Behavior in Government* (Westport CT: Greenwood Press, 1994), 39.

12. Chris Mondics, "Okay, Boys, Dig In!" *New Jersey Reporter* (November–December 1991): 34.

13. "A Small State Can't Help It If Its Politics Seem to Be Cozy," *New York Times*, 6 February 1994.

14. California Legislature, *A Guide to Laws on Official Conduct for Legislators and Legislative Staff* (1 January 1991), 17; also New Hampshire General Court, *Ethics Guidelines and Procedures* (July 1992), 6–7.

15. *Albuquerque Tribune*, 3 March 1992.

16. *Lexington Herald-Leader*, "Givers and Takers," special report, January 1993.

17. *Albuquerque Tribune*, 16 March 1993.

18. Acting Chief Justice James A. Anderson, *Proceedings of the Washington State House of Representatives*, Session on Legislative Ethics, 23 January 1992, 27.

19. Freedman, *Understanding Lawyers' Ethics*, 182.

20. U.S. Senate Select Committee on Ethics, *Hearings on Revising the Senate Code of Official Conduct Pursuant to Senate Resolution* 109 (Washington DC, 1981), 7.

21. "Hard Lessons in Ethics," conference sponsored by the Eagleton Institute of Politics, Rutgers University, Phoenix, Arizona, 23–24 October 1993.

5. Lobbyists and Their Largess

1. Cody and Richardson, *Honest Government*, 91.

2. Elizabeth Drew, *Politics and Money* (New York: Macmillan, 1983), 45.

3. Alan Rosenthal, *The Third House* (Washington DC: CQ Press, 1993), 112–13.

4. Material in this section is taken from Rosenthal, *The Third House*, 99–106.

5. *New York Times*, 25 February 1993.

6. Cited in *State Capitols Report*, vol. 1, 20 May 1993.

7. *Congressional Record*, 11 May 1994, S-5526.

8. John T. Noonan Jr., *Bribes* (Berkeley: University of California Press, 1984), 687.

9. *Lexington Herald-Leader,* "Givers and Takers," special report, January 1993.

10. Schwarz, "Remodeling the Lobby," 30.

11. Schwarz, "Remodeling the Lobby," 31.

12. The following paragraphs are taken from Alan Rosenthal, "Political Protocol," *State Government News* (September 1993): 37.

13. Quoted in the *New York Times,* 19 September 1993.

14. Rosenthal, *The Third House,* 104–5, 116–17.

15. David C. Saffell, "Cleaning Up the Ohio Legislature," *Comparative State Politics* 15 (April 1994): 31.

16. Presentment, Leon County (Florida) Grand Jury, fall term, 1990, 4.

17. Josephson Institute of Ethics, *Actual and Apparent Impropriety,* 13.

18. Washington State Legislature, *Common Sense Guide,* 16.

19. Letter from Alan S. Plofsky, Executive Director, Connecticut Ethics Commission, dated 21 March 1992.

20. What about limitations on gifts under such circumstances? Some states make exceptions for a romantic relationship. They provide that such a relationship cannot be a one-night stand but has to be a "bona fide dating relationship" to be exempt from limitations.

6. Dilemmas of Campaign Finance

1. Josephson, "The Best of Times," 40.

2. Corey Cook, *Campaign Finance Reform* (California Research Bureau, California State Library, July 1994), 25.

3. Tommy Neal, "The Sky-High Cost of Campaigns," *State Legislatures* (May 1992): 16.

4. Moncrief, Thompson, and Kurtz, "The Old Statehouse."

5. Neal, "The Sky-High Cost of Campaigns," 16.

6. Neal, "The Sky-High Cost of Campaigns," 23.

7. Cook, *Campaign Finance Reform,* 29–30.

8. Keith E. Hamm and Gary Moncrief, "Trends in the Costs of State Legislative Campaigns" (paper prepared for the annual meeting of the American Political Science Association, Chicago, 4–7 September 1992).

9. Drew, *Politics and Money,* 45.

10. Daniel H. Lowenstein, "Political Bribery and the Intermediate Theory of Politics," UCLA *Law Review* 32 (1985): 848.

11. Frank J. Sorauf, *Inside Campaign Finance* (New Haven CT: Yale University Press, 1992), 23, 24, 25.

12. Cook, *Campaign Finance Reform,* 17–18.

13. *San Jose Mercury News,* 8 January 1995.

14. Josephson Institute of Ethics, *Actual and Apparent Impropriety,* 5.

15. *Newark Star-Ledger,* 18 December 1991.

16. Josephson Institute of Ethics, *Actual and Apparent Impropriety,* 18.

17. Josephson Institute of Ethics, *Actual and Apparent Impropriety,* 5.

18. See the discussion in Rosenthal, *The Third House,* 123–26.

19. Dean Conley's *Newsletter,* 9 February 1994.

20. Quoted in *Albuquerque Journal,* 19 June 1992.

21. "Hard Lessons in Ethics," conference sponsored by the Eagleton Institute of Politics, Rutgers University, Phoenix, Arizona, 23–24 October 1993.

22. Daniel M. Weintraub, "California Leaders Look at Limits," *State Legislatures* (July 1994): 41.

23. Sorauf, *Inside Campaign Finance,* 170.

24. Rosenthal, *The Third House,* 63.

25. Rosenthal, *The Third House,* 78–79.

26. Rosenthal, *The Third House,* 124.

27. Quoted in A. G. Block, "The Ethics Jungle," *California Journal* (April 1990): 177.

28. Saxon, "The Scope of Legislative Ethics," 202.

29. The project, directed by Lawrence N. Hansen of George Washington University, was discussed by David S. Broder in his syndicated column, "To Reform Campaign Financing—The Voters Must Confront Congress," *Miami Herald,* 17 October 1993.

30. Rob Gurwitt, "The Mirage of Campaign Reform," *Governing* (August 1992): 50.

31. Jacobson, "Political Action Committees," 55.

32. Dave Travis, "Opinion: Public Campaign Financing Could Work but It Doesn't," *State Legislatures* (December 1991): 40; Ruth S. Jones and Thomas J.

Boris, "Strategic Contributing in Legislative Campaigns: The Case of Minnesota," *Legislative Studies Quarterly* 10 (February 1985): 89–105.

33. Neal, "The Sky-High Cost of Campaigns," 19.

34. In 1990 a federal judge declared the law unconstitutional because it gave incumbents an unfair advantage.

35. Donald T. DiFrancesco, "New Jersey's Road to Campaign Finance Reform" (address to the annual meeting of the National Conference of State Legislatures, San Diego, July 1993).

36. Cook, *Campaign Finance Reform,* 23.

37. Cody and Richardson, *Honest Government,* 17.

38. Cook, *Campaign Finance Reform,* 11–13.

39. Sorauf, *Inside Campaign Finance,* 199–203.

40. *Lexington Herald-Leader,* "Givers and Takers," special report, January 1993.

41. *Lexington Herald-Leader,* 8 January 1993.

42. Gurwitt, "The Mirage of Campaign Finance Reform," 51.

43. Travis, "Opinion," 40.

44. Quoted in Eliza Newlin Carney, "FYI: Don't Look Here for PAC-Bashers," *National Journal,* 16 July 1994, 1690.

45. Cody and Richardson, *Honest Government,* 21.

46. Cook, *Campaign Finance Reform,* 4.

47. Josephson Institute of Ethics, *Actual and Apparent Impropriety,* 14.

48. New Jersey Ad Hoc Commission on Legislative Ethics and Campaign Finance, *Report,* 22 October 1990.

49. See Cindy Simon Rosenthal, "Where's the Party?" *State Legislatures* (June 1994): 31–37.

50. Malcolm E. Jewell and Marcia Lynn Whicker, *Legislative Leadership in the American States* (Ann Arbor: University of Michigan Press, 1994), 115–19.

51. DiFrancesco, "New Jersey's Road to Campaign Finance Reform," 10.

52. "Hard Lessons in Ethics," conference sponsored by the Eagleton Institute of Politics, Rutgers University, Phoenix, Arizona, 23–24 October 1993.

53. *Lexington Herald-Leader,* "Givers and Takers," special report, January 1993.

54. *Boston Globe,* 27 May 1993, 18 November 1993.

55. *Boston Globe,* 22 March 1994.

56. See Dennis F. Thompson, "Mediated Corruption: The Case of the Keating Five," *American Political Science Review* 87 (June 1993): 369–81.

57. Josephson Institute of Ethics, *Actual and Apparent Impropriety,* 6, 11.

7. The Management of Legislative Life

1. "The Institutionalization of the U.S. House of Representatives," *American Political Science Review* 62 (March 1968): 144–68.

2. *Saint Paul Pioneer Press,* 5, 6 August 1993.

3. Interview with author, 1 September 1993.

4. Office of the Attorney General, Minnesota, *Attorney General's Report on the Unauthorized Use of Rep. Alan Welle's State Telephone Access Code,* 7 June 1993.

5. District Court, 2nd Judicial District Memo. The reason for the provision was Governor Rudy Perpich, who had been using phone records in a squabble he was having with a few legislators of his own party.

6. *Minneapolis Star Tribune,* 24 March 1993.

7. Office of the Attorney General, Minnesota, *Attorney General's Report.*

8. *Saint Paul Pioneer Press,* 24 March 1993.

9. Office of the Attorney General, Minnesota, *Attorney General's Report.*

10. *Minneapolis Star Tribune,* 5 August 1993.

11. However, he did tell his chief aide in February 1992 that his son and nephew were involved.

12. *Minneapolis Star Tribune,* 5 August 1993.

13. It is interesting to note that twenty-five years ago when a band of male legislators went off carousing to Tijuana it would go unnoticed. Now when a legislator takes his family to Tijuana, he is likely to be on the six o'clock news. Although our cultural standards are more permissive than they used to be, our expectations for proper behavior by public officials are quite the opposite.

14. While the IR party failed to win control of the Minnesota house in 1994, the following year the DFL party weakened itself further. One Democratic senator went on trial for twenty-one federal counts, including fraud. Another was convicted of shoplifting. A representative was accused of having threatened to cut funding for the Public Safety Department after he was refused a State Patrol plane ride to former governor Rudy Perpich's funeral. The three had to give up their

leadership positions, as did another Democratic senator who was charged with slapping his estranged wife in public.

15. See Rosenthal, "The Institutional Fabric."

8. Toward More Ethical Legislative Bodies

1. *Los Angeles Daily News,* 14 June 1992.

2. David E. Price, "Legislative Ethics in the New Congress," in *Representation and Responsibility,* ed. Jennings and Callahan, 129.

3. Jane Mansbridge, "Public Spirit in Public Systems," in *Values and Public Policy,* ed. Henry J. Aaron, Thomas E. Mann, and Timothy Taylor (Washington DC: Brookings Institution, 1994), 149–50.

4. Interview with Representative Bill Lear, Kentucky, 3 February 1993.

5. Josephson, "The Best of Times," 36.

6. Annual meeting of the Council of Governmental Ethics Laws, Minneapolis, 22 September 1993.

7. Garment, *Scandal,* 140.

8. "The Age of Reformation," *Newsweek,* 29 March 1993.

9. For a more detailed account of ethics commissions, see Alan Rosenthal, "Administering Ethics to Legislators," *Spectrum* (summer 1995), 28–35.

10. Callahan, "Legislative Codes of Ethics," 233.

11. Hastings Center, *The Ethics of Legislative Life,* 19.

12. The point is made by Ian Ayers and John Braithwaite, as cited in Mansbridge, "Public Spirit in Public Systems," 151.

13. Hastings, *The Ethics of Legislative Life,* 51–52.

14. Loftus, *The Art of Legislative Politics,* 162.

15. Jean Ford, "An Insider's View of State Legislative Ethics," in *Representation and Responsibility,* ed. Jennings and Callahan, 270.

16. See A. G. Block, "The Reality of Willie Brown Jr.," *California Journal* (August 1995): 6–11.

17. "Gibber & Other Misdemeanors," *Texas Observer,* 14 February 1992, 3–4.

18. *Louisville Courier-Journal,* 2 February 1993.

19. Hastings, *The Ethics of Legislative Life,* 51–52.

20. *Hartford Courant,* 13 January 1993.

21. Gutmann and Thompson, "The Theory of Legislative Ethics," 186–87.

22. Cody and Richardson, *Honest Government,* 35.

23. Testimony of Michele Radosevich, *Proceedings of the Washington State House of Representatives,* Session on Legislative Ethics, 23 January 1992, 13.

24. Loftus, "Legislative Ethics," 28.

25. Interview with Senator Paul Burke, Kansas, 28 January 1993.

26. Interview with Vic Hellard, director of the Legislative Research Commission, Kentucky, 2 February 1993.

27. Loftus, *The Art of Legislative Politics,* 151–52.

28. Interview with Representative Bill Lear, Kentucky, 3 February 1993.

29. A. G. Block, "The Roberti Legacy," *California Journal* (November 1994): 9.

30. Richard C. Paddock, "The Mixed Legacy of a Practical Politician," *California Journal* (March 1992): 144, 148.

31. Block, "The Roberti Legacy," 9.

32. Block, "The Roberti Legacy," 11.

33. Interview with former Senator Barry Keene, California, 5 January 1993.

34. Interview with Representative Pat Sweeney, Ohio, 4 February 1993.

35. Hastings, *The Ethics of Legislative Life,* 7.

36. "Hard Lessons in Ethics," conference sponsored by the Eagleton Institute of Politics, Rutgers University, Phoenix, Arizona, 23–24 October 1993.

37. This is a central theme of the work of the Kettering Foundation. See David Mathews, *Politics for People* (Urbana: University of Illinois Press, 1994).

38. Merton, "Legislative Ethics and Professional Responsibility," 318.

39. Patterson, *Out of Order,* 25.

40. Senator Elaine Szymoniak, Iowa, at "Hard Lessons in Ethics," conference sponsored by the Eagleton Institute of Politics, Rutgers University, Phoenix, Arizona, 23–24 October 1993.

41. See Thomas E. Mann and Norman J. Ornstein, *Renewing Congress: A Second Report* (Washington DC: American Enterprise Institute for Public Policy Research and The Brookings Institution, 1993), 6.

42. Hastings, *The Ethics of Legislative Life,* 9.

Selected Bibliography

Books

Bowman, James S., ed. *Ethical Frontiers in Public Management*. San Francisco: Jossey-Bass, 1991.

Cody, W. J. Michael, and Lynn R. Richardson. *Honest Government: An Ethics Guide for Public Service*. Westport CT: Praeger, 1992.

Drew, Elizabeth. *Politics and Money*. New York: Macmillan, 1983.

Fleishman, Joel L., Lance Liebman, and Mark H. Moore. *Public Duties: The Moral Obligations of Government Officials*. Cambridge MA: Harvard University Press, 1981.

Garment, Suzanne. *Scandal: The Crisis of Mistrust in American Politics*. New York: Times Books, 1991.

Lewis, Carol W. *The Ethics Challenge in Public Service*. San Francisco: Jossey-Bass, 1991.

Loftus, Tom. *The Art of Legislative Politics*. Washington DC: CQ Press, 1994.

Mathews, David. *Politics for People*. Urbana: University of Illinois Press, 1994.

Noonan, John T. Jr. *Bribes*. Berkeley: University of California Press, 1984.

Patterson, Thomas E. *Out of Order*. New York: Knopf, 1993.

Rosenthal, Alan. *The Third House*. Washington DC: CQ Press, 1993.

Sorauf, Frank J. *Inside Campaign Finance*. New Haven CT: Yale University Press, 1992.

Thompson, Dennis F. *Political Ethics and Public Office*. Cambridge: Harvard University Press, 1987.

————. *Ethics in Congress: From Individual to Institutional Corruption*. Washington DC: Brookings Institution, 1995.

Zimmerman, Joseph. *Curbing Unethical Behavior in Government*. Westport CT: Greenwood Press, 1994.

Articles

Boulard, Garry. "Pluperfect Purity." *State Legislatures* (January 1995): 28–33.

Callahan, Daniel. "Legislative Codes of Ethics." In *Representation and Responsibility: Exploring Legislative Ethics*, ed. Bruce Jennings and Daniel Callahan, 221–34. New York: Plenum Press, 1985.

Cava, Anita, Jonathan West, and Evan Berman. "Ethical Decision-Making in Business and Government: An Analysis of Formal and Informal Strategies." *Spectrum* 68 (spring 1995): 28–36.

Gurwitt, Rob. "Deadly Stings—Wounded Legislatures." *Governing* (June 1991): 25–31.

————. "The Mirage of Campaign Reform." *Governing* (August 1992): 48–55.

Gutmann, Amy, and Dennis Thompson. "The Theory of Legislative Ethics." In *Representation and Responsibility: Exploring Legislative Ethics*, ed. Bruce Jennings and Daniel Callahan, 149–65. New York: Plenum Press, 1985.

Josephson, Michael. "The Best of Times, the Worst of Times." *Spectrum* (fall 1992): 34–41.

Loftus, Tom. "Legislative Ethics: The Rules of the Game." *Spectrum* (winter 1993): 27–30.

Lowenstein, Daniel H. "Political Bribery and the Intermediate Theory of Politics." *UCLA Law Review* 32 (1985): 784–851.

Malbin, Michael J. "Legislative Ethics." In *Encyclopedia of the American Legislative System*, ed. Joel H. Silbey, 1155–70. New York: Charles Scribner's Sons, 1994.

Manning, Bayless. "The Purity Potlatch: Conflict of Interests and Moral Escalation." In *Political Corruption*, ed. Arnold J. Heidenheimer, 307–13. New Brunswick NJ: Transaction Books, 1970.

Mansbridge, Jane. "Public Spirit in Political Systems." In *Values and Public Policy*, ed. Henry J. Aaron, Thomas E. Mann, and Timothy Taylor, 146–72. Washington DC: Brookings Institution, 1994.

Merton, Vanessa. "Legislative Ethics and Professional Responsibility." In *Rep-*

resentation and Responsibility: Exploring Legislative Ethics, ed. Bruce Jennings and Daniel Callahan, 303–24. New York: Plenum Press, 1985.

Rosenthal, Alan. "Administering Ethics to Legislators." *Spectrum* 68 (summer 1995).

———. "The Legislature: Unraveling of Institutional Fabric." In *The State of the States,* 3rd ed., ed. Carl Van Horn. Washington DC: CQ Press, forthcoming.

Saxon, John D. "The Scope of Legislative Ethics." In *Representation and Responsibility: Exploring Legislative Ethics,* ed. Bruce Jennings and Daniel Callahan, 197–219. New York: Plenum Press, 1985.

Scott, Steve. "The Legacy of the Capitol Sting." *California Journal* (August 1994): 8–12.

Stern, Robert M. "Ethics in the States: The Laboratories of Reform." In *Representation and Responsibility: Exploring Legislative Ethics,* ed. Bruce Jennings and Daniel Callahan, 243–61. New York: Plenum Press, 1985.

Stoker, Laura. "Interests and Ethics in Politics." *American Political Science Review* 86 (June 1992): 369–80.

Thompson, Dennis F. "Paradoxes of Government Ethics." *Public Administration Review* 52 (May–June 1992): 254–59.

Reports

Cook, Corey. *Campaign Finance Reform.* California Research Bureau, California State Library, July 1994.

Harwood Group. *Citizens and Politics.* Dayton OH: Kettering Foundation, 1991.

Hastings Center. *The Ethics of Legislative Life.* Hastings-on-Hudson NY, 1985.

Josephson Institute of Ethics. *Actual and Apparent Impropriety: A Report on Ethical Norms and Attitudes in State Legislatures.* Marina del Rey CA, January 1992.

Index